BLUE WATER COUNTDOWN
Preparing for long-term cruising

GEOFF PACK

for Allan,

best wishes,

[signature]

JAN '96

YACHTING MONTHLY

Dedication

For Lou Lou
whose trust and willingness has always been an inspiration to me

First published in 1988 by David and Charles as *Ocean Cruising Countdown*
This edition, fully revised, published in 1992 by **YACHTING MONTHLY**,
 IPC Magazines Ltd, Kings Reach Tower, Stamford Street, London SE1 9LS
© Text and photographs: Geoff Pack 1992
© Line illustrations: Yachting Monthly 1992
Cover picture: anchored off Bora Bora, by Patrick Roach

Book Editors Andrew Bray and Peter Nielsen
Book design Simon Firullo
Illustration Mike Collins

Price £12.50
ISBN 1 85277 073 2

Typeset by Ebony, Heathlands Industrial Estate, Heathlands Road,
Liskeard, Cornwall PL14 4DH

Printed and bound by Clifford Frost Ltd, Lyon Road,
Windsor Avenue, Wimbledon, SW19 2SE

Contents

The Author

Geoff Pack was born in 1958 and started sailing a few months later. After leaving college he joined *Yachting Monthly* as a trainee journalist. Three years later, aged 20 and just married, he and his wife Lou Lou bought *Foreigner*, a 35ft Wharram catamaran. After rebuilding and refitting the boat, they sailed her across the Atlantic, arriving in Barbados with little more than the clearance fee. After four years and 30,000 miles of sailing, a couple of them spent running a 40-ton Caribbean charter boat and doing yacht deliveries, they returned to Britain. In 1983 they bought *Euge*, a Rival 34, in which they completed a very successful 11,000-mile 'Atlantic Circuit' cruise to the Caribbean and back. There followed a few years in the Hampshire countryside, Geoff returning to *Yachting Monthly* as Assistant Editor and Lou Lou bringing up their growing family. In 1991 they sold up again and set off to circumnavigate, now with three children under five years old, in their 41ft Apache catamaran *Foreigner 2*.

Introduction to the Second Edition

Laying to anchor here in the West Indies, one year into what is loosely planned as a circumnavigation, I'm very much aware that blue water cruising has had a pull on the tiller, its course has changed. The publication of a book, like taking a photograph, freezes a time frame. In rewriting and updating this edition I've been astonished at how much blue-water sailing has changed in the five years since *Ocean Cruising Countdown* was first published. Just as the '80s was a tumultuous decade in social terms, that in turn created a new breed of blue-water sailor for the '90s. Those five years have seen, for example, the introduction of GPS, whose accuracy has had a major impact on cruising safety (and therefore confidence), as well as a plethora of sail-handling equipment that has tamed slightly bigger vessels for cruising with greater speed and comfort. What hasn't changed, of course, is the cruising life itself; still it relies on resourcefulness and self-sufficiency, thrives on friendship and new experiences.

If there's one comment I hear more than any other amongst the cruising fraternity, it is that people fervently wish they had taken it up sooner. If, having finished this book, you feel the cruising life is for you, seize the opportunity to go before time and circumstance take it away from you.

Geoff Pack
Bequia, West Indies
July 1992

1. Fresh Outlooks

To cast aside the shackles of a conventional working existence and replace them with freedom, time and a yacht to visit faraway places is the passionate dream of many. What makes it such a pleasant dream is that it is an attainable goal for most people who have good health, an adventurous spirit and the ability to make sacrifices and changes. Visit a port like Falmouth, Cornwall in mid-summer and amongst the yachts you'll see craft with the familiar hallmarks of windvane gears, baggywrinkle in the rigging and a boot-top line long since lost under the water. All are heading for faraway places, their crews with a blue-water glint in their eyes.

However, for every one that gets away there are probably fifty which don't make it. Of those which do get away, a good proportion return within a year with plans to do it a different way. In order to understand what makes for successful ocean cruising we must first look at why others have failed to fulfil what seems, at the outset, to be the purest form of hedonism. It may seem cynical, but there is a common expression among those expatriates who live in the West Indies – 'another rotten day in paradise' (I've substituted 'rotten' for the vernacular!).

Too many prospective ocean cruising people concentrate wholly on the suitability and preparation of their yacht when they embark on their project. They don't for a moment consider whether they personally are either suited to, or prepared for, the enormous changes in their life. The first section of the book examines some of the more common worries, difficulties to be overcome, and changes in attitude to contend with. In most cases there are no easy remedies offered, because we are all different and must come to terms with the problems in our own way.

The psychological break

It is said about ocean cruising that when it's good, it's really good, and when it's bad it's awful. For the majority of us living in a conventional way in western society, the margins of both our enjoyment and unhappiness are drawn for us. Barring genuine disasters, there is invariably a buffer of some sort to stop us getting really low, whether it's the support of a family, a doctor to ease our pains, a mechanic to repair our car or supplementary benefit to keep the wolf from the door. But neither does 'the rat race' offer very much in the way of pure joy, supreme challenge and fantastic excitement or experience. There are exceptions, of course, events like childbirth, marriage, professional achievement, running a marathon and so on, but on the whole life is a lot of gradual uphill cycling before you get to freewheel down a brief, steep, hill.

In going ocean cruising you are widening those margins of joy and misery by leaving behind the sheltered existence most of us experience. When you've got a toothache 1,000 miles from land, need to repair the engine starter motor when anchored at a deserted atoll, or come into contact with a corrupt police force, you very quickly realise that it's easy to take for granted the advantages of boring, everyday life in a democratic society. When you're thousands of miles from home you'll have no one to turn to but yourself to solve difficulties. You will need to be adaptable, resourceful and a jack of all trades.

As age sets us in our ways it also makes learning new skills harder, so one must strive to remain flexible and to wholly acknowledge the concept of self-sufficiency. Before you set sail, and during your cruise, you may have to learn skills that passed you by in normal society; they may be the ability to recognise the symptoms of the more common diseases and first aid, the capability to complete a sound fibreglass repair below the waterline, or diplomacy in dealing carefully with a bureaucratic port official. Acquiring such knowledge may be straightforward, but you have to ask yourself if you have the inclination to adapt and learn much that may be new to you.

Self-sufficiency at sea cannot be over-emphasised and although it doesn't matter if many of the conveniences carried aboard yachts today break down, their breakdown can start a chain reaction that puts the yacht and her crew into danger.

An obvious example is the failure of the electrics, a common enough occurence and not usually serious. A few years ago, my wife Lou Lou and I, employing five other crew, took on the delivery of a 40-ton luxury ketch from the West Indies to Bermuda. She was a complicated vessel, as is necessary when designers try to incorporate all the comforts and conveniences of domestic life aboard a yacht. She had no generator and relied on the engine to charge the batteries and keep the fridges and freezers cold. Seven crew consume a lot of food and as her galley was designed to be used in harbour and not at sea, much of the provisioning took the form of frozen convenience foods which could be prepared in the microwave.

Halfway through the delivery the engine went badly wrong and with it in pieces, requiring spares we didn't have aboard, we lost the ability to charge the batteries. We had no navigation lights, no log, no compass light to steer by at night, no RDF, and no VHF to seek help with. We couldn't even get water out of the tanks except by scooping it in cups from the inspection hatches. Being in the tropics, the freezer's contents very quickly went bad, instantly putting us on to basic rations because it was flat calm and we had no idea how long we might be out there. It was May, when the sun's declination was very close to our latitude, therefore right overhead at noon, which made a latitude fix questionable and gave pretty nearly north/south position lines at any other times during the day. As my course was northwards towards Bermuda, with its dangerous outlying reefs, I needed my latitude urgently (there were no sight reduction tables for star sights aboard) and without the log I could not judge dead reckoning with any accuracy. What had one day been a very comfortable, if not luxurious, cruise on a £1m yacht turned overnight into a nightmare. We completed the trip successfully, and subsequently sailed on to the USA, but I took more risks than I care to think about. Apart from the fact the boat was unsuitable, despite her size, for long offshore passages, I was to blame for relying too heavily on her services and not considering the implications of a minor problem (the lack of a spare head gasket and torque wrench) causing a chain of events that left us ill-nourished with attendant low morale, and with little more than a vague idea of our position when making a difficult landfall.

A similar situation could arise on a modern cruising boat, if for instance a drive belt had broken and you discovered that you had every description of belt aboard but the appropriate one. Or perhaps a deck leak had put out the alternator. Unless you have some other form of charging (solar panel, windmill or shaft alternator) you only ever discover the problem when the batteries are low and you decide to charge them. By then, you haven't much power left to conserve, and the voltage will quickly dip below the minimum 11v required by many electronic navigation systems. A staggering number of ocean-bound yachtsmen fit GPS or SatNav and either never get around to learning astronavigation, or learned years ago, but have become dangerously rusty since relying on electronics.

Today we rely heavily on microprocessor technology and on the whole its reliability is excellent. Even if something goes wrong, a technician can easily identify the Printed Circuit Board (PCB) giving the problem and swap it for a good one. The salesman will tell you the reliability of such marine products is exemplary, but always remember that he won't be there to argue with in the middle of the Pacific and neither will the technician. It would be naive, and against the purpose of this book, to

Consumerism pervades boat shows but when you're trying to find spares or maintain that glistening exterior in a jungle rain forest anchorage, Earl's Court and Southampton seem very far away

say that modern electrical equipment is unsuitable on ocean cruising boats. Some is good and some is superfluous, but never be totally reliant on it. Always regard gadgets as an aid and be sure you can operate quite normally, if inconveniently, without them. In this way, never instal a Weatherfax if you don't know basic meteorology. Even simple electrical equipment like a speed/distance instrument must be backed up by a mechanical trailing log. I doubt you'll ever find an experienced deep water yachtsman who wholly relies offshore on anything that requires electricity.

Doing without consumer society

In the past 25 years consumerism has become a dominant aspect of our modern society and economy. The 'throwaway' concept which it embraces started with ball-point pens and has spread widely, to cars with in-built obsolescence and even buildings constructed cheaply in the certain knowledge that they only need to last 20 years before being pulled down and replaced. This is fine to live with so long as the consumer is able to buy the next ball-point pen, or replace a piece of equipment now worn-out or superceded by something better, but in the majority of places where ocean cruising yachts go, it is very often difficult to get hold of the most basic spares and supplies. Therefore the consumer attitude that is easy to adopt when living in England, Europe or America doesn't work well when cruising; you simply can't go out and buy a part or replacement and, in any event, you probably won't have sufficient income to support a consumer lifestyle.

A byproduct of consumerism is the whittling-down of standards and quality. The wheels of modern industry rely on frequent replacement. You are leaving this contemporary thinking behind. Your yacht and all her equipment must be reliable and durable. Anything that starts to wear out, break down or cause problems will be difficult, often impossible, to rectify in a distant port. And it will undermine your confidence in the vessel in rough conditions at sea, when every component is being pushed to the limit.

Quality, not quantity

It is a false economy to fit out with anything less than high-quality equipment for a long-distance cruise. The item designed for occasional weekend use will probably let you down after constant use. The cost of having spares or a replacement sent out to you (not to mention the hassle, time, telexes, telephone calls and customs hold-ups of having it shipped) by far outweigh the extra cost of good quality from the outset. Most ocean cruising projects are working to a strict budget and advice about buying the best can be irritating, but I cannot over-emphasise that in the long run your money is far better spent on a limited number of products of known quality than on a wide range of cheaper goodies. Good examples are sails, where you'll get better service out of a high quality working suit than a full wardrobe bought for a 'special deal', or electronics, where it can be tempting to buy a complete set of economy wind instruments for the price of one really decent speedlog.

This philosophy also goes for the boat itself. The Far East has long manufactured products to a much lower price than Western countries, and yachts are now being built

The ocean cruiser must put up with terrible punishment like pounding to windward for days or even weeks on end: at times like this the quality of her equipment will seem worth paying for

there. Places like Taiwan have produced some fabulous craft, but a fair proportion are constructed of poor quality materials (despite outwardly attractive local teak finish) and they are built by people who have never been aboard a yacht at sea in their lives. The same caution is necessary with amateur-built yachts, especially after the rash of big boats built in back gardens during the '70s when ferrocement construction seemed the ideal way to obtain a lot of boat at low cost. It can be a difficult decision when you are confronted with the spaciousness of a cheaply-built 44-footer for a similar price to a quality yard-built 38-footer. Needless to say, look very carefully and if you're in the least uncertain, engage a surveyor. However, don't immediately write off a yacht with an 'amateur' tag attached to it, for some home builders have high standards and will almost certainly have invested much more love, care and attention in it.

Most yachts sit unused in marinas or at moorings for nine out of ten days of the year. They are the equivalent of a saloon car parked in the drive with a low mileage accumulated on short trips around town. But your ocean cruiser will be your yacht, your home, your car and the tool of your trade. Like a workman's tools, it will be used every day. It won't be sailing every day, but long and often arduous ocean passages will be interspersed with time in port where the pumps for fresh water, shower or heads are used all the time, when the dinghy is a workhorse carrying crew, water containers and provisions around, the varnish is forever being walked over, door latches used, light fittings switched on and off, hatches opened and closed and so on. To withstand that constant use without giving trouble, quality and not quantity must be the watchword throughout.

There are other reasons why consumerism and its disregard for quality has little place aboard the ocean cruiser. Consumerism relies on turnover being generated by high consumption which in turn requires money as its lifeblood, and most cruising yachtsmen must, of necessity, be fairly thrifty. The consumer tinkering with his car on a Sunday afternoon might use half a roll of paper kitchen towel to wipe up grease. Tissues and paper towels are forever useful on a long distance cruiser, but the wily ocean-going yachtsman would probably use rags (washed out afterwards) for his engine cleaning and a tiny amount of paper towel for other jobs because he knows it is precious. He won't be near a shop selling it for a few months yet and such luxuries in poor island communities are three or four times as expensive as in a High Street shop at home.

Another byproduct of modern consumerism is a lack of pride in ownership. Because so many items are here today, gone tomorrow, you don't develop any attachment to them. In the 1950s the average family car was loved, given a name, cherished, and polished every week. Nowadays there are so many cars, they depreciate so quickly and we are encouraged to change them so regularly, that they are regarded only as a utility. The ocean cruising yachtsman must rely heavily on nearly all the equipment he has, and in some cases his life may depend on it. There should be little on board that is superfluous and what gear he chooses to take with him he soon gets to know quite well, whether it is the trailing log he dismantles on a quiet morning watch to lubricate, the sail he has put countless stitches in, the echo sounder whose every rogue flicker is familiar as it alerts him passing over many a reef, the steady thrum of the diesel he knows and trusts.

Everyday life has changed so much that most normal households have many 'conveniences' – the paraphernalia of modern living, from washing machines and tumble dryers to TV sets, computers and videos. When you go sailing, pretty much all of this must go and whilst you occasionally find a boat fitted out with much of this equipment (as often as not by a husband trying to persuade a reluctant wife), very few of them get far because that attitude doesn't normally mix with the simple life of ocean cruising. Alternatively, they find they grow out of wanting such items on board, and the sunset with a glass of West Indian rum in your hand becomes far more attractive than watching the video.

If losing those conveniences seems hard to swallow, remember that many of them came about to save the time spent on household chores, and the one thing you will have in abundance is time. Some of the appliances become redundant anyway when you are living aboard in the tropics wearing swimsuits, tee-shirts or pareos (fabric wrap-around dress/skirts) which dry in no time in the warm breezes. At home the ability to cook a baked potato in the microwave in minutes may seem alluring, but it's not half the fun of cooking them with breadfruit thrown in at an impromptu beach barbeque with friends from nearby boats. Having time to spare puts a completely different complexion on things, and it doesn't matter if a cocktail takes a quarter of an hour to make because you haven't got the blender. A car is another thing you think you'll miss sometimes. We've occasionally hired one to do a lot of provisioning or go sight-seeing with friends. For the rest of the time walking keeps you fit, and you don't begrudge the time it takes because you have plenty. And as every port you stop at is different, even a trip ashore to find the post office is a new adventure.

Successful ocean cruising is, more than anything else, an attitude of mind. You won't miss all those consumer and disposable goods, but you may need time to adjust.

2. The Awkward Decisions

If going cruising was easy, many more people would be doing it. There's no turning away from the fact that some very uncomfortable decisions and heartfelt sacrifices need to be made before you can consider yourself prepared to sell up and sail. It is invariably these decisions that are the insurmountable hurdles rather than a boat not quite ready, bank account not quite big enough, or the countless other excuses dreamers come up with to avoid making the break.

Insurance

Unless a rich old aunt has died, most of those going cruising will have worked hard and sacrificed a lot over the years in order to get into the position to own a boat, equip it, and head off. Those who build their boats themselves make a massive investment in time and effort. Others may have bought a boat through long hours in overtime or putting every hour into their own businesses. Some couples deliberately don't start a family so that their plans and efforts are unimpeded. When the boat finally materialises, the idea of risking those years of sacrifice by sailing away with it uninsured is abhorrent to most people, and yet even the most basic insurance is difficult to arrange for long-term shorthanded ocean cruising, and if is possible, then it is prohibitively expensive. Are you prepared to take this calculated risk ?

The late Eric and Susan Hiscock were never insured in all the years they cruised, and believed that proper precautions, good seamanship and a well maintained yacht make up for all that an insurance broker can offer. There are no two ways about it, cruising without insurance hones one's skills and seamanship, just as being insured can develop a false sense of security. Sailing without it means you don't take risks entering harbours at night, you choose your anchorage very carefully and never fail to be within close reach of a hurricane hole during the hurricane season. The knowledge that a broken mast might easily wipe out your cruising funds means that you don't press the boat as hard as you might have done on weekend thrashes when you were working and the yacht was fully insured. In short, being uninsured is the best teacher of good seamanship and may, paradoxically, prove to be an advantage.

There are compromises which can ease you into the world of being totally

The ultimate horror of coming back to your boat and home, which is probably uninsured, to find she has dragged ashore

uninsured. If you're sailing from Northern Europe, it is usually possible to get insurance cover for the Mediterranean, often out as far as the Canaries, and very occasionally across the Atlantic (although at the time of going to press, an obligatory requirement by most insurance companies was to have three experienced adult crew members aboard). If you plan to stay in the Caribbean for any length of time, you can obtain insurance for this, as you can if you intend cruising up the Eastern seaboard of the States. However, if you've crossed over without insurance it will be necessary to get the yacht surveyed again before even your old company will re-insure (they've had to pay out for items broken or lost during the uninsured period). This sort of insurance is not cheap, organising it from far away is not easy and it usually only covers total loss and third party risks.

The problems increase when you venture further afield and head down to Brazil or perhaps the coasts of Venezuela, Colombia and thence into the Pacific. Some people obtain cover, at great expense, for just total loss, but by far the majority spend the money buying equipment which they feel substitutes for insurance, like extra anchors, better fire extinguishers, more charts, bigger fenders, or perhaps a GPS to assist them in the poorly-charted areas of the Pacific where tides and currents are unpredictable.

Six months' insurance for an average 35-footer will buy a GPS set, whilst a year's insurance will buy that plus some heavy ground tackle and a good quality windlass to haul it up with. It is a personal decision, but my view is that this equipment will look after you and the boat much better than an insurance policy. Insurance is one of the protective buffers of modern life that you are losing by going away and which become less significant the longer you are away. When you have been cruising for a few years in out-of-the-way places, you take the risk of sailing uninsured in your stride, and yet travelling on a bus seems terribly fast and dangerous, and crossing the street is something you do with great caution . . .

The other way of looking at the insurance problem is planning from the outset not to put all your eggs in one basket. If the boat is absolutely everything you own, and losing it would be a catastrophe, you could buy a smaller boat and invest the rest of your capital in a house, which you could rent out to pay the remaining mortgage fees. Then if disaster struck you would at least have something to go back to. Another alternative, and one becoming increasingly popular, is to have a steel or aluminium boat. They are not indestructable, but will often survive a fire, are less susceptible to serious damage in a collision and will withstand a moderate stranding that would write off a vessel built in any other material.

What about the children ?

It is fine for father and mother to have great ambitions to sail across the oceans and live in different places around the world but it's unreasonable to expect your children's education and future prospects to suffer as a result. The idea of not working and a simple life cruising in the Pacific may be pure heaven for you, but your son or daughter's greatest ambition may be to become an accountant, living in a city, buying a new car every year and having 2.4 children. How much would you jeopardise their future by taking them away from the conventional pattern of education? Anybody with children of dependant age obviously has some heartsearching to do.

Cruising with children can produce some great benefits. Youngsters create an instant introduction to locals ashore that you would never normally get to know, especially with the sun-bleached blond hair most cruising children have. They also seem oblivious to bad weather and while mother and father are worried on deck, life carries on as normal down below. Initially, the big plus factor you have in your favour with children is their adaptability. Adults may take time to accept the confines of a boat after a lifetime in houses. Children may moan at first, but soon forget as new challenges and activities absorb them. A dinghy with oars, or, even better, a sail, that they are put in charge of soon helps them to forget the bike they left behind.

When you have children, the influence they have on the choice of a suitable boat is important. It will require a certain amount of obvious customisation that any parent recognises – handholds low down throughout the boat, netting around the guardrails, avoidance of sharp corners, and the positioning of important switches and controls beyond the reach of tiny fingers. In turning the battery isolation switch, one of ours open-circuited the Windbugger wind generator and zapped the boat's electrical system with a high voltage (50v +) spike, destroying over one thousand pound's worth of electronics in less than a second. I was the one to blame.

Ideally children should have their own cabin, a well-lit and ventilated area where they can set up their toys, and the installation of a cheap stereo in here will help no end. The cockpit, their playground, must be well-protected and preferably deep with fine stainless (toy-catching) grilles over the large drains it will need as a result.

Children's safety is a major consideration. It is absolutely imperative that a child is able to swim, as no child will put up with the shackles of a permanent lifejacket or harness. And parents must work diligently and patiently to insure that the child is confident in the water and not scared of it – fear of water is something we are taught, it is not instinctive. This confidence could spell the difference between fun and disaster if a child were to fall in whilst playing on deck, in the dinghy or from a quayside.

Most parents agree that infants afloat are the easiest to cope with, their propensity for sleeping half the day making life a joy compared to later on. A French yacht we met in the Canaries had two children aboard under the age of 18 months, although judging by the number of nappies always drying on the guardrails (they had a huge

Having children along creates a great deal of extra work, but as the author's son Oliver demonstrates, the extra fun they create is worth it

water capacity, 200 gallons, on their 37-footer, and washed nappies in a mixture of half fresh/half salt water) it must have been hard work. Although with children under the age of four months one has to be very careful of infections and temperature, by and large they seem to fare quite well at this age, spending most of their time asleep. As soon as babies start to crawl problems increase because then they need constant supervision. On occasions when both parents are needed on deck, conning through a reef passage, shortening canvas quickly with the approach of a squall, or maybe a tricky harbour manoeuvre, such supervision can be very difficult. Strapping the child into a car seat is about the best option in these circumstances.

The primary years of education are something most cruising parents reckon they can cope with themselves, arguing that a daily hour or two of individual tuition will teach them as much as they would learn all day in a class of thirty at school. The wise ones embrace the rudiments of teaching as part of their preparation before leaving and work to a proper timetable and scheme. However, physically sitting down and doing that teaching when you are cruising requires a great deal of discipline on the part of both parents and children. There are so many more interesting distractions for both, and after the first few months the teaching schedule can easily slide into obscurity. In our experience, and that of most other people we've met, children instinctively hate being taught by their own parents. Another disadvantage is that you do not have the educational aids and equipment which are an everyday part of modern schools, especially for computer training which starts at a very tender age. On the other hand, showing children the world and a different lifestyle is often a reason for wanting to go in the first place and is seen as an educational advantage in itself.

There is no easier way to learn a foreign language than by being in that country and making friends. Geography is more interesting when you have been to the places and seen different rock formations or the special crops of a country growing in the fields. The concensus of opinion among cruising parents is that their children very quickly settle down when they go back to school, and rarely if ever have to go into a class lower than that for their age in order to catch up. There are several well-established teaching schemes specifically designed for children being taught by parents overseas, the two most popular being the Calvert School, 105 Tuscany Rd, Baltimore, Maryland, MD21210, USA and the Worldwide Education Service at 10 Barley Mow Passage, Chiswick, London W4 4PH. The latter scheme, however, is not cheap. In 1992 prices started at around £1,500/child. The Calvert School was recommended to us by parents who'd tried both systems, and our eldest now uses their system. The cost, incidentally, is considerably less at approximately £400.

Most parents consider that by the age of 11 or 12 a child must begin formal education, and that signals the end of their wandering life, unless they can send them to boarding school and go off again. Many children have continued cruising into their teens, but this is taking a big risk with examination results that may be badly wanted for university entry or a future career. Education apart, there can be problems in keeping children happily occupied and it is important to see that they meet plenty of others of their age. Decisions about where to go may often be determined by the plans of other yachts with children aboard who will be company. Cruising often dispels shyness in a child because of the need to make new friends all the time, but a single child on a boat among grown-up company all the time can become prematurely adult and seem to be aged seven, going on 35.

What about home?

It may be that the only way of getting enough money together to buy a suitable boat and get going is to sell your house. However keen you may be to rid yourself of material possessions and adopt the more philosophic cruising lifestyle, getting rid of the roof over your head, the very symbol of all you have worked and saved for all these years, is a harsh decision. It may also be very difficult to reverse unless you are sure of having the finance to buy a property if you should wish to stop voyaging in a few years' time.

Leasing your house is preferable if you don't need the capital, but being a long-distance landlord is not easy. It only requires one flight back from a faraway place to sort out problems before rental profits are whittled away. The ideal is to pay a trusted and competent friend, neighbour or relative to manage the letting of the house. It is not an exceptionally demanding job but does take away problems that could be very difficult for you to solve from several thousand miles away, so it is good insurance to pay them well.

Without such a person to manage the property the obvious answer is to go to a property or estate agent. Impersonal attitudes are the root of nearly all house-letting problems – the tenant not having respect for the property or its contents, and in turn the agent not really caring a great deal either, letting it run down then employing 'cowboys' to do the maintenance regardless of their standards or prices. It might be better to rent the house to friends or family, even at half the normal rent. Otherwise try to deal through agents you know and trust.

Unless you have a very small or non-existent mortgage, or own an exceptionally desirable property which can command high rent, it is unlikely you'll make much money by letting. Agents' fees, income tax on the rent (payable even if you have expatriate status), rates, insurance and essential maintenance will eat up the gross proceeds. At best, the property should at least pay for itself and keep abreast of market values. And it will be there if you decide to return, but do have a watertight tenancy agreement and check up with your lawyer what the legal position is should you wish to re-possess. Some middle-aged couples who do not especially need the extra income ask their grown-up offspring to live in their house while they are away, and the offspring usually are only too glad to oblige.

Even if things go smoothly, renting your furnished house, with all its sentimental attachments, to strangers can be difficult. An alternative may be to sell your own house (which, if needs be, will free some funds for the boat and cruising life) and buy a house or flat in a holiday resort and earn money from short lets. In this way, you avoid any emotions, and have somewhere to come back to, albeit during the off-season, if you make a brief visit home. Again, financially, the gain is not high because you will need an agent to manage it and have to pay cleaner's bills among others. Summer rents are high, but the season may be a short one so compare the probable results with those of a long lease.

The final choice is to sell up and put the money in an offshore investment account. If you do, the hardest thing to resist is drawing on the capital. In fact, if you want to maintain parity with property values against your return to dry land living you should plough the annual interest back into the capital.

The single largest influence on what to do with the house must be determined by the state of the property market. Up to and during the 1980s in the UK it was considered difficult to go wrong financially by keeping a property. The bubble burst at the end of that decade and house prices started to dive. Emotional attachment apart, unless the value of the property is rising at two or three points more than inflation, the money is best invested where you will receive only Statement of Acounts from time to time, rather than urgent telexes informing you the roof has blown off or the windowsills gone rotten.

Family ties

Leaving family behind can be the hardest part of going away cruising and comes high on the list of reasons people give for backing out of cruising plans. For instance few people feel easy about, or are capable of, disappearing over the horizon away from an ageing or ailing parent, but on the other hand it could be very frustrating to be otherwise ready and prepared and then watch the best years of your life slipping by because you feel tied.

The problem can often be eased by frequent contact. Letters every week, telephone calls wherever possible and even ham radio (this is dealt with in Section Three) allows family to know exactly where you are and what you're up to. The advent of the fax machine and its worldwide popularisation means that letters and messages can be swapped promptly. Elderly parents who are still active may be pleased to be asked to handle your affairs while you are away, provided they're not too taxing (more detailed suggestions for this are dealt with in Section Three), which is a practical method of involving them and keeping them in contact. And if they are still fit they may be delighted at the prospect of flying out to join you somewhere for a couple of weeks, perhaps taking accommodation ashore.

Your grown offspring are not often a problem because they will be too busy leading their own lives to worry about you, but you will want to keep in touch with them. An annual trip back home by plane for a month or two will make a big difference.

Grandchildren are also missed but the solution is easier. Many cruising people pay for them to be sent out during school holidays. This is often a superb experience for all concerned. For the kids, delivered by parents on to the plane and met by grandparents at the other end, it's the experience of a lifetime; grandparents get to see them for a few weeks (children can easily enough sleep in the saloon for the period); and the parents have a couple of weeks 'off', perhaps to have a rare holiday together. The cost of a couple of air tickets is a small price to pay, all things considered.

3. Is This the Life for Me?

Removing the safety nets

So far we have dealt with the problems posed by the things you are leaving behind – house, family, modern amenities and so forth. Now it is time to look at what lies ahead in your new life and ask yourself whether you can cope and if it is really what you want. Are you prepared to abandon the safety nets of civilised society and rely on your own resources?

There are a limited number of crutches to help you out of awkward situations overseas, but overall you are on your own. The ocean cruising community invariably help each other out. When my wife Lou Lou's hand was crushed by a barge hitting our yacht in Funchal, Madeira, a well-known cruising yachtsman, Dr Ronnie Andrews, put his departure back long enough to not only make sure the hand was all right, but see Lou Lou through her convalescence. We were lucky that there was a qualified medic nearby, but there is invariably someone in an anchorage who'll be able to help out another 'yachtie' who doesn't know much about a particular problem, perhaps a faulty alternator, a VHF that doesn't work or a refrigerator playing up. Payment is rarely expected, but it is a goodwill fund that must be contributed to.

If you run into legal difficulties in a foreign port, it is unlikely you'll find a shore-based lawyer to help you out even assuming there is not an insurmountable language barrier. The fair and impartial justice we take for granted does not extend to all countries and your national consulate can often provide only limited assistance.

My friend Roger Brake took the law into his own hands when a fishing boat put a 4sq ft hole in the side of his trimaran, again in Madeira. It was six o'clock in the morning, and after being so abruptly awoken, Roger had the presence of mind to chase the offending fishing boat in his outboard-powered inflatable, eventually catching up, boarding it and physically forcing the crew back into harbour. It was only this sort of determination, and the help of the American consulate, that meant he was finally able to make them pay up for the damage, but his is a rare success story.

We were not so lucky. A powerful speedboat went out of control in a Lisbon dock and impaled itself in *Foreigner 2*'s topsides, leaving an 8in x 10in hole. The driver/owner appeared genuinely upset and concerned, spending the afternoon with us discussing exactly how it would all be repaired, before leaving us a false telephone

When his boat was seriously damaged by a poorly-handled fishing boat in Madeira, Roger Brake had no help but his own initiative to sort the problem out

number and disappearing off the face of the earth. We eventually tracked him down, but you can't force someone to part with money and to push through legal procedures would be fraught, expensive and could take months.

The popular yachting areas see many yachts come and go, and in many third world countries the yacht is worth more than a native will earn in a lifetime so the temptation is great. Also, because of their transient nature, yachts provide ripe pickings for thieves. Even if they're caught the culprits are often released because, like us, yachtsmen do not want to stay long enough to press charges and go through lengthy courts procedures.

The only answer is to avoid trouble at all costs, locking your dinghy when you are ashore and taking a lot of trouble to make the boat as thief-proof as possible, so it at least deters the more amateur criminals (suggestions for doing this are in the last section of the book). The reverse of the coin is to make sure you sail with a 'clean wake'; pay your dues, don't leave rubbish on the quaysides, don't throw your weight around ashore. If there are any local projects going on that you can help with, bend over backwards to oblige. In this way the ocean cruising fraternity will enhance their reputation.

Realistic expectations

You will be unusual if you have not already read half a dozen narrative books by ocean cruising authors. Probably what you remember of them are only the beautiful anchorages, the 160-mile days, the friendly customs officials and so on. Force yourself to realise it isn't always like that. If it were Nirvana, there'd be more people doing it. There are rainy days, the boredom of prolonged calms, fruitless searches for spare parts you desperately need or signs of osmosis, gribble or electrolysis when you haul out, and times when the budget is tight.

Don't assume all your dreams will come true as soon as the boat is ready and you depart. Go to any port along the tradewind route and you will nearly always find a broken dream. Money is rarely the root of the problem. People with little money but who have a will to cruise invariably find work before the funds run out altogether. Inexperience is also rarely the cause, unless the crew have lost all faith in the skipper. More often, broken dreams are caused by disillusionment resulting from high expectations at the start and not anticipating the occasional miseries, fears and hardships one must put up with when living in a small boat in harbour and at sea.

Relationships can be severely strained by living in close quarters and an essential aspect of deciding to go must be your confidence in getting on with your companion for 24 hours a day, even if you've been married to him or her for 15 years. Having the responsibility of being skipper can often manifest an aspect of someone's character you never knew before. The Captain Bligh image is common and often tolerated with amusement on a two-week holiday cruise, but the prospect of living with it indefinitely could be unbearable.

Crew harmony, especially when there are only two or three aboard, is made no easier by the fact that at sea you can't pour your heart out on the phone to Mum or a close friend, and even in harbour it's not always possible to confide in a new-found aquaintance.

If you have been working hard for years, wrestling with business or professional problems in a society you feel has you trapped by its bureaucracy and materialism, you may well feel that nothing can put you off becoming an ocean vagabond. But stop and try to visualise the bad times. Sailing with a balanced vision of your new life, will be the best way of ensuring you don't turn back in bitter and expensive disappointment.

Lagoons surrounded by palm trees abound in the tropics, but don't forget the filthy commercial harbours one is sometimes obliged to use

Just how much know-how is needed to keep watch? In fact very little, as long as the skipper has the knowledge and experience to deal with emergencies and awkward situations

Have I enough sailing experience?

It is difficult to know when you are ready and capable to command a small yacht to sail across oceans, but there's a first time for everything and if it makes you feel better, there isn't an ocean cruising yachtsman alive who hasn't faced the same question.

A trap many people fall into is to worry about how little physical sailing experience they've had, and put off the decision to go until they have had a few more seasons' sailing. In short, you'll learn more after a month's intensive full-time cruising (taking in a longish passage or two) than ever you pick up in years of sporadic weekends and occasional week-long trips. However, that comment must be qualified by saying that you must always be cautious, understand the weather and know where you are. Good knowledge of, and confidence in, those three factors are the basic and essential requirements before heading off.

Unfortunately, for those leaving Northern European countries there is a natural barrier for the inexperienced – the Bay of Biscay. This could well be the most demanding sailing you are likely to experience for years, and although Biscay isn't forever bad, it has a tradition of sorting the men from the boys, and over the years has turned back a large number of potential ocean cruising projects, even with experienced crews.

The best answer to gauging whether or not you have the knowledge and experience to go long distance sailing is to ship aboard a delivery passage as crew. Very often made under pressure of time and season, a delivery trip with an experienced skipper offers the greatest likelihood of meeting bad weather in an unknown boat which may give you the chance to test your mettle.

The best age?

One rarely meets anyone who thought they had left too early to go cruising. In my experience, nearly everyone over the age of 28 or 30 wishes they had started sooner, particularly those over 55 who see that a time will come when they have to trim their cruising activities because of age rather than out of choice. Some we have met felt that age was more valuable than money, there being little point in striving for the perfect retirement boat if every extra year you spend working towards it means less time cruising. For younger couples children will be the most important influence and the best time to go cruising is probably before you have children or after they are off your hands.

From making hundreds of cruising friends over the years, and seeing quite a few people who had cruised for too long, I firmly believe that one must consider cruising as a way of life for a limited number of years at a time. Ten seems to be about the maximum before one yearns for a break. The ocean-cruising yachtsman invariably returns to the lifestyle later, but that is another matter. This aspect must be considered when making long-term plans. A couple who burn bridges to retire early, in their late 40s say, should not lose sight of the fact that they will probably find they'll want a break after a few years. If by retiring early they were only able to set themselves up with a modest income for cruising, it may not support a return to shoreside living and at this age it may be difficult to start finding new work.

On the other hand, a young married couple in their mid-twenties who plan to start a family at some point are best to get away as soon as they can, even if it means a less-than-perfect boat. A baby born on voyage, even if you are careful to be in a port with modern medical facilities, will nearly always halt a cruise either for the necessity of a bigger yacht or for more funds. A couple who have young children already will have to work out timing in relation to their education as we have already discussed.

Career planning can be another important factor. A few years' break after university is often the only choice for those intending to follow a professional career and this is a time when very few people without independent means are in a position to buy a boat. For them there are only two serious options. The first is to 'ocean hitch-hike' aboard other people's yachts, stopping ashore to work when necessary. The second is to 'slave and save' long enough to buy something like a Folkboat, which with adaption and alteration is capable of making long offshore passages. Although they may not be particularly comfortable, some of the most ambitious and successful cruises have been carried out in smallish yachts with shoestring budgets (witness boats like *Erik the Red*, *Super Shrimp*, *Trekka*, to name but a few of the well-known ones) so don't immediately disregard this option.

Health

Cruising is a very healthy way of life. You are living in unpolluted sea air, eating more natural foods (in harbour, anyway), swimming regularly, and walking a lot, if only to do the shopping.

Apart from this your body quickly tones up with all the physical aspects of running a boat, whether it's transporting water containers from tap to boat (a 5-gallon jug weighs 50 lbs, and you soon get used to carrying one in each hand), rowing the dinghy, raising the anchor or the invisible constant effort of bracing yourself on a boat moving at sea. This, combined with a rich tan and sun-bleached hair, can make a formerly pallid middle-aged commuter look like Charles Atlas after a few months of tropic cruising. So even if your present daily routine, with not enough opportunity to keep fit, causes you health problems in our damp, cold winters, don't assume that they will necessarily accompany you. Cruising is recuperative and the average non-athletic person will find they have never been so fit. Nevertheless, a thorough medical checkup is a must before you make a decision.

Leaving society behind

It is very easy, when working toward an ocean cruising project, to begin to convince yourself that you can't wait to leave behind many aspects of society. The average '90s person is quite complex and we all absorb and thrive on facets of modern society that are easy to take for granted when you have them, but can be missed when they're unavailable.

You may not read a daily newspaper avidly or take it particularly seriously, but when you haven't seen one for a few months you begin to realise how much you appreciated it subconsciously. When you've been cruising for a few months you devour and savour every last word in a women's or yachting magazine that you might have flicked through in earlier days. The TV set is symbolically something many people long to escape from, although in reality they can easily enough do so by simply not having one in the house - but rarely do you find them doing this...

Cinema, libraries, the local pub, art galleries, evening classes, browsing through bookshops, car boot sales, dressing up for special social functions, window-shopping, craft fairs and even fish and chips are just a few examples of the fabric of modern life that one all but abandons when going off cruising. Don't assume you won't miss it.

The litmus cruise

After years of dreaming about warm tradewinds, freedom, and living away from the ratrace, you may still hesitate at the finality of giving everything up, or your partner, husband, wife or children may have grave doubts. The ideal solution is a 'litmus cruise' where you spend a year away but keep the home fires burning in your absence. It is often said that if God created the West Indies, he must have been a sailor – a 450-mile string of islands running north-south served by a reliable Force 4 easterly tradewind has to be near perfection. However, he also created the surroundings for a perfect mini-ocean cruise for all aspiring ocean voyagers living in Europe or America – the Atlantic circuit.

To take a year off is not always easy to arrange, but with the relaxation of job formalities these days, or perhaps in periods of recession, an employer may regard it a convenient economy. A mid-life change of career, perhaps accompanied by a redundancy compensation, is also much more common and may provide an opportunity to try out the cruising life for a year before picking up the threads of normal life again, without having burned your boats entirely. In these circumstances you have very little to lose by making an Atlantic circuit litmus cruise.

The Atlantic circuit litmus cruise offers an ideal way to get a taste of tropic sailing and the lifestyle before committing yourself and your boat for a long period

In simple terms, the winds and currents of the North Atlantic flow in a constant broad, circular, clockwise direction. The westerly wind prevails across its top edge as the Gulf Stream pushes its way from America across to Europe, and off the coasts of the Iberian peninsula blows the so-called 'Portuguese trades', fairly reliable north-westerly winds with an offshoot of the Gulf Stream flowing southwards. Down towards the latitude of Madeira and the Canaries blows the first vestiges of the famous north-easterly tradewinds as the current starts to build in a southwesterly and then westerly direction, aided the further one goes south by the increasingly constant tradewind. This wind and current continue on to the West Indies. Between the West Indies and Bermuda are the horse latitudes, where the wind doesn't really have any particular characteristics, but once north of Bermuda one can pick up the westerlies and Gulf Stream again.

This makes a very convenient circuit for the yachtsman to sail from the English Channel down to Spain and Portugal, the Canaries, West Indies and then back via Bermuda and the Azores. Not only this, but on the basis of a one-year schedule he follows the correct seasons all the way round and has just about the right amount of time in each of the very different cruising grounds it takes him through. Leaving during the English summer, the first test is the Bay of Biscay, a passage which can be as pleasant and placid as often as it is vicious and dangerous. The carrot at the end of this trip is the fabulous cruising and scenery in the beautiful mountainous rias of northwest Spain. A few weeks can be spent exploring here before heading south through the unspoilt fishing ports of Portugal and striking out for Madeira or the Canaries. Most transatlantic yachts gather in the dry and touristy Canary Islands until late October/early November, by which time the tradewinds are usually beginning to establish themselves. While the Canaries-West Indies run has been dubbed 'the milk run' in the past, it can nevertheless be quite a taxing 2,700 mile voyage. The blasé few describe it as 'setting the twin jibs and self-steering, then sunbathing and book-reading till Barbados comes over the horizon ahead' but it can at times be frustrating for lack of wind (particularly early in the winter) or, conversely, be a wild roller-coaster of a ride downwind with the crew very happy to stop at the other side.

Some people prefer to sample a Christmas spent at sea, but otherwise there are always a series of parties on the congregating yachts in the principal West Indian anchorages which make up for a Christmas away from home and family. One has between December and the end of April to cruise the Caribbean chain of islands and archipelagos before heading north again on your passage homewards. Many yachts stop in Bermuda, itself a lovely place on the route, whilst others prefer to press on directly to the Azores. One can easily spend a month or two in these superb islands before the beginning of August, a prudent time to consider the final 1,200-mile leg back to the English Channel.

The 'Atlantic Circuit' litmus cruise takes around a year to complete and its beauty is the fact that it gives a good all-round idea of what ocean cruising is likely to be like. There's a good chance of heavy weather on the early and late passages but you also sample tradewinds, tropical heat, the calms of the Sargasso Sea and the occasional frustrations of Biscay. A year is quite enough to decide whether or not you would be happy about the life on a more permanent basis. A lot of yachtsmen find that it fulfils their urge to make long passages, while for others it only fuels their thirst for more.

The other major advantage of an Atlantic Circuit litmus cruise is the ability to gauge what you really require in an ocean cruising boat. The best boat to make the cruise in is a standard production boat at the upper end of the quality scale, which you buy (or maybe already own?) on the basis that she will be resold at the end of the voyage. A popular production boat like a Westerly, Rival or Nicholson is usually a good bet in resale terms and, what is more, one doesn't need to make huge changes (and therefore spend a lot of money you won't recoup on resale) to such a boat to make an Atlantic Circuit cruise. A thorough overhaul and refit, and probably a re-appraisal of the sail wardrobe combined with the addition of a self-steering gear, and a collection of spares (most of which you can take with you to the next boat) will, in many cases, be all that is required to take such a boat long distances.

This boat won't necessarily be your eventual ocean cruiser, but she will be a vital yardstick when it comes to deciding what for you constitutes the best boat. If you're very lucky it could be she is broadly right and only needs slight modifications and additions to be suitable for the big cruise. What is more likely is that you will discover that your next boat needs berths to be a little wider, doesn't need as big an engine, the cockpit must be more comfortable and you need a bit more accessible stowage and perhaps a shower. The list is endless (and make sure you compile it as you approach the English Channel on the final leg) but a highly important ingredient to the success of the big project – assuming you still want to carry that through.

The litmus cruise has dozens of advantages, especially for those who have twinges of doubt (or plain fear!) about many aspects of the ocean cruising lifestyle. For the businessman, it gives him the ability to see if his company can function without him, and it will teach the householder some of the ins and outs of leaving the home behind. Finally, the best thing about the idea of an Atlantic Circuit litmus cruise is that learning has never been so much fun . . .

4. The Efficient Ocean Cruiser

The process of designing, building or buying a yacht (in most cases the future ocean cruising yachtsman is confronted by a blend of all three) is a fascinating but at times frustrating juggle of hundreds of requirements and features, balancing one against the other, which must always result in a compromise of sorts. We are no closer to the perfect boat than we are to perpetual motion and the sooner the yachtsman realises this, the quicker he'll reach the goal of organising the best boat for his purposes.

The choice of a new or secondhand long-distance cruising yacht is normally determined by her principal design features; size, mono or multihull, keel configuration, construction, deck layout, self-steering qualities, rig and accommodation plan. However, having found a boat with the major points you want, it's very easy to fall into the trap of disregarding as trivial a number of other details which, in sum, could lead to the boat being as unsuitable as if you'd bought a junk schooner when you really wanted a bermudian sloop.

This is when the Atlantic circuit litmus cruise pays huge dividends in terms of preparation for the 'big off'. The key to shrewd choice of an ocean cruiser lies in appreciating and anticipating what she will have to achieve over and above the straightforward weekend and holiday cruising boat. Obviously, the difference between the two is chiefly the extent to which they are used. This can be broken into two broad divisions which, allowed for and understood, should improve the quality of your choice.

The first relates to the everyday functions and routines of living aboard. Daily living and sailing has got to be smooth, easy and efficient. While ultimate seaworthiness is important, this shouldn't interfere with the in-port suitability and comfort. Even the most active ocean cruisers spend an average of five days in port for every one at sea. Even when they're at sea, assuming they're not sailing to the Poles or circumnavigating south of the Great Capes, the proportion of time they spend in weather that justifies tiny or non-existent ports, tight squeeze-through companionways, back-breakingly heavy gear or decked-over cockpits simply doesn't warrant the discomfort and inconvenience these features cause the rest of the time. In this way the sturdiest Colin Archer, traditionally thought of as a long-distance boat, can be the worst possible ocean cruiser. Therefore the balance between ultimate seaworthiness, comfort and efficiency has to be weighed carefully in the light of your intended cruising parameters.

Consider what you will be doing each day, from getting up in the morning and washing to decanting water containers into the tanks, cooking, reading, navigating, writing letters, and then imagine yourself those things in your chosen boat. That neat little washbasin in the heads looked fine in the brochure, but you probably weren't aware that you have to crouch under the sidedeck with legs twisted around the toilet to try to shave over it. The saloon table might have an uncomfortably high fiddle round it, which makes letter writing difficult, or the largest galley locker may be directly behind the cooker, so the cook risks being burned reaching it.

Details that we can all put up with in an ordinary cruising boat, like underbunk water fillers, fiddly locker catches and gas-bottle turn off switches situated just beyond arm's reach, will soon drive an otherwise content and happy crew member crazy. It's surprising how, when living aboard, simple omissions like a convenient place to put a rubbish bin in the galley can be a continual, if petty, irritant.

The second major consideration of continual use of a vessel is related to maintenance. An ocean cruiser needs a lot of work and attention paid to her to keep in trim. Checks and maintenance are a normal and vital part of a cruising lifestyle and the routine needs keeping up not only for the sake of the ship, but for your own temper. Excuse the dreadful adulteration of the proverb, but procrastination is the thief of efficiency. If something is easy to do, you'll do it. If it's difficult or awkward you'll put it off until perhaps it's too late.

Of the many criteria to be checking a potential boat for, one of the highest on the priority list should be this element of ease and therefore efficiency. A battery hidden in the darkest corner of the engine compartment will be a constant annoyance for the person who has to check the acid levels or take hydrometer readings, so they will

Design features like this, an anchor which fouls the roller gear when it's being lowered and raised, will quickly drive you insane. In choosing a boat, spend time checking the layout of her normal working systems

probably do the job less often. The same goes for the engine dipstick, the accessibility of the water tanks for cleaning, the layout of the ground tackle (if it's difficult to get the anchor up you'll take a risk and stay where you are rather than move to shelter), and even the reefing arrangements. A simple winch that is easy to dismantle will get greased far more regularly than one whose springs and pawls fly in all directions the moment the drum is released.

It is easy to see how the maintenance factor is multiplied by the constant usage when you consider that the heads unit which is used once or twice every other weekend on an ordinary cruiser usually works for years without giving trouble or showing signs of wear, but one used every day of the year by two or three crew will need attention and replacements regularly. If you choose a boat whose heads and attendant machinery and plumbing are artistically concealed between interlocking GRP mouldings or joinery it will probably take longer to dismantle the toilet compartment than it will to replace the work-worn gasket. Ask anyone who owns a boat with numerous or even one-piece interior mouldings if they've ever tried to track down a wiring short-circuit!

When you are looking over that potential ocean cruiser, inspect her equipment, fittings and machinery with an eye to having to work on them offshore or, just as bad, in a place where spare parts and chandlers are unheard of. Will that smart and sophisticated dual switchover double-action bilge pump take your improvised rubber plunger, scissor-hewn from an old sailing boot? Will a locker of tools, modest supply of sheet copper, rubber, wood, fastenings and sealants, plus a bosun's bag of old adaptable sailing fittings, cover most eventualities? Although over-simplification isn't necessarily a virtue, there's nothing more frustrating than carting around a boat full of superfluous broken gadgets and equipment. My earlier story of the luxury-equipped yacht with inoperative electric water pumps and no other way of getting at her full tanks is a typical example.

Many boats these days are built to the throwaway ball-point pen concept. With features like glassed-over keelbolts and all deck fitting fastenings concealed under a permanently sealed deckhead liner, they are impossible to inspect and maintain, and if something does go wrong, butchery is required to get at it. Look at the design of your boat's hull and deck joint (if she's GRP). Consider if, after many thousands of ocean miles combined with tropical heat, it might leak. Would it be possible for you to trace the leak and repair it?

There are a number of other points which, in a normal yacht, are useful features, but have no place in ocean cruisers. A good example is the trend by some builders (particularly those in the Far East) to mould imitation planking seams into GRP hulls. This undoubtedly gives a certain character to a bland GRP hull, but it is very difficult to clean thick harbour oil from it and virtually impossible to match evenly if the hull has to be repaired.

Apart from the wear of full-time use ocean cruisers are also subject to a higher rate of damage. We have found that 90 per cent of this is caused by other craft and people, usually in circumstances over which you have little or no control. Every boat in its lifetime can expect the occasional quayside knock or brush with another boat, but this is a rare occurence if it is kept in a marina week in, week out. An ocean cruiser visiting a host of different ports and anchorages doesn't have this home-base security and is vulnerable to any number of dangers. Several of our boats have been damaged over the years and we don't know of many others which haven't suffered to a greater or

Efficiency is multi-faceted and a feature such as ventilated drawers will make life that much more pleasant in a hot and humid climate

lesser degree. Consequently, the 'maintainability' of gunwales, stanchions, rails and other appendages is imperative. Look at your chosen boat and make sure stanchion bolts aren't all glassed over, or if the pulpit gets torn off it won't take the foredeck with it.

It is better to have a boat whose hull you can repair anywhere in the world. Steel, wood and ferro and to a lesser extent GRP can be repaired almost anywhere, but damaged aluminium is both difficult and expensive to weld in most places. Exotic materials (including special core materials) and unconventional construction techniques have no place on an ocean cruising yacht. Replacements abroad may be unobtainable or sub-standard and expertise may be lacking.

Finally, Robin Lee-Graham, at the time,the youngest-ever circumnavigator and inspiration for hundreds of ocean cruising yachtsmen, once said going cruising was a matter of learning how little you needed, not how much. There's a great deal in this philosophy. The majority of new ocean cruising yachtsmen are guilty of taking everything with them down to the kitchen sink, their boats way down on their marks, lockers stuffed and decks cluttered with gear they'll hardly ever use. Try not to fall into the same trap and learn from the experienced men who often carry little but the bare essentials of living.

The life of the average ocean cruising boat is one full of variety. One month she may be put through the punishment of thrashing to windward for days or even weeks on end. The next month she could be nestled like an egg in a sack of potatoes in a commercial ship harbour, while the next she may be floating in transparent suspension tied to the palms of a deserted lagoon. All the time she is working, moving, functioning. She must be a smooth-running home, and an efficient workhorse, at the same time as being capable of weathering any storm. To select the basic design features of your ocean cruiser is obviously very important indeed. However, it is the easy part and probably only constitutes 20 per cent of the total process. It is the other 80 per cent, which is so easy to overlook, that leads to a suitable and therefore successful ocean cruiser.

5. Construction Materials

The choice of construction material for your ocean cruiser can be a perplexing one. Very often it is decided for you when a boat which is suitable in most other respects turns up. Nowadays, with excellent coatings to prevent rust and taking the difficulty of insuring against damage into consideration, steel takes a lot of beating as a material for long-distance yachts. This is especially so if you are prepared to build or have one built, but buying secondhand in steel can be quite dicy. Other construction materials – GRP, wood, aluminium and ferrocement – have their different advantages and disadvantages.

The ocean cruising yachtsman's priorities are first strength, then maintainability and durability. Cost is an inevitable parameter, and the yacht must also be capable of being repaired comparatively easily anywhere in the world.

The strength of a yacht takes a much bigger testing in ports, anchorages and near the shore than ever it does in the open sea in gale conditions. Most properly rigged modern yachts can easily stand up to wild weather at sea. The real strength is needed in withstanding running on a reef, a severe grounding entering a shallow port, or damage caused by other craft dragging on to you. It is for this reason that heavy-displacement yachts have often been favoured for long-distance sailing. It is more realistic to bear such hazards in mind than the ravages that a gale at sea can inflict on a yacht. In proportion to the numbers of ocean cruising yachts serious mishaps are not that common, but accidents will happen and any experienced ocean cruising yachtsman knows of half a dozen friends who've either lost their boats or come very close to it. For that reason, even if it seems a rather pessimistic outlook, each material is now examined in the context of extreme circumstances.

GRP

Glass reinforced plastic turned the yachtbuilding world on its head within a few short years in the '60s and '70s. Its construction and maintenance advantages are too well known to need repetition here. From an ocean cruising point of view the suitability of GRP is unquestioned, and illustrated by the fact that approximately six out of ten of all ocean cruisers are built with it.

GRP construction has, inevitably, changed over the years as the technology and experience have developed. Early glassfibre boats, those built until around 1970-72, were often massively constructed (for example, the early Nicholson 32s were fully framed as well as stringered), because no one was quite certain how strong they needed to be and the oil-based resins were then cheap. Naturally enough, boats from this era have proved very durable, and as long as other features are right, their construction makes them very suitable for ocean cruising. The mid-'70s oil crisis changed things and as oil prices rocketed, so GRP scantlings came down to a more realistic standard.

For a weekend cruising boat, GRP's lack of maintenance is absolutely ideal, but strange as it may seem, this can be a problem for the long distance cruising boat. She will be taking many knocks, bumps and scrapes that can be difficult to repair cosmetically. A wild and windy night moored alongside a little fisherman's stone quay in the Azores with a raft of boats moored outside you can leave permanent scars on a GRP boat's beautiful topsides. Though it may seem a chore that wood or steel needs complete repainting from time to time, the result seems to be a generally better turned-out boat.

The maintenance of our GRP Rival 34 became a worry after a while because in many ways she was too nice to take into places where we knew she would emerge covered in thick oil which for months afterwards left an immovable yellow stain, or where we knew the harbour was busy and we might receive a bump. The hazards might be minor but they are numerous. In the West Indies for example 'boat boys' come alongside selling their wares. Their dinghies are heavy, wooden and the fenderless capping rail has often long since broken off, leaving the nails sticking out. You generally know of their arrival by the bump as they come alongside... It broke our hearts to let the yacht deteriorate, so in the end we avoided the risky (and likely as not, more interesting and deserted) places and became slaves to keeping the boat looking nice. It changed the character of our cruising lifestyle and we learned a valuable lesson – that unless you can come to terms with the shine and corners being rubbed off your newish or immaculate boat, it is better to invest in a rather older, tattier craft.

One of GRP's huge advantages over wood is its immunity to rot and marine borers like teredo worm. However, osmosis is more prevalent in warm tropic waters, so if you're scanning the secondhand market, a boat which has been appropriately treated and protected definitely scores highly. If you're starting with a new boat, make sure she is coated with two-part epoxy before she even leaves the building shed. For several years there was much unjustified scare-mongering about osmosis and now it seems that yachtsmen have come to terms with the fact that it is not a serious problem if nipped in the bud. All the same, it is something to be avoided by preventative maintenance. Not only can it be an unplanned drain on financial resources, but if discovered while slipped in some far-off location, the chances of finding suitable products to rectify it are slim indeed. Procrastinating about its treatment could be a very expensive mistake.

If you're looking at GRP boats, avoid those with dark-coloured gelcoats. Not only do they show up every scratch and knock but in warm climates the dark colours fade and chalk, so repainting will be required that much sooner. A dark colour also absorbs heat so the cabin temperatures will be higher.

GRP sandwich construction has enjoyed much success over the years, especially where a high strength:weight ratio is necessary (ie in light displacement craft and multihulls). If you hit a harbour wall its impact resistance is very good indeed and it is very stiff. However, having such thin GRP skins on each side of the core material, its abrasion resistance is not nearly as good as conventional laminated GRP and this puts its suitability for long-distance cruising into question. Were you to ground on a coral reef the boat could quickly be quite badly damaged or even lost. If the boat were damaged and repairs attempted in a distant location, finding a suitable core material such as sheet end-grain balsa or Airex foam would be almost impossible.

Timber

Until a few years ago everyone thought timber was on the way out as a boatbuilding material. Most of us still enjoy the aesthetic pleasure of a wooden boat, but the lack of suitable seasoned timber and the many advantages of modern materials combined to eclipse them. However, the development of modern epoxy resins and techniques such as the Gougeon Brothers' Wood Epoxy Saturation Technique (WEST) has given timber a new lease of life and makes it a very strong and light method of construction for custom boatbuilding. As well as its strength, the WEST-built yacht has the advantage of being impervious to both rot and osmosis.

Although traditional wood construction has many good advantages such as the ability to be repaired almost anywhere, it also has drawbacks, of which one is often the initial cost compared to alternative materials. Susceptibility to rot is another, and good protection against wood borers is vital for wooden hulls in warm waters. A protection system can be used but it is important to make sure it isn't breached by nudging a coral head or going aground. Copper sheathing is a traditional protection which blunts teredo teeth and also acts as an antifoulant for much of its life. This is a major expense, although if you plan to keep the boat for a long time, the costings work out well in the long run.

Fibreglass or Cascover sheathing is only a long-term success if it is applied when the boat is new, or when she has been hauled out long enough to be tinder-dry. Thereafter it is an effective protection for five to ten years, before it tends to blister and lift off. It then becomes a regular maintenance routine to grind the affected areas off and re-fibreglass over them.

A good barrier of antifouling paint has worked to deter borers on countless wooden yachts but it is taking quite a gamble and teredo will quite often get a hold in the crevices round the rudder trunking, the base of the keel or deadwood, where the antifoul hasn't reached. It is essential that a wooden boat is hauled out at least twice a year to be checked over and re-antifouled. As hauling out isn't cheap and you can rarely do an adequate job by careening, the price advantages of having a wooden boat become eroded the longer you cruise and always lingering in the background is the possibility of uncovering rot or worm.

In a situation where a yacht goes ashore or is badly stranded, all things being equal wood will deteriorate and the yacht break up faster than GRP, ferro or metal. And of course the longer a boat remains intact the more time you have to leave it safely, or to do something about saving it.

There will always be those for whom the appeal of a wooden vessel is strong. If you are one of their number you should be aware that there are considerably better materials for the hull of an ocean cruising boat before you reach a decision.

Ferrocement

Coming on the scene in a big way in the late '60s and early '70s, ferro was regarded by many as something of a wonder material. Not only did it lend itself to custom designs but it was comparatively simple for the inexperienced boatbuilder to construct, and above all a very cheap way to build a hull and deck. The resulting construction, properly executed, created a very strong hull that was durable, impervious to rot, rust, borers and osmosis.

It all seemed too good to be true and the '70s saw hundreds of hulls being built in back gardens and yards around the country as dreams to sail off around the world were spawned. In a way, ferro's inexpensiveness and simplicity killed it because for every smooth and sound hull produced there were three dippy and bumpy ones, badly faired and plastered, that had been built by complete novices. Then came the more serious problem that tripped up so many builders. Because of its weight (and the early ones were very heavy, with inexperienced builders ladling on the cement) ferro lent itself to boats of 35ft and over. You could build an enormous hull unbelievably cheaply and many people did, dreaming that they could earn their living from chartering their 50 or 60-footer when they got to the South Pacific. The hull might have been cheap but all the other elements of fitting out cost no less, and big boats need a lot of proportionally expensive fitments, from big engines to big spars and big sails. In another section I argue the case for fitting out simply, but to a high standard, a slightly bigger boat than you might otherwise build or buy. That can work as long as you have a reasonable amount of capital to start with and the boat isn't too big. Many inexperienced ferro builders mistakenly thought that once the hull was done, most of the work and

Although ferrocement is an excellent material for hulls if they are built well, commerically it still suffers the stigma of many failed projects

spending was over. Dozens of dreams went sour, and a lot of bare hulls, many built badly, went on the market. This flood had the effect of bringing prices down sharply. Others were finished, but they looked terrible, and the overall result was that ferro got itself a bad name, despite the fact there were many good examples around. A stigma built up around ferro boats and even well-finished ones were not that easy to sell and prices were generally low. You may need to keep the eventual re-sale value of your ocean cruising yacht in mind so it is important to be aware of this history of ferrocement, regardless of the merits of the material.

Nowadays, very few new boats are built in ferrocement because of the commercial implications of their resale value. This doesn't detract from the fact that there are some excellent ferrocement boats afloat and their market price is usually lower than similar-sized boats built in another material. Well-built ferro, and I should emphasise that it must be well-built and finished, has many merits for long-distance cruisers. As I have said, it is strong, durable and doesn't rot, or rust, or get eaten by borers or infected with osmotic blistering. As experience of using ferro progressed, hulls became steadily lighter and many medium-displacement designs were built and even raced with some success, such as the Hartley RORC 39.

The adhesion of paint systems can be a problem with ferro boats. For many years one regularly saw them shedding their paint in sheets. Like steel, it is necessary to shotblast and use modern epoxy paint systems (especially tar-epoxy) to resolve the problem. Ferrocement is otherwise a very low-maintenance material and one need only really think about cosmetics. Any chips knocked off through a graze with a quay are easily filled, sanded and overpainted.

Another minus point against ferro construction is the difficulty of dragging them off reefs in a stranding. If the yacht has pounded for any length of time and the cement has been pulverised out of the framing and mesh, the friction created by this exposed steelwork makes towing off very difficult indeed and many boats, far from mortally damaged, have had to be abandoned for this reason.

If you consider ferro you stand a good chance of getting a slightly larger boat for the available money and one with few problems, but balance this with the knowledge that in Europe ferro boats are notoriously difficult to sell and in America they are almost impossible. In Australia the attitude is different. Their resale value is good and they change hands quickly, although for the foreigner selling an alien boat there are enormous importation fees.

Aluminium

Aluminium is regarded by some as being the very best building material for ocean cruising boats. It is about 65 percent as strong as steel but is only one third as heavy. It also has the great advantage that it doesn't rust, although being low on the galvanic scale it is subject to corrosion with dissimilar metals. You have to avoid, for example, mooring for any length of time alongside a steel boat or pilings without hanging plenty of zincs in the water around the boat.

The owner of an aluminium yacht must also be very, very careful of electrolysis. Stupid errors can be disastrous, as was demonstrated by the owner of a 28ft British production-built aluminium sloop in the '70s. Hoping to save himself some money, he had taken delivery and chose to do the commissioning of the yacht himself. A few

This 30ft aluminium sloop went ashore in the Azores. Although she took a terrible pounding that would have obliterated wood, ferro or GRP construction, ultimately the aluminium split and holed. On a steel boat that is much less likely to happen

months after launching he was disappointed when he discovered she was leaking. He had her hauled out and traced the leak to a small pinprick, but was also horrified to discover that all the underwater hull plating was paper thin and that the leak was the first of hundreds about to happen. The problem was quickly diagnosed. He had antifouled the yacht with some cheap, unlabelled paint which had turned out to be a strong copper-based antifouling. There was a similar apocryphal story about the crew member who lost his small change out of his trouser pockets into the bilge when getting undressed one night. Although he pulled up the floorboards and found most of it, the odd pennies he couldn't find quickly ate their way through the bilge plating.

In terms of raw material costs aluminium is expensive, at between 10-15 times the price of steel. However, it should be remembered that when a labour-intensive metal hull is built for you in a shipyard, raw materials rarely constitute more than 25 per cent of the price. Added to this, the actual hull and deck of a boat is only between 10-45 per cent of the total outlay, dependent on the standard of finish and equipping. So in these terms, an aluminium boat needn't be exceptionally expensive. In comparison to steel, which can be repaired in the most remote outpost, the welding of aluminium is a headache in many areas, although MIG welding equipment is gradually becoming more common in major centres.

French yachtsmen are particularly keen on aluminium and very often they don't paint the exterior but leave it bare. This might not be to everyone's taste, but on this basis it has to be the lowest-maintenance material of all, including fibreglass which requires regular cleaning, polishing and, after a while, repainting or spraying.

When compared to wood, fibreglass and ferro, aluminium is amazingly strong if one is unfortunate enough to run into a reef or get stranded on a shore. It will take an incredible pounding, but it can split and hole, which steel is unlikely to do. The photograph on the facing page shows an aluminium boat we saw in the Azores which had run on to a rocky foreshore on the island of Faial. Fortunately her crew of five (none of whom had been on watch) had got ashore unscathed, and the yacht was later salvaged to be stripped of her gear. A wooden boat would have been matchwood in no time and a fibreglass yacht ground to pulp. However, the sight of those splits and tears in the hull were enough to tip my opinion in favour of steel as the best compromise material for long distance yachts.

Steel

There is a steadily increasing trend for ocean cruisers to use this material and many skippers who go on to commission or build a second cruising boat choose steel – a telling statistic.

One of the more bizarre sights I've seen while ocean cruising was a French steel sloop lying in St Barts in the French West Indies. She had a massive V-shaped indent

Steel is a fine material for ocean cruising hulls, but the quality of finish is all-important if rust is not to be a recurring problem

in her topsides and deck amidships which extended about 3ft (1m) inboard from the line of her original gunwale down to the waterline. She had been run down by a ship and survived it. Her owners didn't have enough money to have the repairs done, so until they'd saved enough they were continuing to cruise in her.

One of the reasons more people are turning to steel is the increasing difficulty of getting insurance for ocean voyaging, not to mention unreasonable premiums and restrictions. Steel's proven strength and durability is comforting for the uninsured yachtsman because there are dozens of accounts of steel boats going ashore and proving almost indestructible. A good proportion are hauled off and live to sail again.

Steel is well suited for amateur fitting out because once the hull and deck structure are finished the interior joinery and bulkheads don't contribute to its strength. Unlike fibreglass, where the integrity of bulkheads and certain interior furniture is paramount, the worst an amateur can do is create a bad joinery finish. The hull itself is a different matter. Experienced welding techniques and correct welding sequences are essential to avoid unbalanced stresses being set up and the plating overheated, which results in it being stretched over the framing and giving a 'hungry dog' look. A steel hull can be built by the amateur and be very strong but unless filler is used, the skills required to produce a fair hull only come after much experience.

For many years the two major disadvantages of steel were rusting and weight. Of course it weighs the same today, but whereas once upon a time hulls had to be built with a reasonable thickness to give longevity against rust, now that the rust can be avoided (with good design and, more particularly, modern epoxy finishes) thinner scantlings can be used, so both disadvantages are significantly diminished in modern hulls. While modern steel-hulled yachts don't have to be of especially heavy displacement as once was the case, it is nevertheless very difficult, on yachts less than 45 feet, to build to a design that is much less than moderate in displacement.

Rust nearly always attacks from the inside, so it is imperative that the interior treatment is the very best from the beginning. Once all the wiring, plumbing, insulation, and domestic fit-out is added, the interior of the hull is unlikely ever to be properly prepared and painted again. Mistakes can be made with the exterior and, although expensive, it is quite possible to grit blast and re-coat, but not so with the inside. Again, modern insulation materials largely eliminate sweating in the hull, which can be a problem in colder climates. It has probably been written a thousand times (and ignored almost as often) but it is vital that all areas of the hull are accessible for wire-brushing and proper painting. It should also be entirely self-draining so water can never collect. If an area, perhaps only one frame, is difficult to paint properly, the chances are that it will not receive adequate treatment and the inevitable result will be rust. Therefore the interior design in this respect is just as important as the general design of the yacht. An experienced steel boat owner will be able to point out dozens of bad points to you, particularly in older yachts. A feature like an angle-capped toerail with wooden capping is not only going to be a problem if moisture ever gets between the wood and steel, but also trying to chip, wire-brush and paint effectively on the underside of that capping piece will be difficult.

In terms of maintenance, the modern steel ocean cruising yacht does not fare well against other materials and an older steel boat comes far and away at the bottom of the list and is a constant maintenance problem. The name of the game is keeping the paint on the steel, and this is achieved in three ways. First, water must never be allowed to collect, or preferably even linger, where there is painted steel. If possible, no external surface on a steel boat should be horizontal or nearly so, as water will remain here and seek out any flaws in the paint, ultimately undermining it. Second, good design will avoid any sharp corners or edges that do not hold paint well. At construction stage, it will pay to look very closely at where radius can be used (either by employing rod, pipe or simply grinding off a curve) to help the paint stay intact. Third, certain areas of a boat will receive hard treatment and more than a normal amount of knocks or abrasion. The most obvious are the cleats and fairleads, but there are plenty more, like the edges of the forehatch where sailbags are dragged in and out or the perimeter of the transom that gets a regular knock from the dinghy. Ideally, these should be capped with stainless steel. Even with these precautions, the cosmetic maintenance of a steel boat will be a constant occupation (some say thorn in the side) of the long-distance cruising yachtsman.

If you've ever been aboard a yacht at sea during an electrical storm, you know the feeling of vulnerability of your mast being the only high metal object (ie lightning conductor) for miles around. Lightning strikes are far from uncommon. A minor one can wreck the yacht's electrics and electronics, a major one can easily start a fire and has been known to shatter topsides between chainplate and waterline to the extent that the yacht has foundered. Because it is the perfect conductor and due to the Faraday's Cage effect, a steel yacht is immune from serious damage during even bad lightning strikes. This has to be a major advantage in steel's favour.

Another point in its favour is the ability to repair, alter or modify it almost anywhere in the world, because even the tiniest inhabited islands have a welding kit somewhere.

It would be foolhardy to assume that steel is an ideal material, because it is not – it only lends itself to certain designs, and care and attention to detail of the original design and steelwork will reflect heavily on its subsequent maintenance and lifespan. Also against it is the fact that its maintenance-intensive characteristics make it less than desirable for the normal yachting market, so there are few production steel boats to choose from. As a result, when buying you will nearly always be looking at a custom boat and the two extreme tendencies are highly expensive and individual custom yachts at one end, or cheap home-builts at the other. Hopefully there is a happy medium, but the choice is quite limited if you have clear ideas on what you want to buy.

6. The Hull

The right size

When we talk of boat size, we always consider LOA, length overall. Beware of this, partly because builders can be blatantly dishonest about the true LOA of their designs, but also because subsequent owners of less well-known designs can round the LOA up a foot when it comes to putting the boat on the market. A friend of mine bought what he thought to be (and the yacht agency's particulars described as) a 43-footer, which actually turned out to be 37ft 3in when a tape was put over her. There are also some 33-footers which are very much more comfortable, by dint of subtle beam and freeboard, than the narrowish 38-footer that initially sounds so much more suitable.

It is quite incorrect to assume that the size of the boat in which you plan to sail away will be in direct proportion to the extent of your finances. When a boat-buying budget is depressingly tight this may seem to be the case, but scratching below the surface, you'll find it isn't the only influencing factor to choosing size.

The clearest way to assess what is about the right size for you is to briefly imagine yourself in the highly desirable (and unfortunately rare) situation of having, within reason, unlimited funds to purchase the yacht. Don't let your imagination run away with the idea that, once the boat is ready to go, you will have any more money than you presently budget for cruising costs. Just stick at assuming you have enough money to buy and equip the boat. This will enable you to assess what would be ideal as a basis to work towards.

The number of permanent crew aboard is the principal influence. If they are a growing family, this gradual expansion is another factor to take into account. Alternatively, if they are teenagers about to leave the nest, you don't want to be left with a large and unmanageable yacht in their absence.

Much depends too on your outlook to the sailing lifestyle. This is underlined by a simple maxim in the cruising world – smaller ocean cruising boats are sailed much more frequently than bigger yachts that are more complicated and more trouble to get under way. If you are an adventurous type who wants to explore every last little bay and islet in an archipelago and take your boat up close to the reefs to dive on them, beware of setting your sights on a biggish yacht.

Larger yachts will be considerably more time-consuming to maintain. They generally have more sophisticated equipment and this too will have a snowballing effect as her crew spend more time servicing or fixing items like the water pressure system or the electric windlass. Sewing a ripped mainsail is a major job on a 48-footer, but relatively quick on a 33-footer. Sophistication also needs feeding from time to time with specialist spare parts, many of which the prudent yachtsman will carry but some of which he will not. Waiting in port for spares to arrive can spoil your pleasure no end.

Having spent two years skippering a 56-footer I was desperate to get into a small, simple boat again, and I was fortunate enough not to have been picking up the bills. Simple things like cleaning round the waterline or scrubbing the decks take so much longer. Keeping the topsides reasonably clean and occasionally polished seemed like a Forth Bridge operation (as soon as you've finished at one end, it's time to begin again at the other). I remember an occasion early one morning (before the sun became too hot) revarnishing the deckwork teak. Friends on a nearby 34-footer had been doing theirs too and we were commiserating. They had finished all theirs, taken a bus to see the nearby volcano and later gone off for a swim and windsurfing session before I'd wielded the last brushstroke.

What might also prevent you getting the most out of your cruising is physically getting a largish boat under way for a short passage, maybe out to a reef or a nearby coral atoll. With her capacious accommodation there is a lot more work involved in making her shipshape – more hatches and ports to close tight, more items to put away

Very nearly an ideal mainstream cruiser for two people, with a good turn of speed, exceptionally spacious accommodation, easily-handled rig and production-built by a reputable builder

in safe places. The awning is not only a fairly big job to get down, but it then has to be folded up and put away (not to mention re-setting when you get to the next anchorage a few miles further on). Getting all the sail covers on and off is time-consuming and rarely much fun. Larger boats generally have bigger dinghies which usually need more powerful and heavier outboards, so that lot will have to be lifted up on deck and lashed down. A bigger boat might well have an electric windlass, which makes raising the anchor easier (assuming the windlass is working and not waiting for a new solenoid to be sent out from home), but if that anchor hauls up a load of mud and weed (and big anchors hold a lot), it's going to need more than one or two swilled bucketfuls of water to clear it as that muck makes its way back aft, clogging up around the stanchion fittings. I am deliberately exaggerating to illustrate the point that there are drawbacks to large boats even if you can afford them. If you and your wife are ocean cruising to get away from hard work and don't have extra crew, you'll be jumping out of the frying pan and into the fire if you look at boats over 45ft (13.71m). With a crew of two or three willing teenagers (and they must be willing) it's a different matter altogether and a larger boat will give you some privacy.

We had an experience recently which taught me a great deal about the right size of boat. At a time when improvements in sail-handling aids are instrumental in per-suading people to buy larger and therefore more comfortable boats, we were very glad not to have too large a boat. A storm in a small harbour in the Canary Islands convinced me I would never want a boat bigger than 40ft. Although in most conditions it is quite possible for a couple to handle a bigger boat, during bad weather in harbour when berths or anchorages have to be changed, it can be a different matter. In those con-ditions, weaker crew simply weren't able to push the boat off to squeeze a fender in, lines were heavily loaded and anchors too weighty to be easily run out in a dinghy. I watched people on large boats realise that their inability to control its mass and windage in bad conditions could lose them their boat because they were being unable to safely move from a dangerous or exposed position.

The other important element of larger boats is cost of running. Running expenses do not rise in proportion to size – a 43-footer doesn't cost 20% more to run than a 36-footer because she is 20% longer (any more than she costs 20% extra to purchase ini-tially). Remember that a medium-sized boat (say 36ft) does exactly the same job as the 43-footer – they are probably equally seaworthy and equally capable of supporting a cruising lifestyle. When the two are motoring along a windless coastline together each doing five knots, the larger will not only be using 50-75% more fuel, but when her engine service period comes up she will probably require half as much oil again, and larger, more expensive filters. Yet they will both arrive at the same time at the same place. The only real difference is the interior volume and stowage capabilities of the larger and marginally more speed under sail, but you will pay a high price for these advantages so be sure you really want or need them.

In the last fifteen years, since ocean cruising has become so much more popular, the trend in the size of short-handed (two or three crew) long distance yachts has been concentrated in the 35-40ft (10.6-12m) bracket, though three or four feet either side of this is common also. There are also hundreds of smaller boats, less than 30ft (9.15m), crossing the oceans these days. Other than financial considerations, there are few real advantages to going below 30ft for extended cruising and most owners readily admit they would like something larger if they could afford it. However, a small, well de-signed, well built modern production yacht can be very seaworthy indeed (with good

Beware of spending the best years of your life saving for an ideal boat; a yacht like this Trintella 1, suitably strengthened and modified, is just as capable of long voyages as a boat half as big again, even though you will have to put up with smaller living spaces

hatches and windows they are good examples of the 'well-corked bottle' theory of seaworthiness). They inevitably create certain discomforts and difficulties for their crews; they are easily and invariably overloaded and with short waterline length passage times can be long. All the same, one regularly sees boats like Vertues, Contessa 26s, Folkboats, Vancouver 27s, Twisters, Frances 26s and Great Dane 28s in far flung ports of the world.   At the beginning of this chapter I argued that you don't necessarily have to determine boat size by the extent of your bank account. It is straightforward enough to suggest to a wealthy man that he and his wife might be happier in a sensibly thought-out 40-footer, rather than the luxuriously appointed 55-footer he could afford. However, it is also possible for the skipper with a limited budget looking, let us say, for an oldish Nicholson 32, to afford a more suitable 37-footer if the real needs are considered carefully. The fact is that it is the finish of boats that costs money, further compounded by the goodies added on. Mirror-finished topsides, shiny stainless steel, a big engine, solid and chunky varnished hardwoods and a navigation table surrounded by electronic wizardry are fine for people who can afford them. Frenchman Bernard Moitessier sailed his *Joshua* engineless for the first season whilst he worked her as a sailing school to raise money. His masts were telegraph poles he had hewn into shape and the rigging was rough galvanised steel. Instead of 'yachty' cowl ventilators, he had one quarter of a tyre inner tube fitted on the deck (which was flattened whenever a wave passed over it, thereby stopping the water getting below).

For some people this is too big a sacrifice and they are prepared to work and save for the standards they want before getting away. But if you have a tight budget and are enthusiastic to get going quickly, a yacht that is very simply fitted out is attainable at a very low price if you are prepared to finish and equip her yourself. She may not be perfect, but she'll get you afloat and sailing long distances.

Lou Lou and I started ocean cruising in this way. By selling our London flat we realised we could raise £5,000. In 1979 it seemed like a small fortune. In those days, £5,000 would have bought something like a Folkboat or Contessa 26 but with not much left over for essential equipment and savings to sail with. Although we were universally considered very foolhardy, we put the flat up for sale and it went immediately. I've always been overweight and reckoned that a small boat like a Folkboat, which with modifications is capable of ocean passages, could be a disaster to live on board for me. Instead we bought *Foreigner*, a secondhand Wharram catamaran, which at 35ft x 17ft seemed like a ship in comparison, and inspired by Moitessier refitted her very basically with 'nothing fancy', living aboard in London at the same time.

We learned from our mistakes (and we made plenty) and I'm sure many people laughed at our rather infra dig sailing machine with her rough appearance, but it nevertheless enabled us to be away ocean cruising without any financial help by the time we were 22 years old. Her outboard engine was hopelessly unreliable and expensive to run so for most of the time she was handled under sail and in the end we became quite proficient at it. I always looked forward to the day I could afford a boat with a diesel, but we, like thousands before us, managed quite happily without. After a couple of years' cruising, including an Atlantic crossing and visiting most of the Windward and Leeward Islands, we sold our much-loved *Foreigner* in the West Indies. She had been far from ideal at times, but had got us cruising on the tiniest budget and taught us an enormous amount that we could incorporate in the next boat.

Another ocean sailor, Nick Skeates, lost his *Wylo* on a Pacific reef and arrived in New Zealand a few months later, almost penniless and with only some gear salvaged from the wreck. Within two years he had designed and built the 32ft *Wylo II* from scratch and was off again, subsequently completing a circumnavigation in her. This was in 1979, so prices are a little different, but she was built and equipped complete for less than US$5,000. I met Nick and went on board the yacht in the West Indies and if she didn't have the glitter and finish of a Boat Show exhibit (he boasted that she didn't have a single piece of stainless steel on her), she had nevertheless been sailed halfway around the world.

Ocean cruising folk's second or third boats are invariably more representative and telling than their first, which is exceptionally difficult to get right without experience of your personal requirements. So it is interesting to look at a few well-known ocean cruising yachtsmen's boats and see how they progressed in terms of size.

Eric and Susan Hiscock. I have huge respect for these two because they were prepared to experiment, go along with the times and if necessary change their published ideas in the cause of progression. For many years Hiscock advocated paraffin for cooking and heating but as circumstances changed, paraffin's quality diminished and its availability thinned, he changed to gas (and wrote an article explaining why and how he'd done it) and never looked back. He started ocean cruising in the

24ft (7.31m) *Wanderer II*, and later progressed to the 30ft (9.15m) heavy displacement sloop *Wanderer 111*. He was later to say that she was his favourite, with her simplicity and easy handling, if a little slow. They then decided to sell their Isle of Wight home and made a big step up to the 49ft (14.9m) Jongert ketch *Wanderer IV*. They owned this very comfortable yacht for some 15 years before finally opting for the wooden 39ft (11.8m) *Wanderer V*, which was something of a compromise between *Wanderers III & IV*.

Bernard Moitessier. Progressed from a tubby home-built 28ft (8.53m) ketch to the 39ft (11.8m) *Joshua*, a heavily constructed steel ketch. In her he made some remarkable passages (including twice around Cape Horn) and she was his home for 17 years. When she was lost on a Mexican beach he replaced her with *Tamata*, a 36ft (11m) steel sloop.

Lin and Larry Pardey. Although they passionately argued the cause of small ocean cruisers, when the time came to replace their 23ft (7m) *Serrafyn*, the new boat was quite a jump bigger at 30ft (9.15m). Maybe their next boat will be around 37ft (11.27m)?

Hull design

While the ocean cruising yachtsman looking for the suitable boat need not know too much about naval architecture, the basic concepts discussed here will help, within

The bulletproof Colin Archer still makes a good ocean cruiser but, benefitting from the last 90 years of design and development, the modern yacht is much more likely to make a better long-distance liveaboard cruising boat

Of necessity, cruiser/racers are built very strongly and even hard weekend racing is unlikly to tire them; many of the less extreme and un-twitchy ones, such as this UFO 34, can be re-arranged for short crew and make superb long-distance boats

limits, in the choice of a hull and displacement. The finer points of hull design are a complex subject, well documented in a number of books for those who want to go into it more deeply.

The characteristics of a hull's design are closely related to displacement, so when considering a suitable boat the two go hand in hand. The merits of heavy versus light or moderate displacement have kept yacht club bars alive with lively conversation for years past. Simplifying matters as far as possible, a heavy displacement boat is built strongly and her design allows her to sail with not only this weight, but a considerable amount of stores as well without being adversely affected. On the face of it, this makes her well-suited for long voyages and nearly all early ocean cruisers were heavy displacement wooden vessels built to withstand the rigours of the sea. In simple terms, the heavier a boat is, the stronger she needs to be built to withstand her own weight being thrown at and off seas. This requirement for strength adds to the weight, which in turn requires heavier sails and gear, stronger hatches, and stouter spars. The result is that she is only likely to sail well in stronger breezes and will slop the wind out of her sails in lighter going, giving her a poor general performance. Her ability to carry a large crew and stores will also be at the cost of extra scantlings in her construction or extra lead required for her keel. She will also be expensive to equip, requiring larger-sized gear, ropes and so on, which also means she will be more costly to maintain.

At the other end of the scale (and I'm deliberately stating extremes to illustrate the point) a light displacement boat is built with trimmed-down scantlings, but is just as seaworthy because the mass being thrown at seas is so much less. Imagine her as a ping-pong ball tossed in the waves compared to a golf ball. She also needs less power to drive her so the rig can be smaller and lighter, which makes her easier to sail and usually faster. Similarly, she will have a smaller engine, using less fuel, and lighter, less expensive ground tackle which needs no heavy windlass. However, the light displacement boat has the disadvantage that her load-carrying capability is limited because stores constitute a much larger proportion of her total weight in comparison to the same stores on the heavy boat. And people on light displacement boats don't eat any less! The result is that she will go down on her marks, and the more that is loaded into her the less capable her structure will become of withstanding the greater mass as she pounds away at sea. The result will be not only bad sailing performance, but, in extremis, the danger of breaking up.

Looking at the two extremes, then, it becomes clear that somewhere between the two will be the best answer. Displacement is generally regarded and simply calculated as a ratio of displacement/waterline length. The table below illustrates the displacement/length ratio of several designs to give you some idea.

Moody 36	205	Rival 34	345
Sadler 32	255	Salar 40	350
Sunbird 32	255	Nicholson 35	365
Pionier 10	260	Giles 38	365
Rival 38	300	Rustler 31	400
Warrior 35	300	Nicholson 32	440
Vancouver 32	310	Bowman 36	440
Bowman 46	325	Endurance 35	470
Vancouver 27	330	Tradewind 33	500

These figures are computed by dividing the displacement in tons by the $(LWL \times .01)^3$. Making sure you have accurate displacement figures, you can easily make the same calculation on your chosen craft. As a rough guide, expect an average ocean cruiser capable of carrying sufficient loads with a reasonable turn of speed to come between 250 and 350. This doesn't necessarily imply that craft outside these figures are unsuitable. It simply means you must anticipate the penalties of limited load carrying at one end of the scale, or, alternatively, high cost and poorer performance at the other.

Waterline length

Waterline length is the next most important aspect of hull design to consider. For an ocean cruiser, the longer it is the better. Not only does a good waterline length mean greater speed, but also much more usable accommodation or storage space for a given overall length. Our Rival 34 *Euge* always drew admiring comments wherever she went with her very pretty overhangs, fabulous sheerline and counter stern. But although an excellent boat in many respects, her waterline length was only 24ft 10in (7.56m) for her 34ft (10.36m) hull length. As a result her accommodation was small compared to others of similar LOA. She was also sensitive to having weights, such as the ground tackle, in the ends, and with a maximum speed of just over seven knots, we had to work that much harder at sailing to keep up respectable daily averages. With a longer waterline we could have relaxed a bit and maintained similar speeds at 60 percent potential, instead of the 80 percent we had to keep up.

Beam

Beam also affects how much boat you get for a given length. There is an enormous contrast between a narrowish yacht with pleasing overhangs and a beamier, full-ended hull which can easily have twice the volume for the same overall length. Some of the popular French multichine steel designs such as the Group Finot Reve D'Antilles have superb accommodation for their length and with sensible professional design manage to maintain good sailing performance and seakeeping qualities too. Their increased beam and therefore form stability means they can trade a little ballast for load-carrying, which, within limits, is a desirable feature for long distance sailing.

Generous beam has a lot of advantages for the ocean cruiser, such as increased deck space which makes for easier working and for stowing a lot of the gear a long-distance boat needs, like running poles, extra ground tackle, liferaft and maybe a rigid dinghy. However, there are snags in having generous beam. The wider a boat, the harder she is to design properly, as heeled underwater shapes can distort badly and create inefficiencies. These not only slash performance but lead to questionable handling characteristics which sometimes don't manifest themselves until conditions are bad, when you most need predictability. Also, for a given displacement, a designer will be trading underwater depth as he increases the beam. The resulting wide, shallow hull has high initial stability which will drop off the further she heels, which is not desirable in a boat likely to meet severe conditions. So generous beam can be a good feature, but be careful that it is not excessive, as has been the case in some production cruisers built in the last fifteen years.

Freeboard

Freeboard is an aspect of design which naval architects have tended to relax in the last few years. If freeboard is too low headroom will be limited, unless there's a high coachroof which is not good for heavy weather work. Also, low freeboard means a wetter (and I don't mean spray) boat, which raises a number of problems, such as safety of crew working on deck, and greater reliance on the integrity and watertightness of hatches, windows and ports. Cabin leaks, combined with a regularly drenched crew, will quickly sap morale in sustained heavy going and it is then that mistakes will be made.

Conversely, while high freeboard will keep the decks and crew drier, it has the ill effect of raising the yacht's centre of gravity, especially if she's a heavily constructed boat with proportionally heavy equipment. The higher centre of gravity works against stability, particularly in extreme conditions, making the boat more susceptible to being rolled over and less ready to self-right. A higher centre of gravity also works against sail-carrying ability and so reduces sailing performance. Increased windage is another drawback to high freeboard, although for a given interior headroom the windage difference between low freeboard/high coachroof and high freeboard/flush deck is not great. High freeboard can be a bit of a nuisance too when getting aboard from a dinghy, passing up heavy shopping or water containers, and high freeboard does make it considerably more difficult to retrieve a man overboard.

Stern shape

The merits of different stern shapes were hotly argued for many years among yachtsmen. The round or canoe stern was often favoured because it gave the following sea an opportunity to break either side of it, but it was not particularly buoyant and cut out a lot of otherwise useful stowage space. It has largely vanished from modern design.

The counter stern is traditional but has gradually blended in with the transom stern, leaving us with the retroussé, which gains the maximum waterline advantages of the former with the practicality and space of the latter. Ultimately, overall hull balance is more important than how the stern is finished off and a hull with the correct distribution of buoyancy fore or aft is likely to be the most seaworthy one. In my experience of running before severe conditions, when a rogue sea is big enough seriously to poop a yacht, the stern shape is irrelevant compared to the boat's ability to resist broaching through the good design of her overall hull shape.

Draught

This really depends on the sort of cruising you wish to do. Some people, while keen to cross oceans, many want to explore places such as the Bahamas or areas of the Great Barrier Reef. The European canal system will require shallow draught and numerous Pacific atolls, especially in the Tuamotus for example, are opened up to a boat drawing little water. River cruising in locations such as the Nile or Amazon is also possible with shallow draught.

However, unless you're a shoal draught enthusiast, the depth of water required is rarely a problem until you need more than around 6ft 6in (1.97m), when you have to start looking carefully at whether or not an anchorage or bay will accommodate you. Draught between this figure and genuine shoal is arbitrary, because anyone lacking the advantages of true shoal draught will tend to anchor or moor in similar places to the 6ft 6in (1.97m) man. In this case case, why not go for slightly deeper draught and gain from its advantages, such as low centre of gravity, better tankage, and quite likely better sail carrying ability and consequent performance.

The importance of performance

Boat speed and performance are not looked on as being particularly high on the ocean cruiser priority list when compared to seaworthiness or comfort. It is common to hear potential voyagers saying that speed or weatherliness are unimportant when crossing oceans. One can only assume these people have never experienced a passage of over 20 days, and base their opinion on short trips where speed difference is not noticeable.

Compared to other forms of transport, a boat travels exceptionally slowly. In proportional terms, a boat that makes five knots against another doing four knots is getting there 25 per cent quicker, which may not seem much on a short trip. But see how that difference is amplified over high ocean mileages. A 3,000-mile passage will take the four-knot boat 31 days and 6 hours, and the five-knot boat only 25 days. Some people (not that many if they're honest) are like Bernard Moitessier and love to spend as much time at sea as possible. But most of us, after two or three weeks at sea, are still enjoying it but greatly looking forward to getting in. If there were a way of shortening the trip by six days, nine out of ten would jump at the prospect of fresh food, plentiful water and a change in scenery and company. On the simple day-to-day routine of a yacht crossing an ocean, the daily position fix is something of a highpoint. An ocean is large and if those crosses only progress across the chart in tiny increments it can noticeably sap morale and crew happiness. A boat that is going well and making respectable daily runs will keep her crew smiling . . .

In this context it is worth remembering that respectable speed is as much a product of the skipper's philosophy as it is of the yacht's capabilities. A skipper who loads her right down on the marks may always be able to produce some special tool needed once in a blue moon, or a can of some favourite delicacy three years into the cruise, but if the sailing passages are tedious as a result, there is not much incentive to leave port and head for the next place. Of course you may be going in the first place to get away from the rush and hurry of modern living, but the performance philosophy still makes sense, because knowing you have the ability to get to places will widen your cruising range and general outlook. A 48-hour beat into a tradewind in a capable and weatherly ocean cruiser might well take you to an atoll that very few other people ever visit. Efficient sailing has great rewards.

There is no single element in creating good boatspeed. Performance philosophy is a combination of many factors. They include starting off with a good boat, not overloading it, making sure the underside is kept clean, the weight well distributed (preferably out of the ends and as low down as possible), and no unnecessary windage aloft. Then, at sea, she needs to be sailed consistently for twenty-four hours a day.

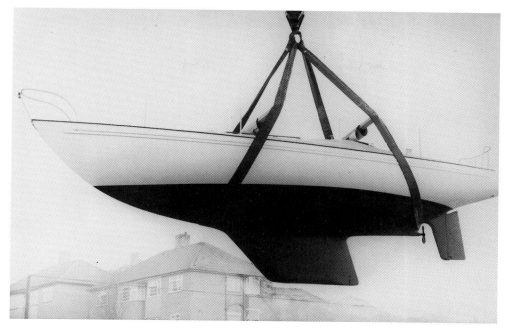

The Rival 34 is an evergreen ocean boat which set the standard as an ideal compromise between the advantages of the traditional long keel and the more efficient fin and skeg configuration

Keels and ballast

Seamen are traditionally conservative because the man who goes to sea with or in something 'new-fangled' might be trusting his life to it. Not surprisingly, therefore, some new ideas take a long time to be accepted and among them is the keel configuration which most of us today take for granted. The keel controversy raged for many years until the yachting boom of the 1970s pretty much established that the fin and skeg worked and was here to stay. That is not to say that the traditional long keel is unsuitable, but modern design and construction methods favour the fin and skeg configuration. Long keels still appear from time to time on 'new' designs, but more to be in keeping with a pseudo-traditional concept than for any practical reason.

The long keel evolved from the days of wooden sailing ships, when structurally it was the vessel's backbone. Smaller workboats such as the smacks and trawlers made it a little deeper for better windward performance. It was the yacht-like pilot cutters, whose competitive livelihood was dependent on their sailing performance, that converted it into the wineglass-stem proportions of the classic long, deep keel. It was soon realised that incorporating the ballast on the end of it instead of in the bilges made a significant difference and in due course the bolt-on external fin keel was tried. Post-war racing successes proved the better handiness and performance of the fin and skeg configuration, and when monocoque fibreglass construction came along and did away with the need for a strong central backbone, the long keel's days were numbered.

For the early ocean cruisers, sailing before Blondie Hasler and others had pioneered the windvane self-steering gear, the long keel was good because it undoubtedly aided the yacht's ability to sail in a straight line. It made it easier for the helmsman and more reliable for sheet-to-tiller self-steering, where steadiness counts. The other aspect that was, and still is, regarded as a great asset is that the long keel is an integral part of the hull structure, so when a yacht is aground or stranded, it spreads the loads over a wider area – a comforting thought if you are starting to pound badly. Another merit is the ability to position the rudder on the after edge, a strong arrangement that protects the rudder enormously. Having the rudder like this, especially one externally mounted on the transom, is still one of the best and most practical arrangements for a long-distance boat, and can simplify the installation and operation of windvane self-steering.

The long keel is gradually disappearing though as the fin and skeg (or even the fin and spade rudder) proves the better all-round arrangement. There are of course wide variations of fin keel. In the early '70s Peter Brett designed the Rival 31 (later to be stretched into the 32 and then re-modelled into the 34) which had a 'long fin' which was accepted as a good compromise between traditional long and modern fin. It maintained good directional stability with the handiness and better performance of fin and skeg. The concept of the long fin is still very good for the ocean cruiser for a number of reasons. First, the keel is mounted on the hull's underbelly over a greater length and in a stranding or heavy grounding the strains are better distributed. Secondly, the reasonable tracking a long fin gives allows the possibility of rigging a basic sheet to tiller self-steering if your windvane or autopilot packs up or is damaged. A sensitive, narrow fin-keeled boat whose helm you can't leave unattended for more than a moment is impossible to make self-steer on any point of sailing other than close-hauled, and this will be a curse if Sod's Law decrees the windvane gives up in mid-ocean.

The question of having encapsulated ballast (ie fitted within the hull or keel moulding) or an externally mounted casting is an interesting one. The yachtsman with encapsulated ballast doesn't have to think about keel bolts corroding (especially when the yacht is taking a pounding). However, the bottom of the keel will nearly always be the first part of a yacht to hit a reef or rock and stands a chance of being damaged. If the damage has cracked the laminate and seepage occurs, a cast iron keel will start rusting and there is nothing you can do about it. On the other hand, if you hit the bottom with an externally mounted keel the worst you will do is scratch the paint off the ballast, which can be wire-brushed and recoated at the next slipping.

If the grounding is a serious one, where the yacht has been pulled off but sustained quite serious damage to the keel foot, the owner of a boat with an encapsulated keel has the worry of the fibreglass being so badly damaged that the keel casting may drop out. You could also argue that an externally mounted keel's bolts would give up, or their attachment within the hull disintegrate, before you could get the yacht off the reef or shore. In a later section I describe a good way of building a sacrificial shoe for an encapsulated-keeled yacht, and with this fitted I think it tips the scales in favour of this ballast arrangement.

Keel design has been in the spotlight since Australia won the America's Cup with a radical wing keel in 1983. It initiated a fashion for wing keels; some of these were good, others were marketing gimmicks. The good thing to have come out of it is the refinement and popularisation of the keel shapes Henry Scheel had been developing for years; slightly bulbed, fatter lower sections which maintain low centre of gravity with shallower draught. These keels are very desirable for ocean cruising because they minimise draught. The various shapes of wing keel, especially the Tandem keel, rely much more on hydrodynamics to operate well and would therefore be at quite a disadvantage on an ocean cruiser which might go for lengthy periods without hauling out and would therefore be fouled.

The design of bilge keels has improved by leaps and bounds over the last few years to the point where the performance difference between a yacht so fitted and an identical one with a fin keel is marginal. An asymmetric aerofoil section and slight toeing in forward creates marginal lift to windward and helps to make up for the wetted-surface disadvantages. However, many of the older craft sporting bilge keels lost a great deal of windward performance. Many owners regard this as a reasonable price to pay for their ability to sit upright when dried out and it made them very popular, particularly in Britain, for coastal cruising. Many parts of the world have too little tidal range to take proper advantage of bilge keels, but they will nevertheless save their owner a great deal in slipping costs wherever the tide allows. Weighed against them is slightly diminished performance and the fact that when you dive and scrub off the underside at anchor, cleaning the inside face of the keels is a horrible job. Although in broad terms a fin keel is better suited to long-distance cruising than bilge keels, if you have found a yacht which is otherwise well-suited to your needs you ought not to turn it down purely on the basis of her having bilge keels.

Centreboards deserve careful consideration. They have always been regarded as troublesome, partly because they can become jammed with mud, sand, shingle, or even barnacles but also because with older materials they were difficult to maintain, which in turn led to breakages. With a fibreglass case one need never worry about rot getting a hold inside, and with the strength of this material movement is minimal and leaks are rarely a problem. Nylon bushes control the board much better these days and modern engineering has made raising or lowering the board much easier.

If you are designing or building a new boat and have the ability to decide, the comparison between the centreplate and daggerboard is an interesting one. The fan-shaped hinging centreplate has always had a popular following, with the advantage that it is possible to locate the board under the cabin sole, or fairly unobtrusively under the saloon table which it can support. The hinged board also acts as a primitive depth sounder which in reefy waters can be a big plus point. However, this type of board is still very difficult to maintain. Removing it to paint the inside of the box or the board itself is a fairly major operation and if it isn't easy to do, it's likely to be a job left until it causes problems.

The daggerboard is in many ways a better proposition if, and only if, you can organise the accommodation around it. With the box left open at the top, it should be possible to remove the board completely using a halyard and get it on deck to antifoul or patch up damage. If you also use a thick-sectioned chord and fit dinghy inspection hatches well above the waterline in the casing, with the board pulled out on deck it will be possible to get an arm inside the box to paint in there too.

The other advantages of a daggerboard are numerous. While a centreplate has always been regarded as a useful depth sounder, they will obligingly raise themselves as the vessel ploughs onwards on to the reef. Time is precious in such circumstances, and the extra few moments or even minutes it takes to wind up the board to get off the reef might result in the boat being driven inextricably shorewards with possibly disastrous consequences. On the other hand, with a stout daggerboard fitted into a very strong box, the boat would be stopped very abruptly and would still be in water deep enough to give the crew time to sail or haul her off.

A strong daggerboard casing extending from hull to deck in the middle is also a desirable structural feature, enormously strengthening both hull and deck, and can also be arranged to take the mast compression loads.

A serious disadvantage of both centreboard or daggerboard keel arrangements is that they raise the centre of gravity much more than conventional keels. There are ways to ease this, but they must be considered at design stage – building the board as heavy as possible, using lead instead of cast iron ballast, positioning the engine, tanks and batteries as low as possible and trimming down heavy top hamper. Wings fitted to the tip section would help a great deal too. The lifting keel for an ocean cruiser would also have to have an infallible method of holding the board in the lowered position just in case the yacht was rolled in severe conditions.

Accommodation can easily be worked around a centreboard case, but it is more difficult with a daggerboard which extends from keel to deckhead. Depending on the yacht's size and beam it is possible to site the saloon aft of the box, but with the case still within the cabin to some extent (as might be a keel-stepped mast). On a larger boat, 40ft and up, the saloon could be positioned to one side of the case. The French Kelt 39 has twin forward cabins with a longitudinal central bulkhead dividing them, which solves the problem.

Most of us have no choice in the material used in the keel of our yachts because it is there already and certainly not worth changing. However, if you are starting from scratch and can choose, lead is far superior to cast iron, but much more expensive. The loading of an ocean cruiser inevitably raises the centre of gravity. By starting off with lead and therefore a lower initial centre of gravity you are effectively increasing the yacht's stability and safety. Lead also has a higher specific gravity, so requires less space, and for the same weight therefore gives you spare room in the bilge for extra tankage or storage.

'Ballast ratio' is a term often quoted when it comes to seaworthiness and stability. Be slightly wary of it because alone it is a meaningless factor – many a boat with 38% ballast ratio is safer and more seaworthy than another with 45%. Ballast ratio can only be judged as good or bad when placed in relation to other design criteria such as beam, centre of gravity and displacement/waterline ratio.

Rudders

Although a skeg-hung rudder is less vulnerable to damage by hitting flotsam or whales, there are nevertheless thousands of yachts fitted with unsupported spade rudders which cruise the oceans without any problems. The spade rudder is generally more responsive than a conventional one because it is more efficient hydrodynamically. This type of rudder usually has a slightly balanced area forward of the stock axis which has the added bonus of easing the weight on the helm, a definite advantage when it comes to self-steering (unless it is overdone and the helm becomes too light, which can throw some windvane gears).

Skegless spade rudders have been around for a long time, with designers like E G van de Stadt using them almost exclusively for the last 20 years on enduring production boats like the Pioniers, Excaliburs and Gallants. They have a very good safety record but the protection a skeg gives a rudder takes a lot of beating. For long distance cruising the rudder, whose operation is so vital, should have this protection and for me this outweighs the disadvantages of slightly less efficiency.

It is very easy to equip boats for ocean cruising with needlessly heavy gear. This is usually a sign of lack of confidence or experience, costs more money and cuts down on sailing performance. Nevertheless, everybody who has experience agrees that rudder fittings (pintles and gudgeons) are one item that must be extra strong. We've all seen articles about how to rig jury steering with floorboards lashed to the end of running booms and such like, but in reality it is very difficult indeed to make these lash-ups work even half efficiently without seriously sapping crew strength, a problem which is amplified for the ocean cruiser which by nature will have so much farther to sail to port.

Although twin rudders have been used from time to time before (for example, 1980 OSTAR entry *Spaniel* used them) they have only recently become popular, developed largely by French naval architects. They were at first regarded as a passing fashion, but proved surprisingly effective in use and have a lot of advantages for the ocean cruiser. One of the reasons for their design was to create sufficient rudder area for centreboard or daggerboard yachts, which otherwise need a complicated lifting blade. Angling them so that the leeward rudder is more or less vertical when the boat is heeled improves the steering ability and sensitivity so greatly that several long-distance racing yachts (ie non-IOR) have fitted them, finding that the disadvantage of marginal increase in wetted surface is eclipsed by the better handling (when heeled the windward blade is clear of the water anyway). For an ocean cruising boat the linkage creates an extra complication, but it is reassuring to know you have a second rudder if one is damaged. The only real disadvantage to the system, other than extra cost, is that close-quarters manoeuvrability under power is limited by not being able to use the prop-wash to kick the stern one way or another.

Finally, rudder positioning needs consideration. A rudder situated right aft is undoubtedly best for long-distance sailing. Not only does this make it easier to arrange a trim tab self-steering gear (should finances be tight and you need to make your own gear) but also it makes trouble-shooting, particularly at sea, much easier. It is possible to dive down and free off a net or fish trap wrapped around the rudder at sea when the rudder is aft, it is impossible when the blade is tucked deep under a counter and the yacht is pitching. And if ever you need to rig basic emergency steering lines to the rudder blade, the job is reasonably simple with the rudder right aft.

Another cunningly simple emergency rudder arrangement is to create a small nick or notch on the trailing edge of the rudder blade capable of holding a link of chain. This is easy on a steel rudder, on a fibreglass one a stainless steel fitting might be necessary. In the event of steering failure a length of chain can be draped over the back edge of the rudder and, held from both sides, pulled up until it catches in the notch. Steering lines from either side can then be taken to the primary winches.

Weight distribution

We have touched on this in relation to other factors but the subject is important enough to need examining on its own. For many years racing boats have avoided at all costs having weight any distance fore or aft of the yacht's pitching centre, approximately amidships. Not only that, but all major weights are situated as low as is humanly possible. The performance difference is remarkable, not only in terms of speed, but also their ability to keep moving into large seas when the cruising monohull, with all her ground tackle in the bows and spare fuel, water and cruising necessities stuffed into the lazarette, is stopped, nodding to a standstill in the trough of one wave.

But what of practicalities? It's fine to say that weight should be kept out of the ends, but how can this be done? Because the best living accommodation is in the middle of the boat it goes against the grain to use that centre area for stowage. However, with a bit of thought and cunning, it can be done. If you are in the lucky position of designing (or having designed) your dream boat, the problem of weight distribution can be borne in mind from the outset. If you're working with an existing boat, similar principles can be applied to ease the problem. For a start, consider what are the major weights within a yacht; the ballast, the engine, water and fuel tanks, ground tackle, tools, stores and individual items of equipment like the liferaft, dinghy and outboard. Clearly, the ballast and engine cannot be moved, but the chances are that they are in the right place anyway. It is a much better idea in the long run to have ample water and fuel in the tanks than it is to carry extra in canisters. The first priority on a new boat then is to design in as much water tankage as possible, and a minimum of 30-40 gallons of fuel, which is just enough to keep you going in cruising grounds where it's difficult to refuel, such as the Indian Ocean route from Australia to Suez. If you already have a boat, make the increasing of tankage one of the high priorities of preparation. The lockerage under saloon berths is usually horrible to use and these spaces are a good place to fit flexible tanks.

Spare anchors should, if possible, be put in the bilge. If not, it is often possible to find a place for them in the engine compartment, especially aft of the gearbox where there's often free space on yachts. The working anchor can be taken off the foredeck and sat in chocks just aft of the mast (where it won't foul headsail sheets), and, if you are able to organise it, the main anchor chain locker could be stowed in the bilge in the mast area, stowed there through a hawse-hole on deck whose pipe leads down below next to the mast or its compression post. The liferaft can be positioned in its chocks just in front of the cockpit coamings or in the forward end of the cockpit. The rigid dinghy, if you have one, should also ideally be stowed aft of the mast on the coachroof or deck. Instead of fitting the dinghy's outboard on a bracket on the pushpit, consider arranging a stowage bracket for it in the forwardmost cockpit locker.

Most living possessions we carry around with us don't weigh very much and these can be put in the lockers forward and aft. Light sails like the spinnaker can happily live in the eyes of the focs'le with heavier ones nearer the centre of pitching if possible.

Correct distribution of weight is only a matter of discipline and a little thought, but the difference it makes to sailing performance, especially if you're about to confront a long windward thrash, makes it well worth the trouble involved.

The multi-hulled ocean cruiser

Throughout the spectrum of ocean cruising there are horses for courses in terms of yacht suitability. I'd happily take a reasonably standard production boat on a tradewind transatlantic passage, but it would be a questionable choice for cruising in high latitudes or for taking on the Southern Ocean passage. Multihulls are much the same.

Most writers on ocean cruising disregard multihulls but it would be foolish to ignore them as a possible choice for they have numerous advantages to offer. Without delving

The Wharram family of catamarans is something akin to the Land Rover of ocean sailing – seen all over the world, rugged, uncomfortable, basic but very capable

too deeply into the history of multihulls, the point to remember is that these craft have had nothing like the time the monohulled yacht has to develop and evolve. They came on to the scene in the 1950s and in the first twenty years (still well within living memory) their designers, builders and sailors had an enormous amount of learning to do. Wild claims were made about their speed and capabilities, and whilst they were undoubtedly faster than conventional monohulls, none of the sailing establishment (who'd probably been overtaken by these strange and unnatural creations) were very sorry to see them come to grief fairly regularly in the learning process. Without much understanding of the structures or how to sail them, many broke up, a good few turned over and regrettably several of those pioneers lost their lives. Always happy to focus the spotlight on a controversial minority, the newspapers have to this day always catalogued every multihull mishap – a monohull sinking does not often make news but in terms of statistics is probably just as common.

By the early '70s multihulls had a firm footing and the learning curve was flattening out. Since then hundreds of multihulls have made successful ocean passages, James Wharram's designs proving the most popular and sometimes referred to as the Colin Archer of multihull sailing. Many notable passages have been made in the tiny 26ft Heavenly Twins class cats, including a singlehanded circumnavigation. Countless Catalacs have crossed the Atlantic and Prout Snowgoose cats have cruised all over the world.

It would be naive to suggest that every multihull is suitable for long-distance cruising – there are good and bad. A serious cruising yachtsman wouldn't attempt a long-distance passage in a contemporary half-tonner and he should no sooner try it in a multihulled equivalent. A catamaran or trimaran can capsize, but it is no more likely to happen than a monohull sinking. In both cases, it is a risk that all yachtsmen have to accept. Sailing a multihull, one should consider the possibility of this happening and prepare for it in the same way a responsible monohuller would consider fitting emergency buoyancy bags.

One of the difficulties of opting for a multihull is the limited choice available. Very few companies have gone into the multihulls field, with the result that there are only perhaps a couple of dozen production classes, plus a wide variety of one-offs and amateur-built cats and tris built to stock plans. In strict investment terms it is a difficult decision. The well-known production boats command good resale prices and the one-offs and amateur-built boats are not so sought after, but this doesn't mean that all the home-built boats are not good. Many are better-constructed than those produced by the professionals, but the investment element must be carefully considered. The alternative, if you're especially keen to have a multihull and can't find what you want

Prout catamarans – the 31 or 33ft Quest or the 35 or 37ft Snowgoose – are probably the most popular production GRP multihulls used for ocean cruising and living aboard

amongst the production boats, is to commit a smaller sum (with the rest invested) and buy a relatively cheap cat or tri that is suitable and, of course, sound, on the assumption you're likely to lose a certain amount on resale, offset by the income from the invested difference.

Ocean cruising in multihulls is a completely different game and it is a common enough mistake to cruise them in exactly the same way as a monohull. They are very different craft (not necessarily better or worse) and they require a new philosophy to overcome their disadvantages and capitalise on their good points. Weight, or more precisely load carrying, will always be a problem, in my opinion of greater magnitude in ocean cruising terms than ever capsize is. The smaller the multihull, less than 38ft say, the bigger the problem. A light multihull, and three-quarters of them are light, cannot carry weight very well so the multihull sailor will have a constant battle to keep loading to a minimum. He has certain advantages on his side though, and with a bit of thought he can make the best of them. Instead of carrying vast quantities of water, which is very heavy, the multihull sailor should convert areas of his large deck space to water-catchment surfaces. With a diverter valve and simple filtering system he can direct this straight into his tanks. Another possibility is to have huge water tanks in the otherwise-empty outriggers. These would be filled in port so whilst you'd rarely see your waterline, there would be ample water for regular showers and fresh water laundry. They would be emptied before putting to sea.

That large deck space can also be used to advantage by fitting plenty of solar panels, thus saving on heavy batteries and diesel for charging.

Different anchoring techniques also gains many advantages over the deep-keelers. The easiest option when entering an anchorage is to head for all the other boats and drop the hook there, whereupon the multihull makes itself unpopular by shearing around on a rope rode because they can't afford the weight disadvantage of all-chain cables. But there are many advantages to anchoring in very shallow water where other yachts can't reach. If a multihull is equipped with approximately 30ft (9.15m) of chain, this will be ample scope to lay in 3 or 4ft (1m) of water under chain only, when she won't sheer as much. You won't have other boats dragging into you in the night and you'll be closer to the shore and won't need a heavy dinghy outboard and its fuel. If the crew has disappeared with the dinghy, you can walk or wade to the beach and put your clothes on there, and if you drop something over the side it will be easy to recover. It may raise some eyebrows, but if you're unhappy about the anchor holding, you have the option of walking out and digging a hole for it! In a hurricane anchorage situation, assuming there is no appreciable fetch, shallow water is by far the safest place for a multihull to lie, geographically protected as she is from deep-keel vessels dragging on to her, for they will go aground long before they hit her.

The sensible multihull sailor will always be watching weight, which can be a bore when you want to collect trinkets and souvenirs from your travels, but the way around it is to package them up from time to time and send them home. The weight problem also means that the multihull sailor can't have the luxury of stocking up for months and months in advance, so will have to provision in small batches with local foods.

The multihull's stable configuration can be taken advantage of in many ways. For instance, it shouldn't be necessary to have more than a single inlet seacock in the entire boat. And one could install a couple of hatches under the huge wingdecks. In this way, in port you could keep the hatches wide open and the accommodation sweet in the heaviest downpour while all the other boats in the anchorage are sweating out below

Sadly, only a few multihull sailors take advantage of their craft's unique advantages. Here the hull of a 60-footer is lifted, using levers, for antifouling in a quiet lagoon. When finished, the hull is lowered, the yacht turned around and the other hull is raised

with hatches dogged tight. Taking this a step further, if you're in a risky area for dinghy thefts, moor it overnight between the hulls. If the wire security painter is then taken from a strongpoint in the middle of the dinghy and up through this open hatch into the cabin, the most determined dinghy thief will give up.

After food, the ocean cruiser's biggest outgoing is slipway and hoist charges. The multihull's light weight can obviate much of this because it is possible to drag it up a beach to antifoul, and also to go into a sheltered lagoon and lever one hull out of the water at a time on to props to work on it. A friend of ours had very strong stainless steel chainplates made so that his 46ft Wharram could be lifted out on them by a normal cargo crane at half the cost of most Travelifts or commercial yacht yards. His next project is to make small removeable axles and rubber wheels to fit at each end of both his stub keels so that using his mainsheet as a tackle, he could pull his cat up a beach unaided with his sheet winch. The cost of the axles and wheels will be about the equivalent of one commercial haul-out, but thereafter he was confident his hauling costs would be at the popular price.

The biggest 'if' about multihulls is the capsize question. This element of doubt puts off many people with little experience of sailing multihulls from choosing this type of craft, which might otherwise be ideal for them. No multihull is incapable of capsizing any more than the Titanic was unsinkable. Given searoom, a monohull stands a good chance of emerging from survival conditions afloat, even if dismasted through rolling, having been left to its own devices. A multihull will always need looking after and the circumstances are rare when in a gale she can be left alone. I write from personal experience, having sailed our 35ft (10.66m) catamaran through such conditions, and I believe that a sensibly-designed and well-built cruising multihull of 33ft and above can survive any conditions if she is sailed attentively and constantly. The crew must always remain alert to nurse her along, but they will have a better chance of cooking and sleeping comfortably when off-watch, and so will be better nourished and rested than a monohull's crew.

It is essential for an ocean going multihull have a comfortable and well sheltered steering position to minimise fatigue and exposure in bad conditions and that the self-steering can quickly be over-ridden. Tyre drogues are a good method of slowing the yacht to controllable speeds when running before survival conditions. Two car tyres should be carried on passages where heavy weather can be expected. They will need at least 400ft (120m) of warp so they are always trailing in the trough behind you. Pat Patterson is a multihull designer and sailor with a great deal of experience, including a circumnavigation at times in high latitudes. He is convinced that a catamaran laying beam-on, with a long drogue led to weather from bow to stern, is almost impossible to capsize, even in the worst seas.

The use of parachutes as sea anchors for multihulls has gained steady popularity, especially in America, amongst some highly respected deep-water sailors. Rigged properly (and this is imperative), it is claimed that they transform extreme weather handling by keeping the vessel head into the wind and minimise drift. Although we carry a 20ft diameter parachute on *Foreigner 2*, we've not yet experienced conditions bad enough to employ it. I would urge anyone planning to head offshore in a multihull to buy *The Parachute Anchoring System*, an excellent book detailing the concept, published by Multihulls Magazine, 421 Hancock Street, N Quincy, Boston, Mass 02171, USA.

I'm often asked why I (currently) sail a multihull. I'm ambivalent about the mono/multi question and can get very enthusiastic about both types. We started with a cat, moved to a monohull and subsequently, as our circumstances (principally the arrival of children) changed, moved back to a catamaran. We don't worry any more about capsize than we did about sinking our monohull, believing that good seamanship ought to protect you from either. If I believed, for one moment, that the catamaran was less safe than a monohull, I wouldn't take my children across oceans in one. For us, the motion at sea transforms passagemaking, and with a horde of young children aboard it is hard to resist the extra space (and deck space) they offer.

Multihulls are clearly here to stay and are chosen more and more for tropic passages. They are not everyone's ideal, but they warrant serious consideration as a solution to a number of cruising requirements.

7. Below Decks

The accommodation area of a yacht has many demands on it, especially as it must meet different priorities at sea than in port. Accommodation on sailing boats has suffered from what Garry Hoyt describes as 'design constipation'. On boats less than 42ft (12.8m), nobody, with the exception of the French, has dared to vary from the well-tried layouts that have lasted for generations. Broadly, these follow a standard plan of a foc'sle with twin vee berths, heads and cupboard opposite, saloon with berth either side and divided by a table, then aft, under the main companionway, the galley to one side and chart table opposite, usually with a quarter berth as well. There are slight variations, such as the addition of an after cabin. In the last ten years, as yachts have sported fatter stern sections, it has become more common to tuck aft cabins in the quarter sections of the yacht. Yards can hardly be blamed for not experimenting when the conventional layout, for all its faults, does actually work for the majority of the market. However, there is no doubt that some aspects could be much better for those who will live aboard constantly, so we will consider what features to look out for and how they can be improved slightly for ocean cruising.

Sleeping

The standard layout works quite well for two people. Most couples use the vee-berth double in port so that they can have a bed made the whole time and there are no arguments about what time each prefers to go to bed or get up. This might sound like a minor point, but a saloon double can be irritating when you want to go to bed and your partner wants to stay up and read, especially as you have the chore of converting the saloon double and making up the bed last thing at night.

At sea, the forward double berth is unusable, and the off-watch person usually sleeps on the lee side of the saloon. This arrangement is not so good because the off-watch person monopolises the best lounging seat in the boat and the crew on watch have to be very quiet and can't use the radio, stereo or VHF. So unless you don't mind sitting on the uphill seat throughout a watch, make sure the boat has a comfy place for the watchkeeper to sit, the most obvious being the chart table where he or she can update the log and position. A separate quarter cabin is more desirable. There, the watch below can be reasonably closeted, but make sure it has curtains for a wedge of sunlight from a porthole scything around a cabin is enough to keep anyone awake during the day. The normal double berth may be better divided into two. The snag with quarter berths is that they are underneath the cockpit where there is a lot of noisy activity by those working the ship. An alternative is a curtained-off pilot berth in the wings of the saloon, which if made snug enough could be used on either tack. If you have more than two people aboard, it goes without saying that proper seaberths must be found for everyone not on watch, and this may mean giving up the saloon as a living cabin, which is a nuisance.

While on the subject of seaberths, it is important to make sure they can be used when the boat is rolling downwind. On *Euge* we found all our berths untenable and just slightly too wide when gyrating down the trades so we ended up sleeping on the saloon floor, wedged between the table and berth front, and waking up four hours later with something akin to rigor mortis.

Another point to look out for is the accessibility of a berth. When the time comes for 'all hands on deck' it's no good if the off-duty watch have been shoe-horned into berths a long way from the companionway.

Leecloths must be fitted to all seaberths. For constant use it is worth spending some time making them easy to use, with snaphooks instead of knots to hold them up. We made ours with two pockets, a big one to stuff the off-watch person's clothes into to pad the leecloth, and a small one higher up for things like spectacles.

Saloon

As the main living space in what has become your home, the saloon must be as large as possible. It should be surrounded by readily accessible locker space to contain all the items you might need here, from letter-writing equipment and board games to books, cassettes, drinks and glasses etc. Don't stow regularly-used items under the saloon settees – for the person who's just got comfortable reading a book, it is irritating to be frequently moved.

Light and ventilation are essential and if you have a boat that has no opening hatch over the saloon, make sure that fitting one is high up the priority list - a single forehatch simply isn't enough for comfort in hot climates. Ideally, there should be access forward to the heads through the saloon without its occupants having to move to make way. Saloons with an offset dinette area are usually good in this respect. If at all possible, do not have a permanent sleeping berth in the saloon. It is a constant source of aggravation to all, though of course it doesn't matter for the occasional short-term guest.

For much of the time in hot weather crews like to live out in the cockpit, but the saloon must nevertheless be habitable, with well-angled seats and backrests so you can sit comfortably for a few hours reading. A standard boat whose seat angles are not so good can be improved with new contoured upholstery, a decision you might think extravagant before moving aboard, but one you will be unlikely to regret once you are living aboard. A couple of large bean bags can also be very useful for curling up in comfort. If your saloon upholstery is covered in vinyl sew up some light fabric covers (only to be taken off in really bad weather), otherwise bare skin sticks to the vinyl with the salt atmosphere and constant dampness. This can cause sores on the backs of legs and bums.

A seamanlike interior with 'captive' companionway steps (which give lateral footholds at sea), comfortably angled backrests and good sea berths. Pillars are essential to wrap an arm around while getting dressed at sea

The saloon table needs to be big so everyone can use a section of it without impinging on the next person. It must also be stout and about the only way of achieving this and maintaining the ability to fold it out is to have a steel frame made for it, which is then firmly bolted in place. In my cruising experience in small boats I cannot remember having ever eaten a meal from plates on the saloon table in anything above a Force 2, so I think that fiddles should be dispensed with as they only get in the way. But a deep box (minimum 6in/15mm) should be fitted in the middle of the table to hold all the accoutrements of a meal – cutlery, condiments etc.

Some very experienced yachtsmen believe in gimballed saloon tables, and they certainly have a lot going for them. Our friends Francois and Pascal Grinberg on *Scherzo* have this arrangement and cunningly use the Reed's Sailmaker sewing machine as a counterweight. A gimballed table is only really suitable for two people facing each other fore and aft with their plates situated on the axis line.

Galley

The design of a galley must be assessed with an eye to working there when the yacht is steeply heeled. Lockers with their doors facing fore and aft are hopeless because all the contents will come out at you when the locker is opened at sea. Better to have all the fore and aft-facing area for the crockery in slide-opening bins, or have the locker

A seamanlike, J-shaped galley like this will be able to continue producing meals in the worst weather conditions or downwind rolling

opening six inches above the cupboard base, which effectively creates a very deep fiddle to hold bottles and so on. Large lockers are little more than useless and are a nightmare when the boat is rolling because it is difficult to wedge all the contents in place. It is much better to have lots of small ones, with just one unit large enough for the few big items. Sliding locker fronts must only ever be sited on the fore and aft line. This may sound obvious, but some very well-known yacht builders still forget that a boat heels. They are better than hinged doors, which may let out the entire contents when heeled over – with sliding doors you stand a chance of opening just a small section.

The sink should be as near the yacht's centreline as possible, otherwise as soon as you are heeled it will fill up with water (or need a hand pump to get rid of waste) and become useless on one tack. Twin sinks are quite useful, because at sea one inevitably becomes a dump for loose items like the detergent bottle. It is very useful to have different sizes, a large one capable of doing the laundry in port and a small deep one for washing up at sea. Both fresh and salt water must be arranged to serve both. Fit the salt water pump to the right of the fresh pump, so when hands are being washed or tea-cups rinsed, the immediate action is to go for the salt water faucet.

If a 'bum strap' is not fitted, try to envisage where one will go. The same applies for a crash bar across the cooker. In an ideal galley, the cook should be away from the main throughfare. Cooking is a thankless task at the best of times so if you change nothing else in the interior of your boat, consider changes to the galley to improve the cook's lot – after you've used it for a while to find its faults. Waste disposal, for example, is rarely ever thought out in galley design and yet it is a constantly irritating thing if the cook has nowhere to place rubbish other than a polythene bag which is falling over regularly.

One idea incorporated into a charter boat we once ran was a drying-up locker. It was a GRP-lined cabinet with drain and wire crockery baskets fitted inside. It was a huge success because it solved a common enough laziness problem – not drying after washing up.

Fiddles in the galley area must be high, at least 2in (50mm), but also consider fitting moveable sea fiddles which break up a large work surface and make it useable under way.

Heads and ablutions

Some question the need to build a commodious heads in the best part of the boat when it is only used for a few minutes each day. Others feel that this essential place deserves some special attention. Many a long-distance cruising yachtsman has ripped out the contraption altogether and used a bucket to simplify matters. Nobody would argue that facilities could get more basic than a bucket, although on Conny Van Rietschoten's Whitbread Round The World Race winner *Flyer* there was a rather classy little seat welded into the pushpit over the stern of the yacht and the crew used that, winter and summer. It all boils down to personal preference, but do make sure that the ventilation is well dealt with – either a little solar-powered vent or, better still, a small aluminium-framed opening hatch.

I have dealt with a wide variety of marine loos and only one stands head and shoulders above the rest – the Blake Lavac. Some people prefer Baby Blakes (and treat them with respect and love rather like old Morris Minors) but I've yet to find one that didn't leak slightly. If your boat is fitted with one of the cheap plastic-component marine loos very common now on European production craft, change it immediately. They are designed for occasional weekend use, and simply don't stand up to prolonged living aboard.

Installations vary a lot, but try to ensure that yours is clear and open all round, partly for cleaning but also for maintenance. If you have a Lavac, try to arrange the pump in such a way that a bucket can be placed under it for when you maintain or unblock it. All the pipes should be accessible for annual de-calcifying (taken out and hit repeatedly against a dock to clear constricting calcium build-up). If the pipes are tucked away in little lockers or uncleanable lining compartments, when they are removed the contents will pour away somewhere. The inlet and outlet seacocks should be at least two feet apart and, ideally, situated on opposite sides of the yacht. I guarantee that sooner or later your marine toilet will need work of some kind, generally as a result of an embarrassing blockage. With this in mind, take it apart and familiarise yourself with all the parts before it needs to be done in anger, when the blockings will be turning your stomach and preventing clear thought. Some heads are easy to clear if you know how. Quite often the blockage is not in the unit, but at a turn in the exit seacock where quite considerable pressure can build up and the user must be told to stop pumping (many skippers subconsciously listen to guests pumping the loo – if the rhythm seems to slow or get harder the effect is electric!). To clear this requires going over the side with a short piece of hooked wire and the ability to swim very quickly afterwards . . .

Which leads us neatly on to showers. Like most ocean cruising people, I have showered shoreside in thousands of places and always longed to have a simple fitted shower on board. The ocean cruising yachtsman is independent by nature, yet still four out of five travel the world looking for showers . . . The need is less in places like the Caribbean and Pacific where you can dive overboard and wash in the sea, but in harbours as opposed to anchorages it is necessary to find a shower.

Many people feel that a shower adds complication to their boats with pressurised water, sump pumps and so on, but this needn't be so. One of the best showers I ever saw was on a small trimaran, and we have since copied it in *Foreigner 2*. The focs'le was the heads and shower combined. A loo sat in solitary splendour in a large and otherwise empty glassfibre-lined and watertight compartment with an opening hatch over, all painted white. Water (hot or cold) was supplied by a portable pressurised garden sprayer. After use the hull sides were wiped and the bilge area sponged dry. This arrangement was used daily with conspicuous success. An added benefit was that when it rained the forehatch could still be left open for fresh air to permeate below decks as the focs'le could be mopped up afterwards.

Unfortunately most boatbuilders insist on prissying up the loo/shower compartment with lockers, shelves and fiddly joinery. The result is that the showers are totally impractical to use and it takes a day for all the woodwork and contents to dry out and even then there are soap-laden puddles lingering. It becomes such a hassle to take a shower in such a boat that everyone searches for one ashore, so beware of being influenced to buy a boat on the basis of a fitted shower, unless it is a spacious and easily-drained GRP-lined module.

Navigation station

For the amount of use they get, most chart tables take up an inordinate amount of prime space. Many skippers prefer to navigate on the saloon table, with a big fitted bookshelf behind them and charts rolled up under the deckhead. However, a chart table and seat is most useful as a watchkeeper's position below, where he or she can sit and read, poking a head out of the hatch at each turn of the page and keeping out of the way of sleeping crew. Have one that is flat so that it can be used for other purposes, such as meal or drink preparation, in harbour. It is amazing how many essential books one accumulates, so aim to increase shelf space, allowing for large publications such as the Sight Reduction Tables. If the table has a seat it is better that it face fore and aft, not, as is often the case, with the navigator's seat is the head of the quarter berth. And make sure that if the electrics panel is situated by the watchkeeper's arm or shoulder, as the majority are, that it has a clear perspex sheet protecting it for when the yacht is heeling that way. This also keeps off any spray flying about.

General

A boat that is lived aboard should not be compartmentalised. Try to maintain an open-plan arrangement by taking off doors and opening up bulkheads with large scallops (making sure they're not structural first). One of the best accommodation plans I ever saw was on a Newick trimaran built by a friend of ours, Jan Ebbing, who had spent the previous 16 years cruising and covered 60,000 miles. Confronted with a bare hull (he'd built the boat himself) with one immovable structural bulkhead, he laid a sole at a fairly high level to give him plenty of stowage low down in the bilge. Then he ran two bookshelves the length of the interior just under the hull/deck join. The floor, hull sides and deckhead were thickly carpeted throughout and the accommodation was completed by three or four big bean bags. That was it. The loo was a bucket (if you wanted privacy you went into the forward compartment or the cockpit) and the sink another (different-coloured) bucket. A simple propane cooker could be used anywhere and the bean bags were comfortable for seating and sleeping. This may sound basic but it was one of the most functional boats I've ever seen, has made several long passages, and has been his home now for several years without modification. Most accommodation plans can be subtly improved to make what was an awkward cabin into a comfortable home. A little thought on lighting (both natural and electric) always pays off, and judicious use of bright, light-coloured paints instead of universal varnishwork can give an impression of space.

When considering stowage don't just look at just the extent of locker space, but consider its accessibility and convenience. Many boats have acres of storage under berths and seats, but this is nearly always inconvenient to use. People have to be moved, then perhaps bedding and the cushions, locker lids and so on. So these areas must be backed up by plenty of door-fronted lockers and drawers (opening, needless to say, on an athwartships plane, not fore and aft). Big lockers should be split up, and it is a good idea to see if a framework cannot be incorporated in one of these to take stacked plastic bins, which are very efficient stowage. A boat we once ran had these bins running on little wooden rails fore and aft in the bilges, an otherwise unused space.

You will inevitably have several sets of clothes that need hanging up. A boat really must have a reasonable-sized hanging locker somewhere. A separate oilskin hanging locker situated right next to the companionway is also desirable, although we can live without one when there are just two people aboard. In daytime in the tropics it's more practical to strip off your clothing if you're likely to get wet, rather than put more on. If you have a decent sprayhood that covers the forward part of the cockpit, the best place to dry oilskins is in the cockpit hanging up under that sprayhood, so that the dampness dissipates outside and not into the cabin. All lockers must also be ventilated. This can be done in a couple of hours with a hole-cutter and fret-saw. The intention is to promote through-flow, so one hole will do nothing. Cut holes or slits low and high in a locker so that during the day, as the air warms up, it rises, escapes, and is replaced with fresh. This stops clothes from getting musty.

Finally, a word on guests. If you have a boat less than 42ft (12.8m) and unless you regularly expect to receive extra crew, don't waste precious space by having a special guest cabin. Most people coming out to exotic locations to join you for a brief cruise will be only too happy to put up with a little inconvenience like sleeping in the saloon. Nobody could call you selfish for wanting to use every inch of the confined volume of a yacht that you have to live in for the rest of the year.

8. On Deck

Centre cockpit versus aft

The choice between a centre or aft cockpit is an important one. I have met many yachts-men who misjudged it and were regretting their choice. When sailing, the centre cockpit is nearer the pitching centre of the yacht and the motion is therefore easier. It is also closer to the mast, which means a shorter time spent moving around on deck. The disadvantage is that being nearer the bows, a centre cockpit catches the waves and spray. This was a snag the Hiscocks disliked on their 49ft *Wanderer IV.* People who've sailed in extreme conditions with a centre cockpit say they feel more secure being planted in the heart of the boat, and that centre cockpits are safer with children aboard.

A centre cockpit usually commits you to having wheel steering and it is more difficult to rig windvane gear control lines in them. For this reason one often finds Hydrovane (the vane gear which requires no lines) self-steering on such vessels.

The main reason for choosing a centre cockpit, however, is usually to divide up the accommodation and create a separate, more private aftercabin. This is a desirable feature on a boat of 37 to 40ft and above, where it is possible to have a walkway connecting this cabin to the saloon. The size of this walkway determines the success or failure of the layout. Be suspicious of walkways on small boats though, because good headroom here will result in a high and exposed cockpit. If the boat doesn't have a walkway, it will be necessary to clamber through the cockpit each time you want to use the loo in the night or brew up in the morning. This is all right in a tropical climate but no laughing matter if you live aboard in less balmy climes. More than one owner of a centre cockpit boat has turned over the cramped aftercabin to stowage and ended up living in the considerably smaller forward accommodation quarters. Another point to bear in mind is that if the after cabin has a companionway and sliding hatch into the cockpit, it will face forward and cannot be left open at sea, and when sleeping there in port the washboards must be put in and hatch slid shut every time it rains. Few skippers sleep well when they are so far from the cockpit, so in any case it is necessary to bunk in the saloon when at sea. Therefore the time a centre cockpit with aftercabin scores is when there are children aboard, because this cabin can be theirs to make as chaotic as they wish without encroaching on the rest of the boat. Mum and Dad can sleep in the forward part of the boat and be just as private . . .

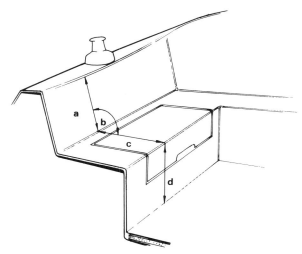

Fig 1 **The comfort of cockpit seats is imperative, bearing in mind the time you will be spending there. These dimensions give an approximate guide to comfortable proportions** *(a) 15in (38cm) (b) 105 degrees (c) 20in (50cm) (d) 15in (38cm)*

Cockpit features

It is absolutely essential that the cockpit of an ocean cruising yacht is comfortable, workable and generally liveable-in. Ocean cruisers spend most of their time in harbour, in a warm climate. Combined with a well-designed awning, the cockpit is the coolest place aboard. It becomes a reading area, the workshop for tinkering with maintenance jobs, somewhere to sleep on hot muggy nights, a place to eat breakfast, survey the world going by or just somewhere to stretch out and relax. Unless it is comfortable you will be relegated to a hot saloon and not be able to look out and take in the surroundings you have just sailed thousands of miles to reach.

The design of a cockpit must also of course be efficient and safe at sea. The ability to self-drain is obvious, but it must empty the majority of the water quickly. Much has been written over the years about small cockpits for ocean cruisers, but the aspect most of these writers have overlooked is that it is the size of just the well itself that is critical, not necessarily the whole cockpit as long as it doesn't have very deep coamings. When your cockpit gets thoroughly filled, through being pooped or broaching, most of the water above the cockpit seats very quickly overspills the coamings and is gone. Normally, if the boat is heeled or rolling downwind all that is left is a well-full. If that well is small, the extra weight of the water will not impede the yacht much and a long drainage time will be more inconvenient than dangerous. However, if the well is a largish size, an extra-big drain will need to be fitted. Some ocean cruisers, adapted from production craft, are fitted with a very large – up to 6in – pipe such as a plastic domestic waste pipe, glassed in from the back of the cockpit right through the lazarette locker to the transom, which is effectively a storm drain. Located centrally, it won't drain the last dregs when heeled over (the normal fittings should do this anyway) but it will clear the bulk of it quickly. So when looking at cockpit size, try to imagine how much water will be actually contained on a bucking, heeling yacht, and judge the volume of the well before the whole cockpit.

Drainage when heeled is an aspect that most modern yacht designers have sorted out, especially as it is easy to arrange with GRP mouldings. However, make sure the the area between the seats and coamings can drain fully when heeled – half an inch of water here is quickly soaked up by the trousers of a crewmember coming into the cockpit and sitting down on the more comfortable lee side. Make sure this water can either drain out on to the sidedeck, or back into the cockpit well, not down into the cockpit lockers as is very often the case. Slight seepage from rainwater while the boat is at rest is not a problem, but in bad weather when a lot of water is coming into the cockpit, you must make sure it is exiting from the drains, not into the cockpit lockers and thence into the bilge. So irritated with this problem was double circumnavigator Leslie Powles that he ended up glassing his cockpit locker lids permanently shut!

The sill of the companionway entrance must never be below the level of the cockpit seats on an ocean cruiser, because in heavy going there will nearly always be a few inches of water in the lee corner of the cockpit draining out and unless you have this high step a lot of water will creep into the cabin and possibly over the engine and electrics through the lower washboard. If you have a boat fitted with a low companionway, screw the first washboard permanently in place very thoroughly, with plenty of silicone sealer around the edge to make it watertight.

Ideally, a cockpit's seats and backrests should run more or less parallel to the yacht's centreline, otherwise with a particularly tapered cockpit (they often narrow toward the stern), when she is heeled over and you are sitting to leeward, you will tend to slide forward. The constant bracing to stay put can be enough to give you a stiff back after a couple of hours on watch or at the helm. The forward ends of the cockpit should really be tried out for comfort because they are usually sheltered by the spray dodger and are the most popular places to sit at sea. The best situation is when the aftercabin bulkhead is high enough to give comfortable support to the back and also slopes forward slightly, as many do.

The size, shape and angle of cockpit seats and backrests are critical if you are going to enjoy being seated there for any length of time. Before the early '70s yachtsmen had to put up with a narrow, hard horizontal bench with a coaming at 90 degrees to it, whose edge invariably hit you in the small of the back. Since then, GRP construction has allowed more comfortable shapes to be introduced. French naval architects have always led the field in cockpit comfort. Figure 1 gives some idea of proportions that work well. If your cockpit seating is uncomfortable it is not a difficult job to remodel it. If you have simple plank coamings their height can be increased in port by having extensions slot over the top. The shape of both the seats and the backrests can be completely altered by cutting comfortably-profiled 'frames' then screwing slats to them park-bench style. When a wheel is used for steering, a 'hump' on the athwartships seat can make a trick at the helm much more comfortable and some classes have this as standard. It is very easy to make such a hump with two plywood contour frames and park-bench slatting and make it portable for use as an ordinary seat in harbour. If all else fails in terms of cockpit comfort, equip it with plenty of closed-cell foam cushions.

A cockpit should also remain clear of fittings as far as possible, because it always becomes the congregating place for crew or friends coming aboard. There is nothing worse than sitting on the coaming only to uncomfortably discover a cleat between the winches, then moving down into the cockpit, tripping over the tiller lines, knocking knees on the tiller itself, and getting yet another cleat or self-steering block neatly in the small of the back. A protruding mainsheet track with its stops and jam cleat can mess up the

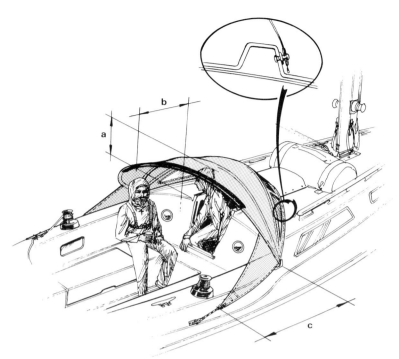

*Fig 2 **If well designed, a sprayhood is a godsend and ultimately, by contributing to the dryness of crew and therefore cabin, can maintain morale when conditions are bad. It should always attach to a coaming and be high enough (a) to not restrict easy access in and out. The length (b) should enable a crew member to sit at the forward end of the cockpit and remain dry in rain. The section of fabric (c) must overlap the coaming and if this part is made without poppers and tensioned with bungy, the sprayhood will absorb seas breaking on it and not split so easily***

forward end of the cockpit seat and the engine gear controls may clutter it up astern. So many of these protuberances can be eliminated. Nothing can be done with winches, but there is no need for sheet cleats. A tugboat hitch on the winch will do all that a cleat can and once accustomed to using them, you'll wonder why we ever had sheet cleats, because they are quicker to use than a turn on a cleat and, tied properly, don't jam up either. When cockpit cleats are needed (for the boom vang lead for example), they should be bolted to the outside of the coaming or on the deck alongside.

Engine controls (particularly the vulnerable key start) should be fitted in a moulded recess so that they are flush with the cockpit and cannot be kicked or have ropes caught around them. If yours are not flush, it is worth investigating the possibility of either moulding a little recess yourself or approaching the builder of any quality production yacht who will normally have a separate mould to make the recess in his yachts, and persuading him to laminate an extra one for you. I once saw a boat whose engine control levers were just inside the cockpit locker. It meant the skipper always had to have that locker lid open when manoeuvring, but he argued that having the controls out of the way meant they didn't catch anything and, away from wind and salt, stayed in much better shape. Do remember though that you need engine controls and

A 'companionway trough' makes an ideal and well protected watchkeeping position with all sail controls led aft and close to hand

instrumentation where the watch-keeper can keep an eye on them while motoring for long periods. Malfunction alarms are often drowned by the sound of the engine, but situated in the cockpit you have a better chance of hearing them.

Tillers are best if they can be unshipped or folded up out of the way in harbour. Wheel steering can monopolise the cockpit and more than one voyager we've met removes it in port, having the boss nut welded with big wings for easy refitting.

The humble cockpit pramhood cover is one of the best yachting inventions for a long time. Well designed (some suggestions can be found in Figure 2), it makes drier sailing probable. A dry crew is a happier and more efficient one and won't bring wet clothing into the cabin. The framework for the sprayhood should be very strong because it will inevitably be used as a grabrail. If the sprayhood extends over part of the forward end of the cockpit, as it should, the watch-keeper can remain fairly dry and if the primary sheet winches are within easy reach the crew will be able to trim the sheets without getting too wet.

Another feature which more modern boats are starting to incorporate is the companionway 'trough', an eminently seamanlike design which not only improves accommodation greatly but also makes a very comfortable watch-keeper's position.

Sleeping in the cockpit is a great pleasure and an absolute necessity in some climates, so the seats must be a minimum of 6ft 6in (1.98m)long and 20in (50cm) wide with their bases angled outboard slightly to hold you in with the boat rolling gently. A cockpit table is a great help when living aboard so find out whether it is possible to have one in your boat. It should be stout and easy to rig and stow. If it is too fiddly it will never get used. A cockpit becomes grubby in no time with a ghastly concoction of breadcrumbs, spilt coffee, jumper fluff, dried salt and short curly hairs, and the common teak grating does little except act as an unhygienic matrix for this unholy mixture. Although a teak grating looks lovely when scrubbed and clean, it belongs to the days when gentlemen had crew to keep it looking like this. Have one on a lived-aboard cruising boat and you will become a slave to it. The best cockpit sole is one left reasonably clear of dirt-collecting slats and one that can be quickly cleaned by a sluiced bucket of salt water followed by a once-over with the deck scrubber.

Anchor handling

One of the differences between the standard boat and the ocean cruiser is that anchoring facilities are gradually diminishing on the normal cruiser, which spends less time at anchor and more alongside. A stroll along an average marina will show a crop of anchors on deck and in rollers that have hardly ever been used. Good ground tackle is most ocean cruisers' insurance policy and it must be complemented with good gear for handling it. When you are in a genuine storm at anchor you begin to realise the advantages of a well laid-out, easily worked and spacious anchor handling area.

The design and arrangement of the bow-roller fitting heads the list of priorities. Basically, the larger the diameter of the roller the easier it will be to haul up the anchor. If the existing roller is less than 2in diameter, seriously consider replacing the whole fitting. Another element is the angle a bow roller imposes on a cable between the person hauling and the anchor itself (see Figure 3). With this in mind, the lower

Lateral-rolling cheeks for a stern anchor roller are highly desirable, indeed there is no reason why such an arrangement can't be organised for the bow roller too

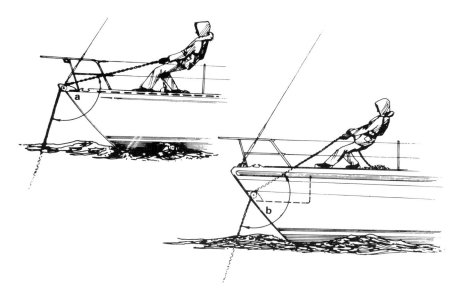

*Fig 3 **The more acute the angle a bow-roller imposes on an anchor chain (a), the harder it will be to haul up. Look for efficient features like the lowered roller in boat (b)***

the bow-roller is situated the better – good examples of this can be found on the Rival 41s and Southerly range of yachts whose bow rollers are actually situated in their foredeck anchor well. The second roller of a double bow fitting doesn't get a great deal of use, but it earns its keep when the conditions are bad and two anchors have to be handled, plus allowing that much more space for each cable's chafing gear. The rollers themselves should be made out of the same metal as the fitting (ie stainless, bronze, aluminium or galvanised). Metal rollers are noisier, but rubber rollers don't last any time at all and plastic rollers (in particular tufnol and nylon) can split, spread or swell in the heat and seize up on the axle pin. The cheeks of the roller must be deep and have a pin to stop the cable jumping out. The cheeks should also splay out to reduce chafe when the yacht sheers. Some production boats, particularly those from France, have started using cast aluminium bow-rollers which can be very harsh on the anchor warp. An hour or so of judicious work with a metal file will breach the anodising but improve the cheeks no end.

An anchor ought to be able to stow within the bow roller, at least temporarily whilst you approach an anchorage or shift to another. If it doesn't, it is tempting to leave it hanging from the bow for a few moments where it stands a good chance of swinging and damaging the gelcoat or paintwork. If you have a roller-reefing headsail, make sure the drum is set sufficiently high off the deck (with a solid spacer) so the anchor can be lowered without the shank hitting the drum.

Whether you have a windlass must depend on a combination of boat size, bank balance and personal strength. Whichever you decide, it must be relatively easy to haul in your anchor otherwise you'll be tempted to stop in a potentially dangerous spot when you should move on. The arguments against a windlass are to keep things simple, cut down weight, and save money for something else. Our two ocean cruisers

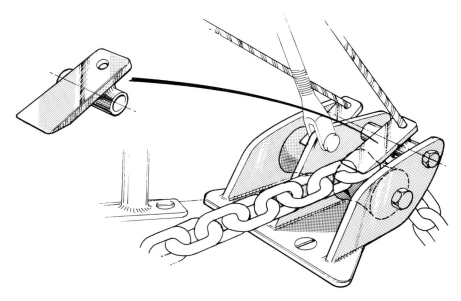

Fig 4 If you have no windlass, a chain pawl will reduce the effort involved in hauling the anchor. With a chain pawl, a 35lb (15kg) anchor and 30 fathoms (55m) of 5/16in (5mm) chain can be handled without difficulty or the need for a windlass

were both 35ft and both equipped with 35lb CQRs and 180ft of five-sixteenths inch chain. It was the same specification of ground tackle which Hiscock used in his *Wanderer 111*, which didn't have a windlass. On the first boat, which was largely engineless, we nearly always sailed out the anchor, which meant about five frenetic minutes of shortening the cable, hoisting sail and then, with sails trimmed, sailing over the anchor, which then had to be hauled up and on deck quickly as by then we were hurtling through a crowded anchorage or harbour. When the anchor fouled, we hitched a line to it and led this aft to a sheet winch to haul up. A chain pawl is an old idea but considerably reduces the total effort required to raise an anchor by holding the chain for you whilst you grab another arm's length of chain, or simply rest for a moment. A grooved bow roller considerably increases the efficiency of a chain pawl, as does a length of shock cord as shown in Figure 4.

I was not disappointed when our second boat had a windlass already fitted. She also had a nice reliable diesel. In practice I found the Simpson Lawrence windlass, highly popular and fitted on thousands of yachts, so slow and uncomfortable to use (you either had to bend awkwardly or kneel) that I hardly ever used it. Instead, we would motor towards the cable, which took all the work out of hauling, then, when it was vertical, put a turn on a cleat and break out the anchor with the motor running ahead. While Lou Lou kept the yacht on station with the engine I had all the time in the world to haul up the anchor. After those experiences I would avoid buying and fitting a windlass on a yacht less than 36ft (needing a 35lb bower anchor) unless it was absolutely necessary, and then make sure it was one of the fast-action types. Having spent many hours and a lot of money repairing electric windlasses as the skipper of a charter boat, I would also look at these suspiciously unless I could afford the very best and a comprehensive selection of spare parts.

The foredeck of a serious ocean cruiser must have at least two king-size cleats and preferably three, for when conditions are bad you need to adjust each separate mooring or anchor warp independently. A lowered foredeck anchor well is useful because it allows you to stow all the cable and anchor in it temporarily while you wash off the inevitable collection of mud, sand, seaweed and kelp. All this muck goes out of the well scuppers rather than being spread all over the decks. However, such a well must have large drains to cope with lumps of seaweed and clear the water which will fill it as you punch into a head sea.

It is easy to forget that the boat will be moored by her stern from time to time, perhaps with the kedge anchor out to steady her in a rolly anchorage or to hold her off the shore while you are tied bows-on to a palm tree. So a stern roller is needed. It will also be useful if ever you have to tow a drogue or warps in bad weather. A good-sized fairlead on the taffrail will do just as well. It is important that there is a fair un-interrupted lead from this fitting to one of the sheet winches so the stern anchor can be hauled tight. This comes into its own if ever you go aground and try hauling the yacht off backwards.

Deck hatches

Until we have sailed in a hot climate, most of us tend not to pay too much attention to opening hatches on yachts. They are seen only as a source of draughts and a danger to seaworthiness in heavy weather. That all soon changes in hot Mediterranean weather and muggy, still, tropical nights. One cannot have enough opening hatches in hot cli-mates. The aluminium-framed opening hatches fitted to most modern boats are very good, but if you've any choice in the matter it's worth fitting hatches which don't have fiddly thumbscrew-tightened support struts. In the tropics, where rain-squalls are a common daily occurrence, hatches are opened and closed regularly and those catches don't last long. And sooner or later someone will fall against or stand on your opened hatch, and an inability to yield will quite likely distort the hatch and make it leak for-ever after. We have fitted Lewmar Superhatches and have nothing but praise for their simple operation and watertightness.

If you are building or refitting and can choose your hatches make sure that when they are positioned on a horizontal surface the water can drain off entirely. If not, they will soon leak.

Fig 5 If a hatch is mounted on a wooden or moulded plinth, when a green sea sweeps it the water is directed up and over the hatch, thus keeping the direct flow of water away from the seal, cutting the chance of leaks

An excellent example of a stern platform, the addition of which gives a boat a much bigger feel on deck whilst providing extra stowage for bulky items

General deck layout

Stowage. Ocean cruisers always seem to accumulate a fair amount of junk and equipment on deck, much of which is better stowed elsewhere. An accumulation of four or five full water or fuel containers, extra anchors, a couple of bicycles, spare gas bottles, and a few heavy drogue warps can have an adverse affect on the yacht's stability. Much of this equipment is seldom, if ever, used and every effort should be made to stow it down low in the bilge or at the bottom of cockpit lockers. Certain items, though, are unavoidably stowed on deck. The liferaft is best situated somewhere aft of amidships to keep it out of the way of solid water forward. When kept in the cockpit well, it serves the dual function of cutting down the cockpit's volume.

The Dinghy. This must have a home on deck and if you prefer to have a rigid tender, make sure it can be accommodated on deck without fouling any important working areas or gear. With ingenuity, dinghies can be adapted to fit on deck, perhaps by

Fig 6 **Heeled ergonomics. The upright cabin and narrowish sidedecks of the yacht on the left make deckwork clumsy, inefficient and quite likely dangerous compared to the yacht on the right. In light of the amount of seatime you will put in aboard your ocean cruiser, make sure the deck is easy to move around on at sea**

building a recess in the transom to fit round the mast or a slit in the bows to snug up to the inner forestay. If the dinghy is stowed on the coachroof you might as well take advantage of its height by bolting handrails on its bottom panels so they can be grabbed when moving around on deck.

Running booms. It has somehow become traditional among ocean cruisers to fit the running booms permanently aloft, either strapped to the mast or taken out to the shrouds. This undoubtedly makes them very easy to use, but has significant disadvantages. Windage is increased a great deal, and the centre of gravity is raised, but more important is their vulnerability in this position. The principal secondary use of running poles is to set up a jury rig if the mast is broken and if they are strung up in the rigging they're unlikely to survive a dismasting without being broken themselves. They are best stowed on deck, as far forward as possible, so the crew can lift their after ends up and hook them on to the mast fitting without fouling the lower shrouds. Running booms are by definition used when running downwind, when the boat will be rolling. If one person is trying to set up the boom it can be very difficult to keep 'one hand for yourself and one for the ship'. So it pays to spend some time establishing a routine and organising stowage for the booms so that only one end need be lifted. My own system uses a simple length of line permanently hanging between the after struts on either side of the pulpit. The front of the boom is disconnected from its deck chock, lifted and placed in this rope sling. With the front thus cradled, the after end can then be picked up and fitted to the mast, completing the operation.

Miscellanea. Keep the sidedecks completely clear of lashed-down equipment and keep all miscellaneous gear like the boathook, scrubber, dinghy oars etc, within a central area on a flush deck or on the coachroof. The less cluttered the deck, the less chance of accidents, foul-ups, or simply stubbed toes.

Heeled ergonomics. How good will your proposed deck layout (and in particular sidedecks) be in providing footholds when the yacht is well heeled over? Figure 6 shows how canted coachroof coamings can be a great advantage in this respect, and contrasts how bad a narrow-sidedecked boat with upright coamings is. Good stout handrails are as useful as footholds when working forward with the yacht heeled over.

9. A Rig for Long Distances

For decades yachtsmen argued the respective merits of the sloop, cutter, ketch, yawl and schooner, but ultimately the arguments were settled, as are many things, out on the racing course. The 1970s saw a fierce leap in the level of racing competition, and considerably more money than ever before poured into the developments of rigs, sails and rigging systems. There was one clear winner, boring though it may seem in the eyes of lovers of the traditional – the Bermudian sloop.

By the late '70s equipment and methods had developed to a stage where it was quite possible for one man to control a large sail area quickly and efficiently. There are, of course, big variations on the basic Bermudian-rigged sloop, from the positioning of the mast, proportions of each sail and the addition of an occasional cutter forestay to make it an inelegant 'slutter'. The efficiency and practicality of this rig has been clearly demonstrated in every BOC Singlehanded Around The World Race, where the sloop/cutter rig holds a virtual monopoly.

For efficiency, practicality and speed, no modern yacht under 55ft (16.75m) needs more than one mast. However, other factors, even emotions, may determine the right rig for an individual. An older couple may well prefer the divided ketch rig with its smaller sails and many still prefer a gaff rig for the atmosphere and character it lends to their sailing.

The ketch has long been a firm favourite amongst ocean cruisers and will probably continue to be so. Its main advantages are that in squally weather you can quickly de-power the rig by lowering the main, and in heavy going you can sail under the snug and well-balanced sail plan of headsail and mizzen. Another is that if you lose one mast (especially the main) you are left with the basis of a jury rig. There is also the facility to set a colourful mizzen staysail and the ability to leave the mizzen up at anchor, ensuring that the yacht lies head to wind.

Our first ocean cruiser was a ketch, and we subsequently went on to run two more, in total logging nearly 30,000 miles under the rig. Without doubt, in heavy or squally weather, with headsail and mizzen set the rig gave an air of confidence, but the disadvantages far outweighed this, especially as an ocean cruiser sailing within normal bounds and seasons shouldn't encounter heavy weather that often. Neither should we pre-suppose that other rigs are poor in heavy weather.

Against the ketch is sailing performance, especially to windward, plus the weight,

The unstayed cat rig on boats like this Freedom is in many ways ideal for cruising,
but is difficult to repair

windage and cost of that extra spar. There are also a handful of minor, but nevertheless significant points against it. It clutters the stern area of the yacht, which is constricting physically (the mizzen boom, for example, nearly always needs to be ducked under), and makes it difficult to set a satisfactory awning. The mizzen also often interferes with a self-steering vane and means an extra sail cover to be taken off and re-rigged.

The mizzen staysail has more value in romantic terms than as a working part of a cruising boat. It's the sort of sail that usually only gets set when you're trying to get a portrait photo of your yacht or perhaps during a regatta. Otherwise, the narrow band of wind direction and strength that allows them to set, combined with only marginally better speed (which always has to be balanced by the increase in weather helm they normally introduce) means that their cost and the space they take up is better used on an ocean cruiser.

Where a ketch does score is if you own a simple, older boat over 40ft (12.1m) that doesn't benefit from the advances in material and equipment made over the last 30 years. With heavy wooden booms and weighty sails, maybe an old-fashioned reefing system, and smallish winches (by today's standards), the ketch is as suitable a rig as it ever was 25 years ago. Efficiency takes on a different context in these circumstances, but performance will be diminished and you will nevertheless have to put up with the disadvantages outlined above.

The yawl is a better-proportioned rig than the ketch, because the mainmast and its sails are more or less the same size as a sloop's, so even ignoring the mizzen, you get almost as good a sailing performance as the single masted boat. The yawl only scores when it comes to close-quarters manoeuvring under sail. At sea, the extra mast's contribution is insignificant and in port you get all the disadvantages of the ketch.

The maintainability of an ocean cruiser's rig is important. Masts, spars and rigging are vulnerable at sea and particularly in port. The ability to make running repairs or even replace a spar anywhere in the world must be considered. In just the same way as exotic materials are unsuitable for the hull of an ocean cruiser, so it is with the rig. The unstayed cat rig on boats like the Freedom and Nonsuch range is ideal for long-distance cruising. It is easily handled, has virtually no chafe and a better safety record than conventional stayed rigs (borne out by the fact that insurance companies offer lower premiums to owners of craft rigged thus). However, generally speaking the masts are either spun-tapered aluminium, carbon fibre or sophisticated constructions of spruce and epoxy. While these rigs have shown themselves to be highly reliable under sail, there are too many potential accidents, particularly in port, that could cause them to break, and once broken there is a high chance they will be impossible to repair. Mast breakages don't necessarily happen at sea. A clumsy crane-driver in a commercial harbour can swipe a mast or you may be unfortunate enough to drag ashore where a mast can be vulnerable if there are any harbour walls. When circumnavigating in *Les Quatres-Vents*, Marcel Bardiaux had a lorry drive over the end of his aluminium mast which was laying on the quayside, ready to be stepped... The chances are thankfully rare, but nevertheless exist. Personal woodworking abilities aside, to find, shape and taper a suitable tree for a mast might be possible on a junk-rigged boat designed to be fitted with one originally, but such a replacement spar would be unlikely to be suitable on a cat-rigged boat like a Freedom.

When our ketch was dismasted off Martinique we were able to locate an inexpensive secondhand wooden bermudian mast of approximately the right dimensions relatively easily, as a hurricane had swept the island the year before and several yachts had been lost and their masts salvaged. If we had had a cat rig with carbon fibre spars we would have had a long wait and a high bill for a replacement to be sent out.

General sail area

Modern materials and related technology means that reefing sails with a small crew has become much easier. So many people are now of the opinion that a larger sail area is to be preferred to a conservatively rigged yacht which comes to a standstill in light airs.

For ocean cruising the ability to sail well in light conditions is much more important than with a weekend cruiser, which you can always motor back home. From time to time an ocean cruiser must contemplate long passages in regions of light conditions such as the Doldrums, Horse Latitudes, and the Gulf of Panama, where heavy, undercanvassed yachts have been trapped for lengthy periods. Being becalmed for

Under the eminently practical Chinese rig, yachts have made countless ocean crossings. Nowadays many of the rig's advantages have been incorporated into the standard Bermudian sloop with roller genoa, so the junk rig is less popular

more than a day or so is no joke, either psychologically or physically, because of the chafe it imposes on gear and rigging. As soon as the wind arrives you can always shorten down, but the frustration of wanting more sail area when your heavy canvas starts slatting around in light going is far from fun. Ocean cruising yachts tend to be on the heavy side (or at least over-loaded), which is immediately against them in lighter going, and it is illogical to have a boat that only starts to move well in a Force 5 when so much satisfaction can be had from keeping her at near hull speed in the much more pleasant conditions of a Force 3. Bernard Moitessier has always been a keen advocate of having plenty of sail area, and it enabled him to drive his heavy-displacement steel ketch *Joshua* consistently over long distances. The disadvantages of a large rig are found when you need to sail in high latitudes or in boisterous tradewinds, such as the Indian Ocean crossing, but this can be overcome by having a smaller, heavier, mainsail bent on during these periods.

For all their popularity in normal offshore cruising, the question of whether to have full-length battens in a mainsail for long distance ocean cruising is a difficult one to answer. Reports from yachtsmen who've used them over long distances are, by and large, favourable, although several have said that the fully-battened sail's main practical advantages (easier regular stowing and no flogging) don't necessarily appertain to an ocean cruising mode. Against them is chafe which, despite greatly improved handling hardware, is nevertheless a problem on a boat which spends most of its seatime off- or down-wind. Another problem with ocean cruising comes when, running downwind with poled out headsails, there is the need to either raise or lower the main. With a conventional soft main this is relatively easy (if pretty unkind on the sail), but much more difficult with a full-battened sail.

I am a great advocate of the fully battened mainsail, having sailed with them for 25 years in my father's cruising catamaran. However, I have to say that after much deliberation, when we ordered a new mainsail for *Foreigner 2*, destined as she was for ocean cruising, we specified a conventional soft sail.

Many experienced skippers prefer to have a battenless mainsail. There are good arguments for this in that batten pockets are the most common area for damage or re-stitching on a mainsail, plus the fact that the battens themselves can quite easily break or be lost. Another good point in favour of the battenless main is the fact that you can haul the sail up and down when the wind is abaft the beam without any battens getting caught in the standing rigging. Against the battenless mainsail is, quite simply, sail efficiency and therefore boat speed. A 'hooked' or J-shaped leech saps speed and causes more leeway. Battens help avoid this and keep the wind flowing off the sail smoothly. With no battens the leech becomes scalloped slightly, and you can expect to lose up to ten percent of effective sail area and therefore there will be a noticeable drop in speed.

To lead aft or not to lead aft

The 1960s and '70s saw a great re-emergence of the Chinese or junk rig which, using modern materials, is still very popular with cruising yachtsmen. The great plus is the ability to handle all the sail controls from one place, usually the companionway area. Junk rig sailors boasted about carpet-slipper passages and not having to don oilskins, and this idea of control from the cockpit converted many people to the rig.

Although the idea of leading one or two lines or halyards aft was far from new, the development of efficient rope clutches and stoppers in the late '70s heralded an upsurge of interest in leading everything aft on Bermudian rigs. In fact, it is nearly impossible to lead absolutely everything aft. Certain sails like the spinnaker and cruising chute have to be rigged and set from on deck, although these aren't part of a normal working rig and are unlikely to be set or lowered by a small crew in bad conditions, or in the middle of the night (when the line-aft arrangement comes into its own).

The main disadvantage of having everything aft is the accumulation of ropes and lines that clog up the forward end of the cockpit. One has to buy more rope and if you are converting from conventional controls at the mast you will need to completely renew all the running rigging. Although one also needs more hardware, like extra blocks at the foot of the mast, turning block sets and a handful of stoppers and/or clutches, the cost of these is offset by the reduction in expensive winches needed. Another disadvantage is the increase in friction in all the lines being led aft.

On the other hand, assuming the boat is fitted with a roller jib, the principal advantage of leading lines aft, and one shouldn't underestimate its implications, is that

Properly arranged with good-quality hardware and rope stowage, leading lines aft to a single winch improves efficiency by taking the danger, wetness and hassle out of conventional reefing, therefore encouraging the crew to set exactly the right amount of sail

it is rarely necessary to go on deck for any sail handling. This is a major safety advantage, particularly if the crew are not particularly experienced at working on deck. A skipper's sleep and rest can be interrupted by many things, but the knowledge that most sail-handling can be done from the cockpit without needing to worry about someone risking going overboard each time the mainsail is reefed is a great comfort. When two people are cruising alone there should be a rule that when one is going on deck the other is always alerted. This is a good precaution, but it often means the off-watch partner loses some sleep. After long experience of this system, Lou Lou and I have decided that our next boat will have lines aft to cut down the number of forays on deck. Having lines aft also means that the chances of keeping reasonably dry are higher, and this makes a big psychological difference on a long trip when salt-encrusted clothes and bodies never seem to dry properly and quickly absorb any moisture present.

The other aspect of lines-led-aft gets back to the old adage aboard yachts – 'if it's easy to do something, you'll get on with it'. The prospect of putting on oilskins and clambering over a pitching, heeled deck to the mast to put in or shake out a reef, standing a good chance of a drenching on the way, will be enough to encourage a watch-keeper to procrastinate and hang on a bit longer with the yacht over- or under-canvassed and therefore straining and sailing inefficiently. If it is easy to reef from the companionway, you'll get on with the job as soon as it is needed. American Dodge Morgan completed a singlehanded circumnavigation in 1985/6 in his massively built 60ft (18.28m) sloop American Promise. She was equipped with every handling aid imaginable, including Hood Stoway mainsail reefing. When I spoke to him aboard the yacht in Maine, USA, after the voyage, Dodge reckoned that because sail handling was simple he hadn't had an incorrect amount of sail set for more than 15 minutes at a time in the entire 27,500 mile voyage. He sailed her efficiently and the rewards were that he not only halved the previous record time (he made the passage in 150 days, averaging 172 miles a day), but gear failures were minimal and he didn't have to put a single stitch in any of his sails.

Many of the disadvantages of a lines-aft system can be eased. Only high-quality equipment will solve the friction problem, although the rope spaghetti can be tamed by using canvas or acrylic pouches. Ideally the coachroof layout, forward cockpit coamings and work areas next to the companionway should be designed with a lines-aft system in mind, but seven out of ten boats can be adapted without too much inconvenience. Used in conjunction with well-arranged lazyjacks (described in Section 3) and a roller-reefing headsail, the lines-aft system has to be the safest and most efficient rigging arrangement for the long-distance cruiser. It has many of the advantages of the Chinese rig, without the windward sailing and speed disadvantage that the junk generally has.

Rigging details

Today the details of a yacht's rig, the gear used and the way it is laid out are far more pertinent than the number of masts she has. In discussing these details below it is assumed the yacht is Bermudian-rigged, although many of the ideas can be adapted and used with gaff rig. They are modern ideas, though, which might go against the grain with some traditionalists.

When a roller-furling headsail is employed, the storm jib can be set up ready for use on a sloop's babystay. It is essential to strengthen attachment points on mast and deck and provide aft support for the mast at the hounds

The roller-reefing headsail

The complication and potential unreliability of roller-reefing headsail equipment has made ocean cruising yachtsmen slow to adopt this particular handling aid. Although far from a new idea, its re-emergence and staggering popularity for normal pleasure use has meant that the products have steadily improved and a number of very good models are now available. Again using the gruelling BOC Singlehanded Around the World Races as a yardstick, all serious contenders fit roller gears, most choosing Profurl, and a handful of others Harken.

The convenience of doing perhaps 80 percent of one's sailing without ever changing a jib on a bucking foredeck is obvious. There are incidental plus points too, including more space in the sail locker and keeping the sail clean by having it off the deck when the anchor is hauled in. The main advantage, though, is the ability of a weaker crew, possibly a child or small woman, to reef down without assistance. The implications are numerous. The crew are safer because they don't need to go forward and change sails (especially at night, when the chances of recovering a man overboard are slight), the off-duty watch isn't called up to help, and the cabin stays drier through not having wet sails and people below. Also, setting a running pole is made much easier by first furling the sail, clipping on the boom, then unfurling.

Against this are two major disadvantages, which can both be eased, if not eradicated. One is the possibility of a jam-up, especially in mid-ocean. There are three ways to avoid the chances of this happening and they are the same as for almost any mechanical item aboard – correct initial installation, subsequent preventative maintenance and correct usage. There are a surprising number of poorly-installed roller reefing headsail gears on boats. The reefing drum is approximately double the diameter of the rolled sail, which means that the line has around half the strain on it that the sheet has. When you compare the sloppy arrangement and skimpy thickness of many headsail reefing lines to the careful alignment given the headsail sheets, leading as they do through expensive sheet cars and turning blocks to two of the biggest winches on board, the contrast is amazing.

Depending on which gear is used, another problem area for those with halyards coming back down the mast rather than to the foot of the forestay drum is the lead and tension of the headsail halyard. One of the few jobs it is worth paying a genuine professional specialist rigger to do is the initial installation of a roller-furling headstay.

The fact that most of these gears are constructed with a combination of stainless steel and aluminium, and happen to be situated on the wettest part of the boat above the waterline, means that unless the gears are completely stripped down, cleaned and greased at regular intervals, electrolysis could freeze all the fittings and make dismantling almost impossible without heat. This regular strip-down will make sure the skipper is completely familiar with the gear and allow him to check the condition of the bearings and any other moving parts.

Using a roller reefing headsail efficiently requires a certain amount of technique, and one should be careful not to fall into the trap of simply letting go the sheet, hauling in some reefing line, then re-trimming the sheet. Similarly, when setting the sail be certain not to simply cast off the reefing line and haul on the sheet, because the loose winding of the reefing line around the drum could lead to bunching and snarl-ups later when tension comes on to it. The reefing line should be led to its own winch and although the sheet must inevitably be eased, the sail should be rolled with just the right amount of tension in it. The sheet lead changes as the sail is rolled, and if you wish to avoid leaving the cockpit altogether it is possible to rig up lines from the sheet car, leading around a block at the front of the track and back to the cockpi. Putting pre-determined reefing marks on the foot of the sail and corresponding points on the sheet track makes the correct sheet lead easy to ascertain, particularly at night.

The second disadvantage of the roller reefing headsail is that when reefed beyond a certain point (normally about 65 per cent of its area) the sail shape starts to go as the foot and leech roll tighter than the middle, resulting in a hollow bag which saps performance, particularly upwind. Over recent years sailmakers have solved this thorny problem by incorporating tapered foam inserts just behind the luff, which work well. Despite this, excepting fairly extreme fractional rigs, there is no such thing as the ideal headsail which will work efficiently in all wind ranges, so the fitting of a roller headsail will always be something of a compromise. Fitting a No.2 genoa to it usually provides a good all-round sail for normal conditions which can be used up to a Force 6 or 7. For light airs, or as part of a downwind rig, a removable forestay (a spare wire foresail halyard can be used and set up with a halyard winch) attaches just abaft the rolled sail. Onto this is hanked a light drifter or, when the wind goes above Force 6/7, a largish storm jib with a row of reef points to take it down to hurricane size. If you have a generous budget, a storm jib can be permanently set up on another roller gear in place of the inner or babystay, meaning that in heavy weather you never have to leave the cockpit to set the storm jib. Either of these systems obviates the roller reefing jib's other pitfall; the headsail's centre of effort moves forward and upward as the sail is reefed, not only making the yacht heel more, but perhaps upsetting the balance and inducing lee helm.

These marks, combined with predetermined corresponding numbers on the sheet tracks, take the hit and miss out of the correct sheet leads for a roller headsail

Properly installed, regularly maintained and correctly used, there is no reason why a modern roller reefing gear should give any problems. What it gives in return is convenience, safety and the ability for one person to reef or unreef a large headsail unaided. The performance loss of having a thick leading edge and, at times, poor sail shape is balanced by the ability to make fine adjustments to the sail area and keep her going at her maxiumum with very little effort. Conversely, anyone who has sailed shorthanded with hanked-on headsails will have confronted many times the situation where you hang on just a bit longer (and a bit more . . .) to a wrong-sized headsail, either too big or too small, with all the sailing inefficiencies and strains that imposes, while waiting to see what the wind will do.

Mainsail reefing

Sail handling is the most common activity in the daily routine of a yacht on a long passage and the ability to easily shorten or increase sail area will not only lead to performance advantages, but will be much kinder on the sails themselves, which means you spend less time repairing them and less money in the long run having to replace them. One can often gauge a skipper's seamanship by the number of sails he moans about 'blowing out'. Modern sails are tough. Kept out of the sun as much as possible they last a long time, but misuse by not reefing in time, or laziness over reefing, or just not keeping an eye open for them chafing, means they will quickly enough be damaged. Her mainsail is a yacht's workhorse. By nature it gets considerably more use than any sail aboard and must be carefully looked after.

Mainsail reefing has come full circle over the last few years. All the old fore-and-aft rigged working boats used point reefing, a more complicated version of what the most up-to-date yacht uses today. There have been periods of popularity for mainsail roller-reefing, but the strength and durability of modern synthetic ropes has done away with the need and a very basic and beautifully simple version of the old points reefing, called slab reefing, has emerged. With well-designed booms accommodating internal reefing lines, spar- and sail-makers have developed this into a foolproof system that is difficult to fault. Practically the only problem is the likely chafe of the reefing pennant as it passes through the clew cringle. Certain small additions can improve the system. My personal preference is to lead all the controls aft to the cockpit, but if you keep them at the mast, a good idea is to build a box around the foot which all the falls can flake into. This saves having to coil them and diminishes time spent on deck. The mast box can also be stowage for oddments like sail tiers, a shackle key, spare lashings etc. Marking the halyard with an indelible pen for the appropriate reefing positions will save a little time, and rope colour coding makes a lot of sense.

If your main is fitted with slab reefing, never tie in the reef points! This may have old seamen turning in their graves, but a clew pennant takes an enormous strain and if anything fails, whether the rope, boom fitting, clew eye or perhaps even a rope clutch or stopper slipping, the flogging sail will be badly damaged as soon as the strain comes on to that first tied-in reef point. Having seen an otherwise healthy mainsail self-destruct in this manner before we could even get it down after the pennant rope parted, I will never tie in a reef, however untidy it looks. Later in this chapter I will describe lazyjacks, which automatically collect a reefed portion of sail. If you don't fit lazyjacks and don't like the reefed section flogging under the boom (in fact, it can be half-tucked on the windward side between the tight new foot and the boom), the best alternative is to arrange a 'bungy cord' tie-down system which will simply stretch if any component of the clew pennant goes. Another point to watch carefully is that the reefed part of the mainsail doesn't get pinched by the reefing pennants. This can quickly cause serious chafe.

Leading halyard and reefing controls aft is gaining popularity and there are a variety of ways of doing this. Many people have tried a one-line system. The reefing line starts at the outer pennant position on the boom, goes up through the reefing clew and back to a sheave at the end of the boom and through the inside, before re-emerging at the gooseneck, going up to the reefing tack eye and then finally coming down to a block at the mast foot and leading aft. The strains on this line are quite considerable and friction usually makes it slow, hard work to pull in this large amount of line. A couple of British production boats, namely the Freedom 40 and Southerly range, have successfully arranged this system. Expensive roller-bearing blocks can make all the difference and if these are shackled to both the clew and tack fittings, further reductions of friction can be achieved. A simple two-line system can operate without a great deal of adaptation from standard spars and their fittings. Having tried both, I prefer the two-line set-up. Against it is the fact that you must have two lines for each reefing sequence, therefore with three reef positions you must have six lines, stoppers et al. However, the friction is minimalised, so the job is much easier for a weaker crew. With this arrangement the ropes split into shorter lengths, which is more practical when they need replacement or end-for-ending as reefing lines tend to. Many prefer to have a mainsail with two generous slab reefs and, when a further reduction is required, change over to a very strong trysail.

During its period of popularity, mainsail roller reefing developed into quite an efficient and quick method of reefing. Eric Hiscock always swore by it and even after trying a modern slab system on his last yacht, *Wanderer V,* he still reckoned it was superior. The speed of the boom turning can make quite a difference and when the simple 'through mast' roller reefing systems came on the scene, and it became possible to roll the boom on a 1:1 ratio (as opposed to the fearfully slow geared rollers), reefing became quick and easy. Pick up any sailing book of the early to mid '70s and you'll see the top ocean racers of the day, *Prospect of Whitby, Quailo, Morning Cloud* etc, all demonstrating that roller reefing can produce a well-set mainsail.

Our Rival 34, *Euge*, was fitted with a through-mast roller reefing mainsail and my first thought was that it would need changing to slab reefing. However, I tried it out, the system worked very well indeed, I never bothered to change it and it never gave us trouble. What was against it was that it took twice as long to reduce sail as slab reefing would have done and I always had to go forward to reef, whereas slab reefing can be led into the cockpit.

In-mast reefing

On the face of it, in-mast mainsail reefing, whether the dedicated variety or the retrofit rivet-on-the-mast variety, would seem ideal for ocean cruising, especially as their reliability has been proven. There is no queston but that it is fabulously easy and convenient to use, and the sail is always protected from harmful ultraviolet rays. The only problem, and it is a major one for an ocean cruiser, is the movement of the sail's centre of effort as it is reefed. Instead of the slab-reefing mainsail's C of E which moves down and slightly forward as it reefs, the in-mast roller mainsail's C of E moves mainly forward and only slightly lower as the sail reefs into the mast. This sometimes causes quite severe lee helm in a yacht, combined as it is with the roller headsail's similar characteristics. For an average weekend cruising yacht, rarely at sea in very strong winds, this is a small compromise for the convenience. For the ocean cruising yacht, quite likely to meet and sustain heavy weather in the normal course of her activities, that lee helm and an inability to make properly to weather when it might matter is not a risk worth taking.

Trysails

When a mainsail is deeply reefed in bad weather, the strain on the leech is enormous as a result of the leverage exerted by the mainsheet, and although tightening the topping lift can take some of the weight off, many a mainsail has been ripped in half in such circumstances. Another disquieting factor in heavy weather is the boom thrashing around. If it can be lashed into its gallows or on the deck life will be much happier. It is also asking a great deal of a mainsail to be the sail for everything from a flat calm to a howling gale. A mainsail heavy enough to withstand several bad gales will be useless in light airs and unwieldy the whole time. Dr Ronnie Andrews, a circumnavigator and past Commodore of the Royal Cruising Club, is one of many yachtsmen who believe a trysail is the answer for heavy going.

Traditionally, a trysail was always approximately one third of the mainsail's area, but Dr Andrews prefers it to be a little bigger, nearer 40 percent. To be practical to use in bad conditions the sail must have its own independent track. Trying to reach a normal slide gate six or seven feet above the deck with a heavy trysail in gale conditions is out of the question. A track can be screwed to a wooden mast or riveted to an extruded aluminium one, but never use self-tapping screws to hold it to aluminium as these can shake loose in bad weather, weakening the track and making it very difficult indeed to get the sail down. By having its own track coming down to the deck, the trysail can be left bent on, in its bag, during passages, simplifying the setting of it. It shouldn't be sheeted on the centreline (the sail will 'cup' and lose efficiency) and twin sheets should be led through blocks aft on each side and taken to spinnaker winches. If you don't have these winches, three-part blocks and tackles can be used, but with these the crew must watch out when tacking.

A trysail should be heavily made (10oz minimum for yachts displacing less than 10 tons) and triple-stitched, with a wire tack pennant that raises it above the stowed mainsail head to avoid chafe. When we had a trysail made for our 35ft (10.66m) catamaran *Foreigner* I stipulated a row of reef points in this already tiny sail. Our friends, and even the sailmaker, thought we were over-doing it, but in a subsequent severe Atlantic gale we were thankful – under whole trysail she was surfing almost out of control, when it was reefed the catamaran became quite docile in comparison.

A running rig

For decades the hallmark of a long-distance cruising yacht was a pair of running booms attached aloft and coming down to either rail. The tradewind running rig of twin boomed-out headsails evolved as much because it is a fairly trouble- and chafe-free set-up for running downwind as because you could take the sheets back to the helm and most yachts would thus self-steer. For the pioneers of ocean cruising with limited crew this was a major breakthrough. Anyone who has used self-steering gear after experience of watch on/watch off hand-steering will understand the significant impact this rig had. It nevertheless had disadvantages. It was expensive in sails and special equipment and inflexible in terms of sail area in fluctuating conditions (and even tradewinds can come and go all the time). The configuration also makes most boats roll dreadfully. Hiscock said that *Wanderer III* could roll from 32 degrees one way to 32 degrees the other in a snappy two seconds! All the same, before the days of self-steering gears these disadvantages were easily ignored for the joy of a free helmsman. Few are fitted today but their broad principle can form the basis of a modern running rig. The first thing to bear in mind is that tradewinds are not the constant-direction, constant-strength dream that many writers have you believe. Even in well-established tradewind belts the wind veers and backs constantly, and can blow anything from a meek Force 2-3 to a thundering Force 7. The demands of a running rig are that it is free from chafe, maintains good balance and is easy to trim as the wind direction changes (ideally, gybing should not be necessary). As well as this, the sail area should be flexible. This is quite a tall order, but far from insurmountable. It should not be necessary to have any specially-made sails, but twin booms, expensive and space-taking as they are, make life so much easier. Unfortunately, the suitability of a running rig is in direct proportion to the amount of money spent on it. There are a number of methods and variations on them, so I shall start with the poor man's version.

Assuming that the yacht isn't a schooner (unless the modern variant with twin equal-height masts), the following will work on most rigs. For running, a mizzen can be forgotten unless you are in very light airs or hand steering. The very poor man's running rig is simple but works well and we crossed the Atlantic with it. A single running boom is a must, however poor you are. If your first tradewind passage is the Canaries to West Indies trip and you don't have a running boom, cut down a small tree in Madeira (Madeira is Portuguese for wood and the island is covered in forests).

It is also important to have plenty of anti-chafe protection on the shrouds. This needn't be permanent but before making a long downwind passage it will pay to cover the shrouds in split cheap plastic hose, taped on at six-inch intervals – any greater distance and the weight of sail against the hose can pull it off. Also, spreader tips and roots must be copiously bandaged with strips of canvas and/or foam taped in place. Alternatively, the old-fashioned method of baggywrinkle is surprisingly efficient. Assuming the trip is mostly downwind, it doesn't really matter about the windage, as long as the whole lot is removed when you get into port.

Undoubtedly the ultimate arrangement for handling running booms is to have them like this, so when they are wanted the bottom end is lifted out to the rail and clipped to the headsail's clew, at which point the inboard end is pulled down to the deck

In light airs the poor man's running rig uses the mainsail eased out a fair way, but vanged down heavily so that the sail doesn't press against any part of the rigging. The largest headsail is then boomed out opposite this (goosewinged) and the next largest headsail fairly well sheeted on the same side as the main, hanked, if possible, on a twin forestay (running is one of the few times twin forestays are efficient).

The first sail to come down as the wind increases is the main. This is not a simple job running downwind and we have found the best way to do so is by sheeting it flat amidships, with somebody on the helm, before lowering it. The sail is then stowed and covered. Because the smaller jib is no longer being 'fed' by the genoa it will need a wider sheeting angle, so the sheet should be led through a block on the end of the eased-out main boom (which normally needs lowering on its topping lift), taking care not to let the stowed sail or its cover chafe against a shroud.

Depending on sail wardrobe, these two headsails can be changed as the wind increases. The main disadvantage (and it really is a drag at 3 am or after the fifth squall of an afternoon) is that the rig cannot be sailed by the lee and is best from a run through to broad reach. When a squall comes through or the wind changes direction and one needs to gybe, the whole lot has to be reversed, which can be quite a procedure. I vividly remember one watch during a particularly squally afternoon when, after three complete gybes with all the work that entailed swapping sails and booms over, I decided that when the next squall came through with its 60 degree windshift, I'd keep the wind over the stern by altering course and wait for the hour it generally took for the squall to lose its force. As the big black cloud approached and the wind increased we were soon hurtling along at great speed, now uncomfortably across the wave train and rolling more. We made great progress towards Brazil (we were aiming for the Caribbean) for an hour. Then another hour. Finally, after three hours the wind looked as if it had changed for good so I reluctantly gybed over, mentally working out how much distance we'd lost. Twenty minutes later the wind had swung back to its original direction and the whole lot had to be gybed back.

A roller-reefing genoa is a great thing to have as part of a tradewind rig, because you can exactly tailor your downwind sail area for the right speed and the reefing control line quite literally becomes a throttle cable in boisterous running conditions. Our Rival 34 made a very respectable passage time on our second Canaries-West Indies transatlantic crossing by judicious use of the roller-furling genoa in this way. The only running boom was standard IOR size (when attached to the mast and held horizontal it extended a foot or so in front of the forestay) and was left permanently attached to the roller genoa. Even when the sail was rolled right up – all except that last foot – the boom was left attached and ready to go. The storm jib was set on its inner cutter headstay and boomed out with a temporary boom concocted of awning battens, dinghy oars and even the deck scrubber, all lashed firmly together. It was a rough crossing, with the wind rarely dropping much below Force 7, and for the greater part of it we ran under storm jib with a couple of feet of genoa unrolled opposite it. This rig was a hassle when it needed to be gybed, but because of the roller we were able to keep set exactly the right amount of sail, and we adjusted it several times each hour as the conditions fluctuated. The result was an 18-day crossing of which, on a 24ft 10in (7.56m) waterline, we are very proud.

For running downwind it isn't necessary to have a perfectly shaped headsail. So a useful setup is to have a very simple roller furling gear, rather like the old Wykeham-Martin, where the sail, set loose-luffed, rolls around itself (in the olden days, the luff was lashed to a light chain to give a thick edge to roll around). It is possible to make this roller yourself out of plywood with two bought swivels. Hoisted at the beginning of long downwind passages, the sail is used only for running or reaching in combination with and opposite your normal roller-reefing genoa, which it should more or less match in area. The ability to have two infinitely adjustable roller jibs would be a Godsend on a long downwind passage and would increase efficiency by enabling the watchkeeper to have exactly the right amount of sail out the whole time. Another system can be used when your standard roller-reefing extrusion has two luff grooves. Using a similar sized sail hoisted in this groove, it would be possible to have twins which rolled on one furling line. If the wind came round on to the quarter and you could no longer hold one of them poled to weather, the sail would be eased to leeward and both used two-ply until the wind hauled back aft again.

As mentioned above, two running booms make life much easier if they can be afforded. If they are approximately 1.3-1.5 x J (ideally telescopic) it is possible to rig them with outhauls and the jibs can be used with the wind on either quarter (see figure 7), which really then gives you as flexible a rig as a squaresail and needs no gybing – a significant step. So the Rolls Royce of running rigs would be twin roller-reefing headsails of the same shape and area, with over-length running booms to enable you to sail with the wind from one quarter right through to the other quarter without gybing, or even leaving the cockpit.

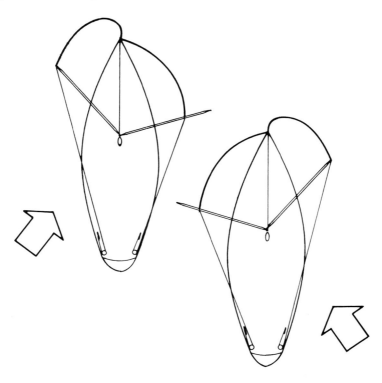

Fig 7 **Extra-long poles are very desirable for controlling downwind headsails, enabling the wind to veer through 45 degrees either side of downwind without the need for much deckwork**

A sail that is also as adaptable as the squaresail going downwind is the spinnaker, especially if it's used with twin booms. The spinnaker used to be regarded only as a racing sail, but now that a variety of bell-mouthed 'throttling' devices have become available, it makes a very logical downwind cruising sail. It is inadvisable with a small crew, however, unless it does have a 'throttler' of some sort. As a long-distance running sail its weakness is that it can't be reefed, so you must be very careful not to get caught out in a tropical squall with it up, and you must be able to resort to another running rig in conditions when the spinnaker can't be used. Another disadvantage is that even with twin booms and a throttler, it is not a sail that you can comfortably leave up overnight with a short crew.

Chafe on the halyard must be watched carefully if you use a spinnaker over long distances. Have a few extra feet of halyard so the top end can be trimmed back from time to time. Also, adjust the position of the 'nip' over the block every 24 hours and always use a large-diameter block. The choice of spinnaker for cruising is critical, because you are only likely to have one, which must be used in a variety of conditions. There are two broad cuts, tri-radial and radial head. The tri-radial is designed more for reaching than running. On a run it can be twitchy and need a lot of tending. The radial head is around 20 percent cheaper, and is more stable when running. Don't go for too heavy a cloth (no more than 1.5oz US for less than 40ft LOA), because in light airs the extra weight will make the sail hard to fill and it will oscillate, possibly causing a wrap-up. When using a spinnaker, never put a figure-of-eight knot in either the halyard or sheets and guys. Racing men follow this rule so the sail can be jettisoned if it is holding them up at a leeward mark. For the cruising man there is a weightier reason – so the sail can be immediately dumped in a man-overboard emergency.

A final option is the cruising chute. These were heavily promoted in the late '70s and early '80s as the cruising man's answer to the reaching spinnaker. About one-third smaller than the spinnaker, and supposedly needing no pole, they were bought by the hundred and the majority of yachtsmen were disappointed. Rather like the mizzen staysail, the band of both wind direction and strength they can be used in simply doesn't justify their existence and to use them safely requires almost as much hardware as a conventional spinnaker, to which they are much inferior.

Lazyjacks

The humble lazyjack is one of the few details that you will find aboard modern ocean racers which was also used in sailing ships 100 years ago. As we have seen, one of the biggest advantages of the junk rig is the ability of the sail to self-stow between lazyjacks when reefed or lowered. They can be fitted just as effectively to a standard Bermudian mainsail.

For the uninitiated, lazyjacks are lines that run down either side of the mainsail, from the top crosstrees to various points along the boom, so that as the mainsail is lowered it flakes itself into the cradle of lines they create, stowing itself. The reason lazyjacks are used on big racing boats is that the sheer size of their mainsails otherwise make them almost impossible to stow for the shorthanded crew. They are just as useful on smaller boats because they immediately tame the mainsail, which might be a handful in strong winds. They are also invaluable to the singlehander, particularly if the mainsail halyard is led aft to the cockpit. With a downhaul line from the headboard, also led aft, the singlehander can lower his mainsail without leaving the helm. Another advantage of lazyjacks is their ability to support the reefed section of a sail surprisingly neatly, making it unnecessary to tie in the reef points.

An important point to remember when fitting lazyjacks is that they should pass immediately under the mainsail and not under the boom. If they pass under the boom, the sail will collect there and look sloppy. If you have a mainsail with slides on the foot there is no problem, but if you have a grooved boom it will be necessary to either fit eyelets along the foot of the sail or screw eyes to the top of the boom. In order to make the lazyjacks easy to adjust or dismantle, make them in separate lines which are reef-knotted together as they join at the boom. Also, when you attach the blocks at the spreaders, position them 6-9in (12-18mm) away from the mast so that the down part doesn't frap against the mast in the wind. This also takes the upper parts of the lazyjack lines away from the sail, so there is less chance of snagging.

When fitting the slightly more complicated system of lazyjacks in Figure 8, it's well worth mocking them up first in thin orange line that will stand out against the sky. After plenty of adjustment and standing back you'll be able to get it looking right, with all

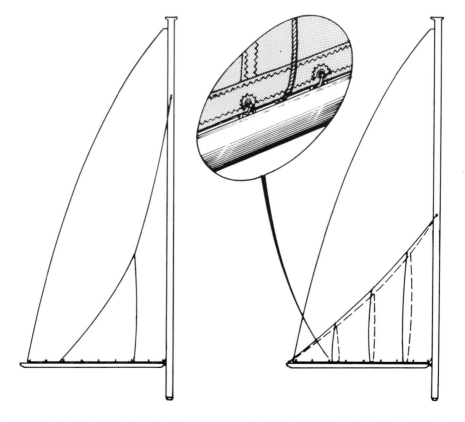

Fig 8 **Properly set up, lazyjacks are a wonderfully simple mainsail handling aid which enables one person to handle a mainsail on yachts up to 70ft (21m). Either of the illustrated methods can be used, but make sure that the tails pass above the boom (inset), either as shown or through eyelets in the sail**

the downhauls parallel, before cutting and splicing (remember to add a couple of inches at each end for the splice). For boats up to 35ft, 4mm line is quite strong enough, but be certain to use pre-stretched otherwise parts under greater load will distort first and reduce the effectiveness of the lazyjacks.

When sailing they cause no detectable chafe to the sail as long as the lines have plastic pipe sheaths where they pass under the mainsail. When the sail is about to be lowered, be sure to keep the lines taut for a neat stow.

Mast-steps

Mast-steps are being increasingly used and the benefits are numerous. One of the most significant is the ability of one person to go aloft without having to be hoisted. As I am well built, my wife isn't able to haul me up in a bosun's chair so she used to have to go aloft and detested every last second of it. Many couples must be in the same position. *Euge* had steps, and when going aloft for any length of time I would wear a bosun's chair and climb up the mast with Lou Lou taking up the slack in the halyard

Mast-steps make a significant contribution to the efficient running of a long-distance yacht, allowing for easy and regular servicing checks as well as the ability to con through a coral pass sitting atop the crosstrees, from where colour contrasts are better

as I went. On reaching the position where I wanted to work, she would make off the halyard and I'd sit back in the bosun's chair, comfortably working with both hands.

Foreigner 2 has no mast-steps, although I would like to fit them one day. Instead I use a Whittall Mast-Climb, a simple stirrup jammer device which allows me to get myself aloft quickly and efficiently.

There is a case for mast-steps extending only to the crosstrees, thereby cutting down the number of holes drilled in the mast, cost, weight aloft and windage. You can use them there for reef eyeball navigation. Certainly steps are the best encouragement to go up the mast and make regular rigging checks, which prevents future problems. They also keep you fit! The need to go aloft at sea is thankfully rare, but if you fit mast-steps the job is a thousand times easier. The best type are those with a stirrup support above the footplate, otherwise they are dangerous to use at sea. An essential addition when you fit mast-steps is to make up a cradle of very thin lines above the crosstrees to prevent halyards getting hooked around the steps. We learned this one when the mainsail halyard looped right around the front of the mast and caught a step on the opposite side. It was a good job we had mast-steps, I'd never have untangled it otherwise . . .

10. Water Supply

Capacity

Ultimately, water is the sole commodity required for survival, both in terms of last-ditch subsistence and for everyday cruising. The quantity of fresh water you have available is a surprisingly good gauge of your standard of living and enjoyment. Anyone who has ever tried cleaning a scrambled egg pan with cold salt water needs no reminding of the joy of washing up in fresh, and the ability to shower regularly and have clean hair rather than a matted, salt-encrusted mop definitely adds a few notches to the pleasure scale.

Of course some washing can be done ashore, but it can be slightly degrading to sit by the water tap on the jetty doing your laundry, and certainly in some places the locals are far from keen about it.So while one of the attractions of the ocean cruising lifestyle is the ability to trim down normal requirements and strip away the comforts you've always been accustomed to, it is wise not to be too stingy with water provision.

The multihull designer John Shuttleworth changed my thinking about water capacity and usage. When I sailed with him on his Spectrum 42 catamaran, I noticed that her central beam was hollow and could take a staggering 400 gallons (1,818 lit) of water. Under no circumstances does the yacht ever put to sea with any water in that tank (she has normal tanks for 100 gallons [454 lit] anyway), but when she arrives in port after a passage with the prospect of a couple of weeks' stay, she goes alongside and fills up the big tank. They say goodbye to their boot-top line, but who cares in harbour? In this way her crew can happily shower, wash-up and do what they like with fresh water until it's time to go, when the normal tanks are topped up (gravity fed) and the remainder is jettisoned before putting to sea again. Water is such a luxury aboard, and yet it is usually completely free. So good an idea is Shuttleworth's that we have emulated it in *Foreigner 2*, which uses gravity feed and carries a total of 375 gallons of water.

The practicalities are not always so simple as space is always at a premium, especially on a monohull. But, if you look upon high water capacity as being a harbour-only luxury (at sea you must impose the normal restrictions) it opens up several options. The very ends of boats are the last place you should put water tanks because they will make her pitch terribly, and yet it doesn't matter one jot as long as those tanks are empty when you're at sea. It is the same about the boat's trim, it doesn't matter if she's down on her marks a bit in harbour, or indeed where her centre of gravity is. The dark corners of the lazarette and focs'le are not normally the most convenient places to have general stowage. Is it possible to re-arrange the existing junk stored there and then construct and install a big tank in these places? Or what about having big flexible sausage tanks loosely set up over the coachroof in harbour? As soon as you go to sea they would be emptied, rolled up and stowed away, but in harbour they would provide a generous supply of water, which could gravity-feed into your main tank fillers and therefore need no extra plumbing. For instance, Vetus supply a 61in x 30in (156cm x 76cm) tank which holds 58 gallons (263 lit). Two of these would look no different to an inflatable dinghy stowed on the coachroof but the comfort they would create aboard would be worth it.

Water catchment

In many of the West Indian islands there is no central water supply – the islanders rely solely on what they can catch from their (often corrugated tin) roofs, which is then directed into a big concrete tank under the house. They call it 'skyjuice'. The houses are not particularly big, but their roofs provide sufficient water all year round to supply such water wasters as regularly-flushed toilets. For them, the trick is large tankage; it can rain hard for a couple of days and their gutters work overtime diverting the water into huge tanks which could keep them going for months afterwards without a single rainfall. Unfortunately a yacht could never emulate this, but thought given to water catchment may save you a lot of trouble and make you more independent of the shore. On the other side of the coin, there are many regions of the world where water is very precious and you'll need to catch your own supply because the locals won't let you have any of theirs.

I have tried many different systems over the years – collecting water is a bit like catching fish, the satisfaction far outweighs the value of the end-product – and in the end it became something of a hobby. The aims are that the system be fruitful, reasonably self-tending and that you remain dry whilst doing it. At sea, where there is likely to be some spray flying about, a bucket lashed under the boom gooseneck takes some beating, but it fails miserably on the convenience and keeping dry stakes. An easy modification, though, is to lash a large funnel under the gooseneck with plastic pipe from its snout leading direct into the water tank filler cap. In harbour, an awning (the universal design is described in the Preparations section on page152) can collect good quantities of water – in a reasonable shower we can get 15 gallons (68 lit) an hour and in a decent downpour two or three times that amount. If the ridge topping lift is taken aft to a cleat on the backstay, you stand a reasonable chance of keeping dry while setting this one up.

If your water filler cap is situated on or near the deck edge and you have continuous toerails, one easy way to collect water from your deck is to make a small dam (a wedged piece of wood with some rags will normally suffice) on the downhill side of the filler so a puddle is formed over the filler cap and eventually the water starts pouring into the tanks.

For our next boat I plan to install the Pack Mk9 system. In fact it's not original, I've seen it used on several ocean cruising boats before. The deck has just one drain each side, at the lowest point. This water runs through a pipe inside the hull with two-way diverter valve fitted. The water can go to a skin fitting and drain overboard, or the valve can be switched to direct it into the main water tank. The weakness of the system is that the decks must be kept clean and this isn't always possible. What we plan to do then is have a standard awning which, if the decks are dirty, will be used as normal for water collection. If the decks are nice and clean though, we'll let the rain rinse them for a few minutes before switching over and using the entire deck area for water collection – which should be very efficient indeed. The Mk 10 version will no doubt have the switchover valve right next to my bunk, so there is no need to get out of bed at night when I hear the rain start!

Methods of water supply

A feature becoming more common aboard yachts is pressurised water, and it is a pleasant convenience. However, you pay the price, not only for initial installation and continuing spares but also electricity used and, more importantly, wasted water. Although I have argued the case for having plenty of water it still shouldn't be wasted and run out of the sink unused, and this is unavoidable with a pressure system, especially if you have hot water, where gallons of cold water are lost waiting for it to run

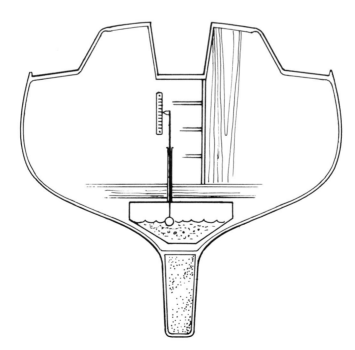

Fig 9 If the tank is situated next to a bulkhead, this system of gauging (seen on a French Amel design) is both simple and accurate

hot. If you have a really large water capacity this is not so important, but you will increase your average water consumption by between 33% and 50% by employing a pressure system as opposed to a hand or foot pump.

If you prefer to have electric pumps, try to standardise them if at all possible so a range of spare motors, valves, diaphragms, bearings and even bodies can be used for all your pumps. The best system I saw was on a charter boat where a mini 'pump room' housed the identical PAR pumps for water pressure, two shower sumps, a refrigerator sump, and two independent bilge pumps. Each pump was bolted to a small piece of ply which in turn fitted into slides, and the electric cables had crimped bayonet terminals. The skipper always had one spare pump (on its plywood base) refitted and ready to go. Whenever there was a pump failure, and there were many, it was a two-minute job to disconnect the pipes and electric cables, slide it out and replace it with the newly rebuilt pump. Speed was of the essence to him (charter guests don't like standing in showers half-washed, waiting for the water to come back) but the system relied on a single range of spares and like most of us charter skippers he knew the pumps inside out.

A water pressure system must be backed up with a hand or foot pump as well. Another modification that we found prolonged the working life of the pumps and motors was fitting an accumulator chamber. This simple device keeps the system under pneumatic pressure, which not only halves the work of the pump, but allows it to run fully and properly when required, rather than the wearing sporadic action when a tap is only turned partly on or when there is a slight leak (or the valves release the pressure back into the tank).

Without doubt the most successful, convenient and efficient water system I've ever seen on a boat was on Francois and Pascal Grinberg's 43ft (13.1m) cutter *Scherzo*. It combines the convenience of a pressure water system with the simplicity and economy of conventional pumped water. They have two generous water tanks in the bilge and from these water is pumped (with a high-capacity bilge pump) into two 5-gallon (22 lit) tanks, one in each cockpit coaming. There are conventional domestic faucets at the galley sink and in the heads compartment, and water to these is gravity-supplied from the cockpit coamings. In other words, they have the convenience of being able to turn a tap to get water, but the pressure is minimal so little is wasted, and there is no noisy pump or electricity used. Finally, the best thing of all is that they are able to log their water consumption very accurately on passage by noting down each time the cockpit coaming tanks are re-filled. The system is pure genius . . .

Gauging water isn't all that easy, although neither is it particularly necessary except on a very long passage. Commercial water gauges sold at chandlers do not work on tanks that are anything but rectangular boxes, and such tanks are few and far between on yachts. It is desirable to have your water split up into three or more tanks, independently tapped from each other. A mental note of which tanks you've used and which are full is usually quite sufficient to keep track of consumption. A system superb for its simplicity is fitted on the French Amel range of yachts, and can be adapted into certain other boats (see figure 9). It is calibrated by pouring in five gallons at a time and marking the scale. Although its accuracy is suspect at sea, it is nevertheless an easy method of gauging water if you are in a dry area and are concerned about consumption.

Even if you are unable to increase your in-port water supply, the boat's water capacity in general is a point of heated discussion. Everyone knows that it's best to have as much as possible, but how much? Both our ocean cruising boats had 45 gallons (204 lit) total capacity and we managed quite adequately. As long as we were able to catch water regularly this small amount was no special inconvenience, although like everyone we always wanted more (like you always want a bigger boat, bigger headsail, bigger wage packet . . .).

Water makers

To convert salt water into fresh is a slow process that requires large amounts of electrical energy. In the past water makers required a generator to produce 110/220V AC, but more recently 12 and 24v models have become available. They still have voracious electrical appetites, combined with the fact there are very few places in the world where you can't get potable water. For large yachts with ample (or maybe surplus) generating capability, the watermaker will be useful as long as it continues to work. For the mainstream ocean cruising boat described in this book, they have no real place.

11. Electrics

For years, the traditional opinion of electrics and small boats has been that the two were uneasy bedfellows and needed to be kept apart as far as possible. The opinion still lingers, but so much has changed over the last twenty years that it would be backward indeed to consider a boat totally without electricity. But all things in moderation . . .

If there is one philosophy that we've seen work time and time again for most aspects of ocean cruising it is the KISS principle – Keep It Simple, Stupid. Generally speaking, the most successful cruising boats and people are the ones who have trimmed their lives down to basic necessities which they find are quite adequate and give them time to enjoy themselves rather than waste pointless hours doing frustrating repair work. This philosophy couldn't be more appropriate than when applied to electricity on boats. A house is connected up to the National Grid and we are all encouraged to use lots of power. To generate smallish quantities of electricity on a boat is not a problem, but as soon as your demands increase you can very quickly become a slave to electricity generation, with a noisy and smelly engine or generator running for many hours a day and ruining everyone's peace.

Some yachtsmen can't cope without huge quantities of power and we have seen many a boat more resembling a small power station than an offshore liveaboard cruising yacht. Their owners believe that a boat should be no different from a house, with electric toasters, microwave ovens, TV and video sets and so on. If I've seen one sweaty, bad-tempered and foul-mouthed yachting consumer hiking some broken electrical fitting around uncomprehending shops in distant ports, I've seen dozens. Their lifestyle and happiness falls apart as soon as some part of the electric system does. If you feel you, or any of your crew, can't live without many of the domestic appliances and conveniences you have at home, you should would seriously re-consider the concept of worldwide cruising.

It is a false impression that such creature comforts will make life aboard that much easier and therefore prolong the cruise. Quite the contrary, they will surely add to the frustrations and costs and spoil the prospect of a free and simple existence. Some electricity will of course be necessary, and we will look at the best ways of supplying it.

Battery capacity and stowage

It is straightforward enough to calculate your amperage requirements over a 24hr period (amps=watts ÷ volts). Work it out carefully, then add 50% to make it realistic. A yacht should have a three-day capability between charges, so if she is using 30ah daily (+50% = 45ah), a 135ah battery should suffice. Unfortunately it doesn't work like this, batteries are not particularly efficient and only when he becomes fully conversant with their operation will the yachtsman be able to create a properly balanced electrical system. For a start, most normal regulators will only let a battery charge up to around 70% of its capacity. At the other end of the scale, when the battery is discharged to less than 40% it doesn't supply enough voltage to operate much of the electrics and electronics the yachtsman relies on it for, and anyway letting a battery discharge much below this level on a regular basis will shorten its life considerably. In other words, for a given 100ah capacity battery, we've only got 30 useable amp hours.

Getting back to our 45ah daily consumption for three days, instead of 135ah total capacity, a yacht will actually need 450ah if it is to stay within that 40-70% workable battery sector. These figures are practical examples and, more than anything else, illustrate the need to charge the battery in such a way that the 70-100% sector is also used, which will effectively double the useable capacity of the battery or halve your amp hour storage requirement. This can be done in two ways; either by using alternative, non-regulated, charging methods such as solar panels and wind generators, or if your engine is your principal charging source, to fit an intelligent regulator, or bypass the regulator altogether (see page 109 for details).

Positioning the batteries deserves some thought. If they are low down they help lower the boat's centre of gravity. But then, if they are too low in the bilge they may be under water if the boat is badly flooded and this might just be the time their loss could be disastrous – if lights are needed to find a leak, the engine needs starting or a Mayday signal has to be transmitted. The engine starting battery also needs to be close to the engine for minimum starter cable runs. However, it shouldn't be so close as to be affected by engine heat, so don't have batteries in the engine room.

The batteries must be in leak-proof boxes and well strapped down in case of a knockdown. If you have the opportunity to build the battery compartment, make it bigger all round than your existing batteries so that in future when they need replacement, you don't have to search for identically sized units. Wooden shims or wedges will hold the batteries in place. The locker or compartment for the batteries must not be shared by any other equipment unless the battery box has a fastened lid, otherwise there is a danger that something like a spanner or length of wire could short across both terminals and cause a fire.

If, as I prefer, you have an engine room extractor fan to improve the general running of the engine and cut down on fuel consumption, then have an offshoot of this sucking the air out of the battery compartment too, so there is no chance of a build-up of gases.

Battery charging

Above all else, the essence of an efficient electrical system is to create the correct balance between what you use and what you put back. This may sound obvious, but there are a surprising number of yachtsmen who don't observe it, whose lights are forever going dim and who spend a small fortune buying new batteries in the hope it will give them a new lease of electical life.

Having assessed your electrical requirements, and matched them to your battery capacity, the next move is to make sure that the charging side of the equation can easily replace all you use, plus the 10% extra required of batteries because of their internal losses. By and large, if you are relying on an engine you will want to keep running hours down to a minimum and on that basis there is no substitute for a reasonably-sized alternator in the 55-90amp range. In the short run, this is the cheapest way of upgrading an electrical charging system, especially if combined with an intelligent marine regulator or bypass. Bear in mind that a battery can only receive 25% of its remaining capacity in charge rate, so there is no point in fitting a large alternator with an insubstantial battery bank.

Alternatively, if there is space one can fit a second alternator. This provides a belt-and-braces approach but is more work, requiring engine brackets to be fabricated, a second (or even third) pulley fitted on the crankshaft, and extra wiring.

The ocean cruising lifestyle revolves around self-sufficiency – one should never have all one's eggs in one basket and this is particularly pertinent to electrics, unless nothing essential is reliant on the system. Two independent banks of batteries reduce many potential problems. Also, it is much better to have extra sources of auxiliary charging if the engine will not work.

Solar panels

There are horses for courses, and there is no question but that solar panels are better on certain boats in certain locations than other alternative charging devices. For Mediterranean cruising for example, a solar panel knocks a wind generator into a cocked hat. We recently spent four months in the Canary Islands, barely saw our wind generator spin half a dozen times and rather wished we'd bought solar panels; this is being written in the West Indies two months later, where that same Windbugger wind generator has kept our batteries topped up (and the 12v fridge frosty cold) permanently, something the same money's worth of solar panels would be hard put to achieve.

But a few words of warning first. The hotter the panel gets, the lower its output voltage and therefore its charging ability, so a panel taken into the tropics is going to be quite substantially less efficient than one located in temperate climes. Also, don't be too optimistic of what you will actually get in terms of daily charge from a given panel. As a rule of thumb, five times its hourly rated output will be the absolute maximum you will get in a day. A 30-watt panel will therefore produce 12.5ah on a very good day when the sun doesn't go behind a cloud or it is not shaded by any of the boat's rig or awnings. Although the very frugal could live on this amount of power, doubling to 60 watts-worth of panel makes more sense for a still frugal, non-refrigerated lifestyle.

When you start trying to convert sunrays into ice-cubes (ie powering the fridge on solar power) you are going to be getting close to running out of space to fit the panels required, on a monohull anyway. When one starts getting to these circumstances you must also make provision for when the boat is left for a period. If your panel's output

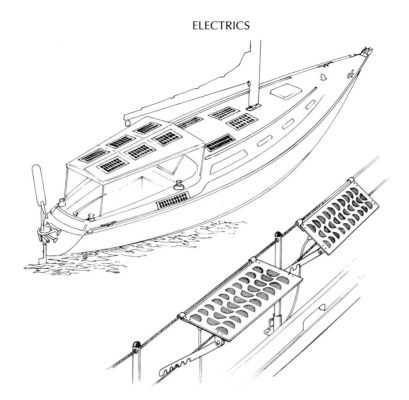

Figs 10a & 10b **With a little ingenuity solar panels can be fitted in a number of ways which, by adjustment every hour or two, increase their output markedly**

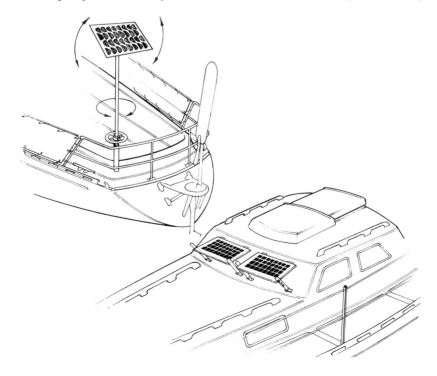

at 14v is greater than 0.5% of the battery capacity, one should either fit a shunt regulator, or a switch (which gets remembered).

Diodes also require consideration. Because, during the night, a solar panel will take power back from the battery, diodes (electrical one-way valves) are often fitted. These will drop the voltage by 0.6v, further limiting the panel's output. On a boat left on a mooring week in, week out, a diode is sensible, but on a liveaboard cruising boat a simple switch in the line is much better, as long as somebody remembers to turn it off in the evening and on again in the morning . . .

The installation of solar panels deserves careful consideration. Although they can be bolted on to an area of the deck and left there, solar panels work better angled directly at the sun's rays so if the installation is adjustable, so much the better. In this way they need tending every few hours, but the charging input is considerably improved. Figures 10a and b show a variety of ideas to make the best from your solar panel. What the majority of ocean sailors now do is leave the panel unattached and propped up in various locations around the deck depending on where the sun is. Awnings can be a nuisance and we've seen more and more yachtsmen fit solar panels to an antenna arch across the back of their yacht.

In terms of watt/£, solar panels are the most expensive way to create electrical power in the short run, but if you plan to cruise for a length of time that initial investment will pay off compared to the ongoing costs of diesel fuel and engine servicing. If you plan to be away for many years, solar panels will pay for themselves, which has to be an efficient way of going about things. They can happily support a yachting lifestyle without refrigeration, but will struggle to make icecubes in most circumstances. However, if you don't plan to rely wholly on solar panels, but have them in conjunction with a wind generator and perhaps occassional engine running, they make a worthwhile contribution.

Wind generators

There are two broad categories of windmill generators – big and small. The most common are small commercially-available ones such as the Ampair and Rutland Windcharger, which use a fairly small propeller and can sometimes be adapted to tow an impeller at sea. The other versions, available and more popular in America, are the large-diameter (6-9ft [1.8-2.7m] prop span) windmills, the Windbugger being by far the most popular and well known, that can be hoisted in the yacht's foretriangle or pole-mounted aft.

The Ampair and Rutland windchargers are the only two small commercial versions made in Britain that are sufficiently durable and reliable for full-time use, although there are several others on the market. When the wind is really blowing the power output of these models is up to 5-6 amps and unlike solar panels they work for 24 hours a day. In 20 knots of wind, the output is nearer 2.5-3 amps. However, one should always remember that many anchorages are desirable because they are sheltered from the wind. Also, when running downwind on a tradewind route, the apparent wind is reduced and these units then don't put in as much power as you might expect.

The large windmill generators like the Windbugger can pump in a really significant charge, up to 20 amps. As mentioned above, we fitted a Windbugger from Florida and in the tradewinds it provides for all our electrical demands, including 12v refrigeration and ham radio. We have found that the Windbugger is the perfect tool for the steady tradewinds of the tropics, but in more varied weather it is not as efficient, with a comparatively narrow envelope of operation. It doesn't start to charge until there's approximately 15 knots at the masthead, giving 7-9 amps at 22 knots, but then needs to be shut down completely at around 32 knots, at which windspeed it is putting in close to 20 amps. The latter factor, that it needs to be shut down, means that the boat cannot be left unattended for any length of time with the Windbugger charging.

The noise wind generators make can be offputting. The smaller variety tend to drum and vibrate (particularly if you have a light craft such as a multihull) and the big variety, turning at lower speeds, make a constant swishing sound. In the light of their power contribution, it seems a small price to pay and after a while you stop noticing the noise. The danger of windmills mustn't be underestimated. Under no circumstances should their propellers be allowed to operate within arm's reach of anyone on deck. Indeed, when the wind starts to blow hard one must lower the large variety on to the deck, taking great care when manually turning the windvane across the wind to depower the blade.

Propshaft generators

The propshaft generator has mixed blessings. They tend to be used on larger boats with props big enough to drive them and the requirement for the sort of power they can produce. It has been scientifically proven that a turning propeller creates more drag than a fixed one, so the boat is going to be slightly slower when you let her prop drag. The noise of the propshaft turning the whole time can be irritating down below, especially as it will have to turn the gearbox in neutral (which creates extra wear on the cutless bearing and gearbox mechanism and is a questionable undertaking with hydraulic transmission).

In its favour, a propshaft generator can pump in a lot of power, up to 35amps, at good sailing speed, and can be quite cheap to rig up using a car alternator. It also works when you are motoring, although you must be careful not to cook the batteries. However, they don't work on propellers less than 18-20in (45cm), unless there is a clutch mechanism fitted between the shaft and gearbox.

The normal setup is a wheel on the propshaft, belted to an alternator. The ratio of wheel diameter to alternator is critical and depends on three things:-
1. Speed of propshaft rotation at around 5 knots. This can usually be physically counted (over 10 seconds). It varies considerably, but a figure of 200 rpm is about average.
2. The lowest operating revs of the alternator you use. This is generally in the 1,100 to 1,250rpm range (but check it).
3. The upper operating revs of the alternator, usually between 7,000 and 11,000. You won't be able to count your propshaft's revs under full engine power, but it's easy enough to calculate if you know your engine's rpm and the gearbox reduction ratio. An engine running flat out at 2,800rpm through a 2.5:1 reduction ratio will be turning the propshaft at 1,120rpm. After the step-up ratio of the propshaft alternator is allowed for, this must fall within the alternator's working range.

It can be seen then that a 6:1 ratio wheel attached to the propshaft in the above circumstances would drive the alternator at 1,200rpm sailing at 5 knots, when charge would be minimal, but when the yacht is motoring fast the alternator would still be within its limits, turning at nearly 6,800 revs – and putting out a great deal of power, especially bearing in mind that the engine's own alternator will be pumping in the amps.

Water generators

Using your existing propshaft with a cheap alternator is one thing, but spending good money on special charging equipment that can only be used while the yacht is under way seems to me slightly cock-eyed, in the light of how little time a yacht spends at sea.

There have been several water generators on the market, looking rather like small outboard motors strapped on the stern. They can contribute up to 10amps, but as far as I'm aware none have lasted in the harsh marine environment perched over the stern of a boat, even when they could stand up to sailing speeds of six knots or more. Dodge Morgan had two aboard his *American Promise* and both lasted a matter of days. If you have money to spare, until a really reliable water generator is brought out I think it would be much better to spend it on an extra solar panel that works in harbour and at sea.

Intelligent regulators

One of the best things to have happened to the cruising sailor in the last few years is the development and refinement of intelligent alternator regulators such as the TWC in the UK or Ample 3-Step from America (marketed in the UK by Ampair). These regulators allow an alternator to put out its full charge for longer, tapering the charge much later than a standard automotive regulator, and thereby cutting down battery charging times markedly. If you're planning to use alternative charging methods like sun and wind then one of these regulators can come low down the priority list, but if you are relying on the engine as primary charging, be sure to fit one.

The rub is that operating at up to 15 volts, they will test your electrical system to the full and quickly uncover its weak points, occasionally in an expensive way. There's a good argument that this is no bad thing, but be prepared before you fit one to go through all connections and wiring with a fine-toothed comb.

Wiring a regulator bypass

This is an incredibly simple operation and the difference it makes to engine charging hours is remarkable. Why then don't we hear of it being used on ordinary boats? Quite simply, it is not foolproof and automatic, and if you are stupid enough to forget that this bypass is operating, at best you will ruin your batteries and at worst your boat will be on fire. Never forget this, and if you're an absent-minded person, do not consider making this adaptation.

A regulator is a small, usually sealed, device sometimes incorporated on the back of the alternator, sometimes fixed to a nearby bulkhead. It senses the battery's state of charge and adjusts the field current into the alternator appropriately. The result is that as the battery 'fills up', the alternator gradually tapers away the charging current it

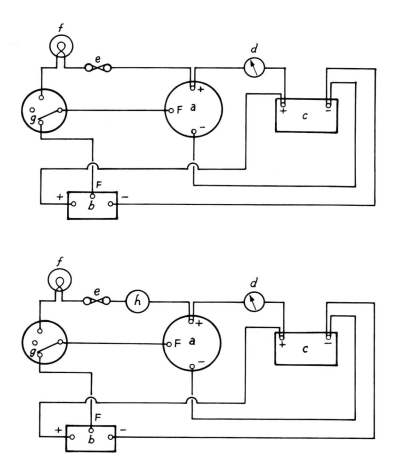

Fig 11 **The wiring diagram for bypassing an alternator regulator and thereby significantly increasing your battery charging ability. The system works well and is used extensively, but it is very dangerous if forgotten. (a) alternator (b) regulator (c) battery (d) ammeter (e) 10A fuse (f) conspicuous red light (g) three-way switch (h) optional potentiometer**

supplies to the battery and thereby protects it from overcharging. The frustrating thing is that these devices tend to work conservatively and even when the battery is only half charged, an alternator will only be putting in a small proportion of its charge, never anywhere near its full output capacity. As a result, the batteries rarely get above 70% of their charge capacity.

When it comes to battery charging in harbour, when you want the engine to be running for the shortest time possible, it can be pretty maddening to watch the ammeter reading that the 55amp alternator is putting in only 10amps after an hour or so, when you know you've taken about 40 or 50 amps out of the battery in the last couple of days.

Figure 11 shows the wiring diagram needed to bypass the regulator and feed the battery's full field current into the alternator, which in turn will pump out its maximum capacity. There are two ways of arranging this bypass (Figure 11). In both, the original regulator facility is still maintained, so if you want to motor for any length of time, it is still quite possible to let the system be automatically regulated as normal. Method A is to have a three-way switch, the middle position being no field current at all, in which case the alternator will spin freely and produce no charge. The other two switch positions are for normal regulated field current and for 'boost' unregulated field current, when the alternator pumps out full charge. It is advisable to have a bright red light in the unregulated circuit so you are always aware that the batteries are on boost charge. The second method is slightly more sophisticated and also uses a three-way switch but instead of having full field current being fed to the alternator, the current can be manually regulated by a potentiometer, so by watching the ammeter and turning the 'pot' you can decide for yourself how much field current goes in and therefore how much charge is produced by the alternator. Although the cost of a potentiometer system is slightly higher, this method is best because you can manually taper the charge into the battery as it fills up with charge and avoid damage.

Bypassing the regulator does not damage the alternator at all – its maximum output is designed to be well within its temperature bounds and anyway, the alternator will probably only be charging like this for a maximum of an hour or two at a time. Anyone can make this simple modification easily for the cost of a three-pole switch, a light fitting and some wire, but it is absolutely essential to remember these rules:-

1. Always have a prominent bright red light to constantly remind you that you are using the boost charge facility (this will also remind you to turn off when the engine has stopped, otherwise the current will flow back from the batteries into the alternator, with possible damage).
2. Watch the voltmeter like a hawk, and switch over to normal regulated field current as soon as the voltmeter is reading 14.3V.
3. To reduce the possibility of 'force-feeding' the battery and causing it damage, make sure that this charging current is being distributed into all the banks of batteries (remembering that a battery, or a bank, can only withstand 25% of its remaining capacity in charging rate).

This system has a further long-term advantage. Diesel engines thrive on hard and constant work and it is very bad for them to run for long periods under little or no load. Unfortunately, this is exactly what the ocean cruising yachtsman does when he runs the engine just for charging in port. By fitting and using a regulator bypass, the engine is having to work harder to pull the alternator around pumping out its maximum capacity, which helps the engine to some extent.

Shore power

Hooking up to a shore supply when one is available is quite a temptation. All of a sudden you don't have to worry about your power consumption, you can charge your batteries full to the brim and all manner of convenient domestic appliances can be used. The trouble is that shore power spoils you, and ridiculous as it seems, it is almost like a vice. After you've been living with it for a while it becomes quite hard to cut that umbilical cord. Once you've got used to a few of those conveniences, useless as they are without mains supply, cruising can start turning into a constant search for a shore power supply, which will limit your options. Your costs will escalate because you will always have to be at a marina or dock, which will cost more on top of the charges for the electricity. 'Alongside living' puts a new complexion on cruising. You can't go for a swim whenever you feel like it, you have no privacy and you become more vulnerable to bugs, rats, thieves and drunks.

Despite this there are occasions when an ocean cruiser can take advantage of a shoreside mains supply, especially if you are wintering over in a port in cold weather and can use a mains heater to keep you warm. Mains supplies vary throughout the world, although generally there are more 240v countries than 110v. The most practical shorepower rig is simply a long electric cable whose plastic insulation is flawless and undamaged. We nearly always end up buying (or borrowing) a suitable plug and if the supply is 110v we don't use it, because a step-up transformer doesn't justify its cost, weight or bulk aboard for such infrequent occasions. We carry aboard an electric drill, jigsaw, a domestic battery charger and a 2kw blower heater.

A comparatively recent development in battery chargers which are of particular interest to the blue water sailor are switch-mode technology chargers. They are compact and lightweight, but more importantly will accommodate any electrical input, be it 110vAC or 240vAC, at any frequency, and convert it into a smooth 12vDC charging supply. The most practical aspect of these switch-mode chargers is their ability to cope when you are hooked into an inefficient shore supply, perhaps at the very end of a long jetty where voltage drop becomes a problem for normal chargers.

Finally, if you find yourself thinking of ways of plumbing in a shorepower circuit and appliances to your boat or becoming hooked to the joys of a mains supply while you're away, think seriously about your cruising lifestyle, because it's the best sign, deep down, that you really want to be living ashore.

12. The Engine

Do you need an engine? Our first year or two of ocean cruising was conducted, to all intents and purposes, without an auxiliary for our large and unwieldy catamaran – for purely financial reasons (although I kidded myself I had a streak of purism). It put a completely different complexion on our cruising standards. On one side our level of seamanship was undoubtedly higher and we developed an ability to quickly assess situations ahead, to see if a harbour, bay or anchorage could be sailed out of, or was suited to us.

On the negative side, we were always a long way behind all our cruising friends, because although the cat could sprint over open distances quickly, we would always be caught becalmed under a headland or in the lee of an island. We once spent 26 frustrating hours trying to make up the lee of St. Vincent in the Windward Islands while our friends motored, charged their batteries up, and did the trip in three or four hours.

On another occasion, trying to leave Bayona in Northern Spain, where long periods without a breath of wind and hazy visibility are common, we went out and spent two consecutive days drifting off the entrance trying to get away, drifting into the harbour and anchoring each night. All the other cruising yachts turned on their diesels and 30 miles down the coast found a good wind, eventually arriving in Madeira a week ahead of us. Sod's Law being so prominent in sailing, we would always turn up within sight of a port an hour or two before dusk and get becalmed. With an engine we'd have been safely at anchor within an hour, eating supper surrounded by our friends. As it was, we generally spent several hours helplessly running the gamut of shipping leaving and entering the port, took the risk of entering an unknown place in the dark and finally dropped our anchor at 0100, tired and impatient.

As we have seen in other respects people's second or third boats are much more revealing than their first, and you very rarely find anyone going on to a second engineless boat. A properly installed modern auxiliary diesel engine is compact, economic to run and highly reliable, and to cruise without one is like shooting yourself in the foot. If you have purist ideas, there is nothing to stop you cruising as if you have no engine and manoeuvring under sail as much as you wish, but the day a strong current is taking you straight toward a coral reef, the ability to fire up the diesel is a fail-safe insurance policy.

Engine choice

The type and size of engine in a yacht would strongly influence my decision to buy her, largely because of this safety factor.

To give an example, we were anchored in *Euge* in St Georges Harbour, Bermuda when a deep and spiteful depression brought a fierce south-easterly gale. The following night, the British barque *Marques* was lost 70 miles north-west of the islands. Our anchorage suddenly became a lee shore, with a three-quarter mile fetch across the harbour for the wind and seas to build up, and all the yachts were jumping and leaping at their cables. Several crews were stranded ashore, unable to launch their dinghies. We were anchored near the shore and had a dozen yachts upwind of us, one or two of which were starting to drag. By 11 o'clock at night the wind was up to 50 knots and we felt decidedly vulnerable with only 50 yards (45m) between us and a particularly unyielding concrete quay. Though we had confidence in our ground tackle, it only needed one of the yachts upwind to drag on to us and we would have been in serious trouble. We didn't even know if the engine would be able to get us out of the situation if we dragged. In the height of the storm we decided that we were relying too much on luck and must move, awkward and wet as it would be. We got some encouragement by motoring up to the anchor. Not sure quite how much power our 25hp Volvo would have if a squall came through, we reefed the mainsail right down and made it ready to hoist within seconds if needed. To our amazement, and with spray driving right over the boat as she plunged into the seas, the diesel could just about get us to windward and to safety. We re-anchored with lots of scope and swinging room and were able to sleep the rest of the night, while other yachts close inshore hung on, praying nothing would give. Although some people say that there should be approximately one engine horsepower per foot of overall length, displacement is a more important criterion than size. As a guide you should have between 4 and 5hp per ton for the engine to have the power to cope occasionally with conditions like those described above.

It is a gross oversimplification, but serves our needs, to say that there are, broadly, three types of diesel engine. The early-style slow-revving, high-compression 'thumpers' like the Sabbs and Listers have been used for decades in everything from fishing boats to concrete mixers, and threaten to be with us for ever. They run slowly and steadily and can be rebuilt time and time again. They generally only have two or three cylinders and it is usually possible to hand-start them. They are also very heavy, tend to be tall, noisy and in many cases will rattle your teeth out. They are expensive to buy initially, but their simplicity leads to low maintenance and if you are planning to go away for a long time and are looking for sheer durability, the initial investment will pay off in the long run. The middle range of engines rev up to around 2,500rpm, generally have more cylinders and although they are more compact than the 'thumpers' are still fairly bulky. The new breed of modern diesels are high-revving, up to 3,500rpm, and are often taken from industrial and even automotive uses. They are half the weight of a 'thumper', half the size, and run like sewing machines. They also only last a fraction of the time, sometimes as little as 2,000 running hours.

For tropic cruising, despite its extra complication, a freshwater-cooled engine is more desirable than raw water cooling because with the higher ambient seawater temperatures there is a danger of salt encrustation in the engine cooling system bores and chambers, leading to gradual overheating. To clean them out is a major job and not undertaken lightly. On a freshwater-cooled system don't forget to use antifreeze, because although you're not likely to be cruising in areas where it needs to stop the water freezing, this fluid also acts as a rust inhibitor. Your cooling system must also have plenty of pencil zincs to avoid electrolysis and these should be pulled and checked frequently.

Most engine manufacturers seem to be fairly reliable but the availability of spare parts overseas is vital. Perkins (or Westerbeke – usually the same thing) are by far the best because they are used in tractors and industrial plants the world over. Much the same applies to Yanmar and Ford. Old-fashioned slow-running engines like the Sabbs and Listers don't seem to need as many spares, which is fortunate because availability is not generally good. There are snags with Volvo, despite the fact that they've cornered a big chunk of the sailing boat market. For years their engines have undergone frequent minor changes with the result that stockists rarely have the part you want, no matter how basic. Not only are spares difficult to get, they are very expensive. This is a great shame, because the design of Volvos is good. With their 2000 series (18-43hp) all the servicing points of the motor are easily accessible on the front of the engine block, and the earlier models could be hand-started.

Starters

The ability to hand start a diesel is highly desirable, as there will always be times when batteries are low.

Lucas Marine in England produce what they call a 'spring starter' for diesel engines. It looks a little like a starter motor and turns the flywheel in the same way as an electric starter motor. One operates it by winding a handle on the side fifteen times, winding up very strong springs. A release lever is then thrown and the engine started. A lot are sold for starting emergency generators in places like hospitals. They seem like a sailor's dream until you learn their price, which in 1992 was over £1,100. A sum like this could be better invested in other items of equipment, or perhaps a spare starter motor and portable generator.

Maintenance

Good access to the engine is absolutely imperative or you will always be tempted to put off vital maintenance jobs. If your chosen boat doesn't have this, come up with ways to improve it, even if it means that some of the sound deadening has to be permanently removed – better a noisy engine than an unserviced silent one. Bigger hatches can sometimes be cut from the yacht's quarter area. Certain ancillary items like fuel filters, battery and even alternator can be re-sited slightly to improve access. If the panelling is large or complicated, cut small access hatches in it to allow you to make the basic checks – engine and gearbox dipsticks and fanbelt tensions. A perspex inspection window next to the water filter bowl could be useful.

One of the most common jobs is changing lubricating oil, and yet it is nearly always difficult to do. Think about this problem before you sail. The ideal is if you can get under the engine and reach the sump plug, but this is rare and it is even less likely that you can also fit a container under there to catch the oil. Several engines, including Perkins and Bukh, include an oil sump pump as standard equipment and as long as

An engine installed with this standard of accessibility is likely to be cared for and serviced much more often than one shoehorned under the cockpit

this is situated in a convenient place, well and good. If not, re-route it to somewhere you can sit comfortably (because thickish oil doesn't like to be dragged up thin pipes so it's quite a physical job) and where a reasonably-sized receptacle can be placed underneath to catch the old oil. The portable pumps available nearly always leak, but it is possible to buy good quality hand sump pumps and this is a good investment for future happiness. Working in the confines of an engine compartment is never fun in the tropics.

The majority of problems with diesel engines come from dirty fuel, so make certain you have at least three big filters (one of them with a water separator bowl) and plenty of paper replacements. If your fuel comes aboard initially through a fine gauze conical funnel (mentioned in the fuel section) and then passes through three more filters before it gets to the injection pump, many potential problems will be avoided.

Though dirt in the fuel will stop a diesel, it is unlikely to hurt the engine much, but if water is allowed to get in it can do a great deal of permanent damage. A teaspoonful of water reaching the injection pump can wreck it in a matter of seconds. It may be just as bad if the pump survives and feeds water to the injectors, for they will be ruined too. If you can, fit Racor water filters with drainable glass bowls, regarded as the Rolls Royce of diesel water filtration systems.

A safety feature beautiful in its simplicity, fitted to most French boats, is the fire-extinguisher hole. In the event of an engine-room fire the worst thing you can do is pull away the casing to aim the fire extinguisher, because this will feed the fire with air and aggravate it. The fire extinguisher hole is an approximately 1+" (40mm) diameter hole cut in the engine casing, with a plastic plug. In the event of a fire, the plug is pulled out and the extinguisher let off through the hole into the engine compartment. It is highly effective.

Designers seem to take pride in the way they can shoehorn an engine into a tiny space, then wrap it up in sound-deadening foam so that it can neither be seen nor heard. As well as fuel, engines need air to run on, in fact for every gallon of fuel consumed the average diesel also consumes 12,500 gallons (56,826 lit) of air! Make sure there are plenty of locations for the air to enter, otherwise the engine will lose power, use excessive fuel and run hotter, causing more wear and shorten its life.

One of the best pieces of preventative maintenance for an engine is to paint it, the engine room and the sump brilliant white. Not only will a clean engine run cooler, but you will immediately know if there are any oil or fuel leaks, especially if you also install some bright engine room lights. Once you have got the engine and engine room clean, a wipe over with paraffin cloth from time to time is no chore. Also, unless you want quite revolting bilges and even perished rubber bilgepump parts, the engine should have its own bilge sump to catch any stray diesel or oil.

Don't leave the country without an engine workshop manual, and also a schematic spare parts list with all the appropriate numbers. Not only does this list bridge most language difficulties, it also makes ordering spares from a faraway spares stockist one hundred percent more efficient.

Engine monitoring

In the interests of economy, some engine manufacturers have stopped supplying proper monitoring instruments and simply fit warning lights instead. A serious cruising yachtsman needs to know exactly how his engine is running and this can only be done by the inspection of proper instruments. With practice they help you diagnose problems and quite often nip them in the bud more than can be said of a light, which will only tell you after the problem has occurred. The system should also be backed up with a loud alarm for oil pressure and temperature.

Engine hours should be logged, if you want to take care and maintenance seriously. Note down engine running hours, any servicing done or adjustments made. Engine hour meters are easy to fit and are a small price to pay to remind you to service the engine at regular intervals.

Fuel

Carry as much fuel as you can without overloading or sacrificing other vital storage space. There are often spaces under the cockpit or in the bottom of deep cockpit lockers where extra fuel tanks can be fitted. Filling up with fuel can be quite a chore alongside commercial wharfs or rough little quays, and the less you have to do it the better. As well as carrying as much fuel as possible, don't be wasteful with it. A motoring range of 400 miles (approximately 25-35 gallons [113-159 lit]) is the bare minimum and as long as you don't squander fuel this will generally see you through parts of the world where fuel facilities are scarce. When there isn't a fuelling berth it is often possible to get a lorry load delivered to a quayside to be split up amongst several yachties. Always have a 5-gallon (22 lit) container of diesel on board, not only as spare, but also because you might have to buy small quantities and 'jug-it' back to the boat.

The fuel filler design and location can be a source of continuing aggravation and if you have any doubts, change yours now. In some places they are used to giving commercial vessels several tons of fuel in a short space of time and the attendant will pass you down a massive pipe out of which will spurt diesel in huge quantities. Before you go alongside, even if you learn nothing else of the local language, find out how to say 'slow down' and 'stop'.

If at all possible, have a 2-3in (76mm) fuel filler pipe fitted and back it up with a 1in (25mm) breather pipe leading from the tank so there is no risk of blow-backs. The breather pipe must exit next to the filler so you can tell when the tank is full. No matter how much care you take there are nearly always spillages when a tank is being filled, so the fuel filler pipe should be out on deck, preferably near the scuppers, and well away from any untreated teak. If not, be sure to put a bucket of water over the teak before opening the filler and taking on fuel.

Rule No.1 for reliable diesel engines is to feed them only clean fuel. To this end, either buy or have made a really good gauzed funnel that is always put in the filler hole before you take on fuel. It is amazing how much grit, muck and dead insects (plus water) you buy along with your diesel in most foreign ports. This funnel alone will cut out 50% of potential engine problems.

You will need to know how much fuel you have aboard, but don't bother with commercially-made fuel gauges. They are never accurate with yacht tanks which are always irregularly shaped. A sight gauge, which you calibrate by filling the tank in five gallon increments, is by far the simplest, most accurate and reliable system and it can be fitted to any nearby bulkhead.

Propellers

Sailing performance must be good if you are to keep a happy crew and this is a strong argument for fitting a folding prop. Over long distances the small contribution it makes to the boat's speed is amplified, and an ocean crossing could be made several days shorter as a result. However, a folding propeller's weakness is its inability to create much power going astern. This may not seem much of a problem until you go aground, when a fixed propeller (preferably three-bladed) will stand a better chance of getting you off before much damage is done. This safety factor alone makes the drag of a three-bladed propeller worth putting up with for the rest of the time.

13. Navigation Aids and Communications

Electronic navigation

In the last fifteen years micro-chip technology has revolutionised the button-pressing element of yachting. While it is a sad state of affairs that more people are starting to sail and buying aids such as Decca without bothering to learn the basics of navigation, it is easy to see why when the electronic wizardry we all use ashore is so reliable. For the experienced yachtsman who does realise that none of these systems is infallible, such aids can be of great value as long as they are kept in perspective.

One of the most common navigation aids used to be the radio direction finder. Obviously, out on the ocean its value is nil, but on the approach to land it can be very handy to home in on an RDF station, even though it is rare to have a cross beacon to fix your position and judge your distance off. The 'homing-in' ability of an RDF can be most reassuring for your first few landfalls, when you may not have been too confident of your astro navigation. Outside Northern Europe and America the RDF coverage is not good, although most of the principal Atlantic islands have one or two aero beacons. The Caribbean has several RDF beacons but their reliability is questionable and anyway, 99 percent of navigation there is done by eyeball. In the Pacific, particularly the more interesting cruising areas, coverage is poor and your RDF will have very little, if any, use.

Satellite navigation systems, in particular GPS of late, have made a big impact, opening up places like the Tuamotu Archipelago where in the past many fine seamen have lost their craft to erratic currents. GPS is now taking over from Transit SatNav, a system which is being allowed to degrade and therefore become unreliable.

An astounding thing about satellite navigators which you must remember is that, paradoxical as it may seem, their very accuracy can make them dangerous! Many charts, especially in the Pacific, were made before such pinpoint fixing was possible, so land masses and islands are often not in exactly the right place. Atolls are regularly misplaced by up to five miles, and reefs can often be a mile or two from their charted positions. Your very accurate GPS will tell exactly where you are on the surface of the globe, but plotted on to the chart it may put you in quite the wrong place, and you

If possible keep the electrics and electronics down to good-quality basics – the chart plotter on this yacht could not be classed as essential equipment, though many cruising sailors are turning to GPS

may be about to plough up a reef when the GPS has put you off the harbour entrance. It comes back to the fact that all equipment is no more than an aid, and should never take the place of good honest seamanship and a keen pair of eyes.

My own initial scepticism about SatNav was dispelled by a quite intrepid and highly experienced cruising couple, Tom and Nancy Zydler. They've cruised the high latitudes of Spitzbergen in the north and Cape Horn in the south and rarely have I met anyone with such depth of experience. Their 37ft (11.27m) yawl *Mollymawk* was a pure seaman's boat – massively strong, utterly reliable, exuding efficiency and simplicity everywhere. They didn't even have an engine but handled the boat impeccably. I didn't expect their instrumentation to extend beyond a Walker towing log but on going below I was amazed to see a SatNav over the chart table. Tom couldn't praise it highly enough and said that it had changed the face of their sea-time because not being absolutely certain where you are, particularly in the proximity of land, causes a lot of worry. Now SatNav has taken that worry away entirely, leaving them to enjoy themselves more and to concentrate on the seamanlike operation of their boat. They were realistic about its shortfalls. It was likely to need to be sent back to the manufacturers annually for some repair or other (in which case they could carry on cruising without it), and they needed to buy a solar panel and run their little petrol generator more often. This was a small price though for the peace of mind it gave them.

Other instrumentation

A variety of precise wind and water instrumentation has been developed by the racing field. Their accuracy is generally very good but in the Grand Scheme of things they should be tacked pretty low on the priority list. Basics are undoubtedly handy – the echo sounder and speedlog – but none of the other modern instrumentation is really necessary for ocean cruising, nor will it contribute very much to the seamanlike running of a yacht at sea. At the height of an Indian Ocean gale it might be able to tell you that it is blowing exactly 52 knots, at 78 degrees off the bow and the boat is making 1.78 knots VMG to windward, but your real priorities must be in the strength and quality of your rigging, the integrity of openings and hatches and the reliability of your bilge pumps. In short, instrumentation must come a long way down the priorities list and only be fitted when essentials are well catered for and there is a first-class complement of basic seamanlike equipment aboard, like anchors, good rig and sails, and high-capacity pumps. All on-board electronic aids should be regarded as just that – aids. If you have to rely on them in any way you should not be going to sea.

Radio communications

Good receivers are fairly cheap and even to set yourself up with an amateur radio transmitter is not particularly expensive. Some people argue that the element of safety that transceivers introduce to an ocean crossing backfires when, for whatever reason, you can't maintain a regular scheduled call and people and authorities immediately start worrying, possibly unnecessarily. Certainly the large majority of ocean passages take place quietly without any radio communication and while this gives a certain peace of mind to the skipper and crew, those at home would far prefer an occasional reminder that you are still afloat.

To the uninitiated radio frequencies and terminology can be very confusing, with short waves, medium waves, AM, FM, long waves, medium frequency (MF), high frequency (HF) and of course VHF. It is much easier to forget all that (with the exception of VHF which most people understand anyway) and think in terms of kilohertz only.

Basically there are two broad divisions – AM and FM. FM is the same as VHF and only used for small distances, usually less than 75 miles. Yachtsmen will be using AM solely and the bigger the frequency number, the further away it can be heard. Something like BBC Radio One broadcasts in the UK on 1,053kHz can be heard for a few hundred miles. The kHz radio frequency scale goes right up to 29,999 and that can be heard worldwide on the right equipment. As you run up the scale so certain sections are allocated for general broadcasting use, for amateur (ham) radio and for marine communications.

Receivers

These have several uses, probably the most important one for ocean yachtsmen being the ability to pick up time signals, either from BBC World Service or the US WWV stations. Whilst modern quartz timepieces are highly accurate, it is nevertheless necessary to check them frequently if you want good astronavigation positions.

WWV broadcast continuous times signals on 2,500, 5,000, 10,000 and 15,000 kHz. World Service broadcast on dozens of different frequencies all over the world, from around 3,915 kHz up to 21,710 kHz, and these ranges are embraced in most 'short wave' portable radio sets available from High Street shops. Don't buy a set that can only be powered by dry cell batteries - you'll find that if you start listening to something like BBC World Service regularly, you'll use dozens of batteries and although they're not usually hard to find, they can be very expensive. Alternatively, use nicads and buy a small 12v charger for them. Transformers which plug into car cigarette lighter sockets and which step down the voltage from 12 to 4.5/6/9v can be bought, although they are rare abroad, so if you intend to listen to the radio regularly, get one before you go.

Technology and models are changing very rapidly but one of the best general receivers for yachts is the Sony ICF 2001, which will pick up all AM radio frequencies from 150kHz through to 29,999 kHz. In other words, as well as serving as a normal 'kitchen' radio, it will also pick up all the marine frequencies such as 2,182 kHz and the US high seas weather forecasts. It also embraces all the ham radio bands so that although you obviously can't talk to others using ham, you can listen in. This can become quite a hobby and very informative at times. The Sony is supplied with an invaluable Wave Handbook, which catalogues all the radio stations throughout the world with their transmission times, languages, areas and frequencies. I spent many a night watch fiddling with the radio, listening to Radio Australia for a while, then Voice of America, and so on. The Sony is very sensitive to moisture, so be certain to look after it carefully.

During our years overseas we became quite hooked on the BBC World Service and particularly at sea we looked forward to hearing our favourite programmes. The BBC publishes a monthly magazine catalogue of programmes and frequencies, *London Calling*, which is very useful. We subscribed to it for several years. They send it out airmail six weeks in advance of the month it covers, so it stands a chance of reaching you before going out of date wherever you are. Details can be had from BBC London Calling, PO Box 76, Bush House, Strand, London WC2B 4PH.

Single sideband radio transmitters

A single sideband radio transmitter, operating between 2,000kHz – 22,000kHz, enables you to contact shoreside marine operators and other ships over a range of up to 6,000 miles. In theory, this allows you to make telephone calls through coastal stations such as Portishead and WOM in Fort Lauderdale whilst you are sailing in the Atlantic. In practice it is a difficult operation which you don't do unless it is absolutely necessary. Commercial and naval ships are duty bound to listen in to 2,182 kHz, which has a range of up to around 150 miles and is the international distress frequency, so this is a safety factor.

For all these advantages, the SSB/MF-HF radio is designed for big ships and is not a very practical or popular radio transmitter for yachts. Although one quite often comes across yachts fitted with them, their crews say they are rarely if ever used. They are also usually between two and three times the price of an amateur radio set.

Amateur/ham radio

Ham radios are highly popular on ocean cruising boats and for very good reasons. There are dozens of regular 'nets' organised - these are simply a regular time and radio frequency that a number of yachtsmen call in on. There is, for example, the Atlantic crossing 'net', which is co-ordinated by amateur radio enthusiasts in England but which yachts sailing in the Atlantic tune in to every day. Those on passage usually call in their position and the weather and will have a chat to the co-ordinator or maybe some friends who are also crossing over. It becomes a friendly daily chat session where people chip in with a bit of help and advice (I remember one crew having trouble with their Aries self-steering which they subsequently rectified by someone else's helpful tip) and as a cruising grapevine it is great to learn the whereabouts of friends.

There are many smaller networks such as the Caribbean Net where perhaps just a dozen hams participate, and of course private ones where you arrange to speak with a particular set of friends maybe once a week. The friendliness of it is of course very pleasant, but ham radio can provide very practical information too. A friend of ours was in Barbados and needed to slip his boat fairly urgently. Rather than sail up through the islands trying to find a slipway that would take him straight away for a reasonable price, he was able to talk to his friends on the Caribbean net who were anchored in the islands with slipways. By the next day he knew the best place to haul, asked his ham friend there to book it, and he sailed directly there. I could quote many other instances.

Many is the time I've tried contacting passing ships through the international distress frequency of 2,182kHz and not picked up any ship within hundreds of miles. The one thing about ham radio is that there is always somebody listening out for an interesting chat. They may not be able to help directly, but in an emergency they could instigate help. There have been several instances of yachtsmen in serious medical trouble being able, through a ham, to contact doctors who have been able to diagnose the problem and advise treatment.

Another practical use for ham is talking to friends back at home. Nobody is allowed to use ham without a licence, but an easy arrangement is to strike up a radio contact with a ham radio operator who lives near family or friends at home. Although passing messages to third parties is against the strict laws controlling ham radio, you can talk to your contact weekly and the folks back home will know you are safe and well.

Ham does have its disadvantages. For a start you need to be officially licensed and this requires taking an examination proving your capability to use the radio properly and within the rules. This exam is not difficult, but it is not so easy as the VHF operator's exam. If you plan to have a ham set aboard, make sure you take an evening class for the operator's exam the winter before you leave.

The other disadvantage with ham radios is the heavy current drain while you are transmitting – commonly between 20-50 amps. This is only intermittently, whilst you are actually speaking, but it is the reason why many yachtsmen do considerably more listening than transmitting.

We listened in to the ham nets very regularly on the Sony ICF 2001 and found them most informative. The chit-chat would often give you information on the best place to buy fuel, or perhaps customs officers to avoid, and we were often able to find out where friends were and so on. The biggest contribution it made though was when we crossed the Atlantic from the Canaries to West Indies. By listening to the daily weather reports of the 14 or 15 yachts which had already set off we were able to wait in the Canaries until we were absolutely sure that the tradewinds had set in for that year, then head off ourselves. By plotting the other yachts' positions and their weather we were able to head just far enough south for the best winds. When we were actually out on the crossing it was somehow comforting knowing there were others nearby rolling as much as us, or when a gale came through, having a worse time of it than us. Listening in to the Atlantic ham net became one of the high points of the daily routine – our only frustration was that we were unable to talk back as we would dearly have liked to on occasions.

VHF

This is nearly universal among ocean cruising boats nowadays. Many people use it purely as a telephone to talk to friends in port or report their departure or arrival to the habour master. We find that the VHF's greatest value is at sea, when we are able to talk to passing ships. On our first catamaran, *Foreigner*, we had no radio at all, and after we'd been at sea for a couple of weeks we longed to have a chat with someone else. *Euge* was fitted with VHF and it was always a pleasure to talk to the crews of tankers, liners and coasters. In the Bay of Biscay on one occasion we found ourselves feeling rather like a tiddler when we struck up a conversation with the QE2!

We were never too proud to ask for a weather report or SatNav position (chat-nav!) just to confirm our astro either. By talking to ships that we were on collision courses with we were able to exchange gentlemanly suggestions which took any possible danger or aggravation away from the situation. On one occasion in a gale we asked a ship heading straight at us to alter course, because for us to have done so would have been dangerous in the circumstances. As it turned out, in the white and broken water of the gale he hadn't seen us, either visually or on radar, and was only too happy to take avoiding action.

Computers

Laptop computers are seen more and more aboard ocean cruising boats, more for the fun factor than real practical contribution. Most people use them primarily for word processing, linked to one of the small 12v portable printers such as the Canon or Kodak Diconix. However, there are a variety of astro navigation and tidal programs that can be run on them. They can also be connected to a short-wave receiver and, through a modem, be used for weatherfax or morse reception. This can be a useful aid and costs a tiny fraction of a commercial weatherfax.

We have a Toshiba portable aboard *Foreigner 2*, it being essential for my work as a writer. I have to say that I see it as an expendable toy in a salty, humid marine environment and will no doubt replace it from time to time as our present extended cruise progresses.

14. Ground Tackle and Self Steering

There is no logical reason for dealing with these two subjects in the same chapter except that they are two aspects of an ocean cruising boat on which no expense should be spared, because one or the other should be looking after you all the time. While a standard-sized anchor with either chain or rope rode will suffice most of the time, there comes a time on all ocean cruises when the anchor becomes the lifeline, the insurance policy and sometimes the life insurance.

Anchors and rodes

The size and extent of ground tackle is one of the few things that most long distance yachtsmen agree about – the gear must be big, but at the same time fairly easy to handle. There is no point in having a big anchor and chain ready to go out as you drag backwards across an anchorage if you have no roller for it, or the pulpit is too cluttered to allow it to be passed through.

The late Bob Griffiths of *Awahnee*, a man of huge cruising experience in high latitudes, had some interesting theories on anchoring. He believed that the correct anchor and rode for specific bottoms was more important than sheer anchor size and he carried no fewer than 10 anchors on this 53ft (16.15m) cutter, and none of them over 45 lb (20kg) so they remained manageable. This may seem over the top, but he said those anchors had saved his boat on numerous occasions. He also said that if he had to choose one anchor it would be the CQR, and this is an opinion echoed by the majority. Three quarters of all yachts are fitted with them. Unfortunately, the CQR is expensive and has a large number of cheap imitators, generically known as plough anchors. The latter are nowhere near the calibre or construction of the genuine Simpson Lawrence CQR.

The Danforth or Meon anchor comes next in the popularity stakes, although I've damaged two of these in the past by bending their shanks. For all that, for a straight line pull (ie used as a kedge) there are few to beat it, and of her five anchors, *Foreigner 2* is now equipped with three of these types, including the much-vaunted aluminium Fortress, which has become our favourite. We carry the diminutive FX23 model, weighing just 23lb, as our storm anchor and the only time it served this purpose,

When choosing or upgrading your ground tackle, remember that in many places there simply aren't protected anchoring areas or harbours and you might have to put up with conditions like this *(Mark Fishwick)*

temporarily holding *Foreigner 2* beam-on in near gale force winds, the only worry it gave us was quite how we'd break it out afterwards. I can't recommend it highly enough, especially for multihulls where weight is critical.

The Bruce anchor arrived amid a storm of publicity in the '70s, but is an anchor that people either seem to love or hate. For me, the fact that there is never a happy medium casts this anchor in doubt when so much depends on it.

Although the traditional fisherman anchor is still available in large sizes, these three patent anchors today dominate the scene. Although various sailing books mention anchors like the Northill and Herreschoff, they are not universally available.

In mooring terms, an ocean cruiser needs adaptability – sometimes she will not only need to anchor but maybe a long line will have to be taken to a far harbour wall, or tied to a coral head or mangrove swamp. To carry ten anchors is overkill (bear in mind Griffiths cruised in some wild and windy places) but an ocean cruiser should have a bare minimum of three good anchors - two similar-sized bowers, preferably of different type, and a good-sized kedge. The most practical system of rodes is to have 180ft (55m) of chain on your favourite bower. This gives ample scope for the majority of anchorages, with a bit of spare to ease out in rougher conditions. In a separate chain locker, there should be 90ft (27.4m) of the same-sized chain (both lengths having a good eye welded in each end) used with the second bower. This can be added to, if necessary, by a 400ft (121m) length of polypropylene. A further 250ft (76m) of nylon should be used with the kedge, with 20ft (6.1m) of chain also attached. The kedge has to have this long length of nylon line for when it is used either in a running moor or stern-to a beach. At sea these two long ropes can be used as drogues or with parachutes if necessary.

With this set-up it is possible, in very bad conditions, to have two big anchors out and a third line taken to a fixed point ashore or on the seabed. (We also carry a couple of old spare 10ft lengths of chain with big eyes at either end which can be used when mooring lines pass over a rough concrete jetty edge, or when a line needs to be made fast to coral. These have been invaluable on occasions). A system we've used with some success in bad conditions is to shackle the kedge and chain to the crown of the main anchor then lower the two in tandem.

We've found that this ground tackle rig has been totally practical and adapts to most conditions, although it should be said the strongest conditions we have tested it in are Force 10 in moderately exposed anchorages with generally good holding.

A chain claw is a useful piece of equipment to have aboard. Most of the time it is shackled to a 6ft (1.8m) length of nylon led over the bow roller, used as a snubber on the main cable and to stop the chain graunching in the roller and keeping everyone awake. You can still hear if the anchor drags. It can also be attached to a long length of rope which is led aft to a sheet winch. If the anchor is fouled, or the windlass inoperative, it's possible to get the anchor up using this rig.

Self steering

The self-steering system of a long distance cruising yacht is the single most important piece of gear she carries, and yet it never fails to amaze me how little thought some first-time ocean cruising crews put into this essential aid. Hand-steering is quite feasible for a day or two, but if your self-steering gear fails halfway through a three or four week passage, you'll never again underestimate its significance to small boat sailing. It has been described on countless occasions in the past as a non-eating crewmember who doesn't answer back and doesn't suffer from the cold, wet or lack of sleep. The increase in rest and therefore watch-keeping efficiency, navigational accuracy and general on-board content means that the self-steering gear should be selected with great thought and it is one of the few areas where money should be no object. It will pay you back a hundred times over.

The sometimes perplexing question is whether to go for a windvane gear or one of the many modern electronic autopilots available today. To differentiate, I shall call all windvane mechanical gears 'self-steering gears' and the electric/electronic devices 'autopilots'. The autopilot is not only cheap in comparison to a self-steering gear, it is also very neat, light, and, if set up properly, uses surprisingly little power. It is also very easy to initiate quickly. However, I can't urge you strongly enough that as a primary gear, don't rely on any sort of autopilot. Most long distance sailors agree that none of the modern range of electronic autopilots is yet anywhere near durable enough to rely on as a main system for ocean crossings.

Every year long-distance race fleets set off on OSTAR, AZAB, Round Britain and so on, and time and time again the biggest cause of problems are autopilots. Some long-distance yachtsmen are forced, through the size and shape of their yachts, to have just autopilots but they generally have two or three back-ups and have many a tale of having to hand-steer. A self-steering gear may be heavy and unsightly, and perhaps difficult to mount on some boats, but it's the only way to go if you don't want to be let down sooner or later.

Originally coming on the scene in the early '60s, the self-steering gear rather went

The Californian-made Monitor vane gear has picked up where the now-discontinued Aries left off. It works on identical principles, but is made in stainless steel throughout

out of favour 15 years later when autopilots became cheap and reliable and were used extensively for coastal weekend and holiday sailing, for which they are very effective. Without a mass market, self-steering gears rather went through the doldrums and although one or two new ones came and went, only the enduring models survived – the Aries, Navik, and Hydrovane. To many people's disappointment, the Hasler (whose creator, Blondie Hasler, developed self-steering gears) went out of production. In the last five to eight years there has been renewed interest in windvane self-steering gears and a couple of interesting new ones have become available.

A big disappointment has been the (voluntary) demise of the Aries Vane Gear, whose designer and manufacturer Nick Franklin decided to quit when he himself set off long-distance sailing. For me, the Aries continues to be the gear by which others are judged, and if you are lucky enough to own one, hang on to it! However, all is not lost, as the American-made Monitor (working on identical principles) will, I'm certain, pick up the baton. Being constructed entirely in stainless steel, the Monitor doesn't experience the problems common to all Aries gears – that of mixing aluminium and stainless in a saltwater environment and therefore freezing very solidly together.

The neat and well-engineered Hydrovane has enjoyed success for many years and has been used extensively. Its principal advantage is that the horizontally-pivoting vane mechanically operates a servo rudder and this means that the yacht's main rudder can be locked, which not only saves on wear and tear but also obviates the need for steering lines coming from the gear to the cockpit – sometimes a nuisance with centre-cockpit, wheel-steered boats and always a source of chafe. It also means that the yacht has a second rudder if you have problems with the first.

The same can be said of the Swedish Sailomat, except that it uses a separate servo-pendulum blade to operate an auxiliary rudder so, in theory, is very efficient. Despite being beautifully conceived and engineered and by far the most expensive of all self-steering gears, the Sailomat has never caught on and has been heavily criticised by some who have used it.

The German-made Windpilots (imported into the UK by Pumpkin Marine) have come to the fore recently. They have become a popular successor in Europe to the Aries and are seen extensively on modern ocean cruisers. Three versions are available, each with different sizes for larger or smaller boats.

Combining a small tiller pilot with a vane gear provides one of the best self-steering arrangements it's possible to have – providing high power from the servo-pendulum and course accuracy and low electrical consumption from the tillerpilot

Last, but far from least, is the Cornish-made Auto-Steer, which has received a great deal of favourable comment from those who've used it. Two versions are available, the same head unit, with horizontal-axis vane, operating either a servo-pendulum with tiller lines, or a trim tab on the trailing edge of transom-hung rudders. Other than being beautifully engineered, one of the big advantages of the Auto-Steer is its portability – it is very simple to remove and stow below. For those who feel that vane gears detract from the looks of their yacht this is a boon, on a more practical level it divorces the fatal attraction that dinghies and vane gears have for each other.

While autopilots are not to be recommended as a primary method of steering, they are nevertheless useful on occasions, because wind-vane self-steering gear is not infallible and refuses to operate well in certain conditions. Properly set up and kept well away from any moisture or water (ie either covered or rigged to operate the steering or rudder stock from within the cabin) an autopilot can be used in very light airs, especially with the wind astern, or when you are motoring for any length of time. We had an Autohelm on our Rival 34 to back up an Aries, and made a little watertight bonnet to protect it from the rain and dew. We only used the Autohelm in very light conditions, but it was kept bone dry and served well for a year. We like to think that the bonnet prolonged its life, but whether or not it did we'll never know.

We gave the self-steering arrangements for *Foreigner 2* a great deal of thought because with several small children aboard we rely on it very heavily; having one parent hand-steering and another asleep would leave the children totally unsupervised, which is unacceptable. The primary gear is an Aries, but it has limitations in light airs; because of steering friction it won't work with less than 6 knots of wind over the vane, or 3 knots past the servo-pendulum. For those light airs, for motoring and for when the helmsman is needed quickly, perhaps in or leaving harbour, we have an Autohelm 3000. The two broad systems work well, but we improved the armoury before leaving the UK by adding a small Autohelm 800 tillerpilot rigged to push a plywood stump where the windvane of the Aries would normally be. In this way, we had an electronic brain with a minimal electrical appetite supplying the course reference, but the brawn of the Aries servo-pendulum physically steering the boat. It works brilliantly, steering the boat on precision courses during conditions in which the Aries was operating marginally such as lowish windspeeds and especially quartering winds/seas, when *Foreigner 2*'s propensity to surge back and forth in speed would bend the apparent wind cyclically, more than the Aries could cope with.

Finally, a word about multihulls and self-steering gears. Short-handed racing multihulls experienced many problems with their highly fluctuating speeds and therefore the varying apparent wind that their vane gears used as a reference. The electronic autopilot came to their rescue. For some reason cruising multihulls got tarred with the same brush. Other than the conditions described in the last paragraph, the usually well-loaded cruising multihull's speed does not skitter back and forth enough to confuse a vane gear which, by and large, works just as well on a cat or tri.

15. The Ocean Cruiser's Dinghy

Never underestimate the constant use and hard work your dinghy will receive once you are living aboard. It is a workhorse, often left banging around with a dozen others at a concrete quayside, regularly dragged up and down beaches over sand, stones and coral, often overloaded, and rarely out of service for long enough to be maintained properly. Durability is therefore essential, but it must also be light enough to be easily manhandled, and preferably need little routine maintenance. The other major feature that marries a dinghy and yacht is the ability to stow it conveniently aboard.

Amongst the dinghy's essential functions will be to serve as a ferry between yacht and shore and as a cargo carrier, loaded down with water containers and provisions. A good one can be used for exploring further afield or as a base to go diving from. In some cases it may be the ship's lifeboat too. It must certainly be seaworthy enough to get you out to the yacht when the weather has deteriorated while you have been ashore and to take out an extra anchor when conditions are bad, or even in a surf with the yacht piled up ashore.

To satisfy all these criteria, it becomes fairly obvious that there is no perfect solution. As ever, it boils down to a compromise, and the chief debate is between the inflatable and rigid dinghy.

Inflatables

Approximately two-thirds of ocean cruising boats have inflatable tenders. Their major advantage is the ability to stow them on a boat where it isn't possible to have a rigid dinghy. The inflatable is also very light (so you can carry it up a rough beach), it carries loads well and doesn't knock against the topsides or under the counter. The great buoyancy of an inflatable is also a bonus when it comes to carrying the full crew complement or lots of stores. If you are concerned about overnight theft, it is a simple and easy matter to haul it up on deck out of reach. Inflatables cannot be rowed into a strong wind or sea, but when powered by a small outboard they are highly seaworthy and even when half full of water can still make progress when a rigid dinghy has long since given up for fear of being overwhelmed. The inflatable is also much better as a diving and snorkelling platform.

Fig 12A wire bridle encased in plastic tubing should be fitted as a matter of course to inflatable tenders, to ease their painter fittings and provide a secure point to padlock a security painter

Against the inflatable is its poor rowing performance, high windage and light weight. This means that if you want to get the best out of it, you're tied to having an outboard engine, which further increases the considerably higher initial cost of buying an inflatable. An inflatable will require more maintenance than an average rigid dinghy and doesn't stand much abuse. It will need patching from time to time, and must be washed out regularly to avoid abrasion from sand. Cleaning weed and scum off the bottom is another chore, though this can be avoided by always turning it upside down at night. An irritating aspect of using an inflatable is that one nearly always gets wet, either from spray over the bow or from puddles collecting around your feet. A final disadvantage of inflatables is their attraction to thieves. In many places an Avon or Zodiac is almost as good as cash. Make sure you sketch the bottom of your dinghy and keep a record of the 'geography' of its patches for evidence of indentification.

Inflatables can also be customised and improved for a lot of work. Never rely on a bow eye or fitting, it is much better to wrap a rope (or wire encased in plastic) right the way around the dinghy (see figure 12), or, if the dinghy has a wooden transom, take the wires to eye fittings in the transom. Floorboards are something of a hassle to fit when you're cruising from day to day, but if you're stopped in a place for any length of time, they will help maintain dry feet, make the dinghy row and motor more efficiently, and keep shopping bags dry. If your inflatable dinghy has a transom, it is worth cutting a sculling notch into it, just in case you are unlucky enough to lose an oar (at times like this one generally picks up the technique of sculling very quickly . . .).

Rigid dinghies

A rigid dinghy will generally cost less than an inflatable. It can be rowed efficiently without too much effort, which further cuts your running costs and keeps you fit. A rigid dinghy will also last longer than its inflatable cousin. Many can be rigged for sailing, adding to your enjoyment of an anchorage, though in practice they are seldom used this way unless there are children aboard. I doubt we'd bother taking a sailing rig along again, it simply isn't used enough to justify the cost, weight and space, unless you can find one exceptionally simple to set.

The main problem with rigid dinghies is finding suitable deck space for them on a boat less than 38ft (11.6m) or so. If you go for a smaller dinghy that fits the available

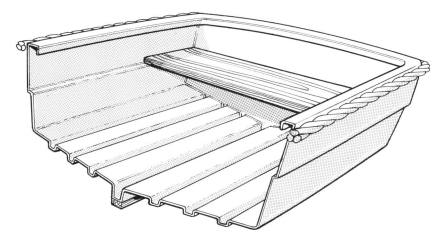

Fig 13 **When choosing a dinghy, the first priorities are strength and lightness. The builder can achieve this effectively by utilising many curves and ridges within the moulding**

space it becomes a nuisance having to make two or three trips ashore each time because you can't fit everyone in, and it is useless for exploring. Rigid dinghies also invariably weigh two or three times as much as an inflatable and this weight is carried high up on deck, which is not good for the centre of gravity. Another point against a rigid dinghy is its seemingly magnetic attraction to your topsides. No matter how well you protect its gunwale with fendering, sooner or later it starts to bump.

On both *Foreigner* and *Euge* we used rigid GRP dinghies. They were always very cheap, never costing more than £100, generally tatty, and for this reason we had less worry about them being stolen. They were never locked up. Maintenance was straightforward – we kept them clean, never let them leak, and made certain the fender was always well attached. Otherwise they received no attention in terms of painting or varnishing, but, being fibreglass, they lasted well and stood up to terrible punishment. We took a different route for *Foreigner 2*, equipping her with a 10ft aluminium dinghy which was modified to double up as a liferaft (see later in this chapter). It has all of the above attributes, except cheapness, but with the children in mind we needed a largish dinghy light enough to be dragged up beaches. Again, with the children in mind, it is virtually indestructible and we hope it will last pretty much forever.

A pair of long oars is essential for easy propulsion, used in galvanised (never plastic) rowlocks which must be secured with lanyards as the right-sized galvanised rowlocks are irreplaceable overseas. The oars must have good protection from the rowlocks or they will get chewed up rapidly with the amount of use they receive. The best way of doing this is by splitting a 9in length of plastic pipe, 'glueing' it in place with silicone and working a turk's head over each end.

The dinghy we had on *Euge* was the best small tender I've ever come across. At 7ft 6in (2.28m), it's great advantage was light weight (75 lb/34kg) but high strength. This is achieved by the simple process of incorporating ridges and angles throughout the GRP mouldings, creating stiffness but at the same time allowing a light lay-up (see figure 13).

If a rigid dinghy doesn't quite fit on deck, it can often be adapted with a recess, either in the bow transom or stern, to fit around the mast.

The best fender material is a thick rope wired on with copper loops. These need replacing from time to time, but the materials are easy to find anywhere. The dinghy bumping problem is often best solved by attaching the end of the painter to an eye in the transom and shackling the spinnaker halyard in the resulting vee to hoist the dinghy out of the water. As long as there isn't too much swell or a very strong wind, the dinghy will lie quietly against the guardrails at deck level until needed again.

Most cruising people would choose a rigid dinghy if it were possible to stow one of 10ft (3.05m) or more on deck. As it is, they are deterred by the fact they can fit only an 8-footer (2.43m) on deck, which with more than two people is crowded and doesn't have much freeboard. One solution is a nesting dinghy, the stern portion of which disconnects and stows in the forward part. In this way, it is possible to have an excellent 10 or 12 foot rowing and sailing dinghy that has the buoyancy and much of the seaworthiness of an inflatable, and comes close to an ideal compromise. The snag is that these are not built commercially so you would have to make your own. This subject will be enlarged on later in this chapter.

RIBs – the perfect compromise?

The Rigid Inflatable Boat, ie an inflatable with a fixed GRP floorpan, comes pretty close to being an ideal compromise between the rigid dinghy and inflatable one. Tougher than an inflatable, and able to be dragged up beaches, the RIB also rows better than its floppy-bottomed sister and keeps the shopping bags and feet of its crew dry. It still requires deck space to stow, but a good deal less than a rigid dinghy of equivalent volume.

The rub, of course, is the high initial price and the related problem of theft. If you're prepared to always lock it up, I believe the RIB makes a first rate tender, and that if you look at the cost in the Grand Scheme of Things, the years ahead of everyday useage and convenience make the extra money well worth spending.

Outboard engines

Modern outboard engines (and I stress modern) are very good nd the best thing you can do to an outboard is to use it regularly as an ocean cruising yachtsman is likely to. The little 2hp or so 'egg-whisk' engines such as the Suzuki, Mercury, Yamaha or Mariner are so cheap, light, reliable, economical and even quiet that it's hard to resist having one aboard if your dinghy is less than 9ft (2.74m). Many was the time in our early cruising days I regretted not having one when there was a long row to pick up water or dive on a wreck. We have a 5hp Yamaha these days, deliberately going for the little extra power or: our 10ft dinghy as an insurance policy for the emergency situation where I might need to run out a kedge quickly to pull us off a reef, or run a line across a storm-ridden harbour to warp us into a safer place.

On the other hand, rowing helps you keep fit and rowing past a neighbour's boat provides ample time to chat, whereas an outboard buzzing away at the stern puts paid to any social contact. The Hiscocks gave up their outboard for just this reason. All the

Probably the most popular tender arrangement amongst blue-water cruisers is a small rigid-transomed inflatable with a 2-4hp Japanese outboard. They are vulnerable to thieves and must always be locked up, but are light enough to be hoisted on deck at night

same, having an outboard is much like having an auxiliary engine – you can be a purist, but choose to use it at will.

Speed is a matter of personal preference. Some people like to flash around an anchorage quickly on the plane and we have come across cruising boats with 20hp outboards for skiing. They rarely made many friends in the anchorage. For most cruising folk, time is the one thing they have in abundance and two minutes getting ashore in a dinghy propelled with an egg-whisk is no sacrifice, even if a 9.9hp could get them to the dock in 15 seconds. The smaller motor uses a fraction of the fuel and can be passed up on deck with one hand.

Like popular inflatables, outboards of all varieties are like a little cache of money attached to the back of your dinghy and must be well protected from the thief. Make sure that it is securely locked to the tender and the dinghy is well locked to mothership or shore. If the dinghy isn't locked as well, an outboard thief will take this too (no matter how disreputable) and either break the outboard off at his leisure, or use a knife to remove an inflatable's transom.

In terms of spares availability the widest-used outboard worldwide is the Mariner, which is a close relation to the Yamaha. These two are used in many Third World areas on dug-outs and trading craft. If you have a larger dinghy, or want the ability to plane in a smaller one, arguably the best outboard ever built was the Johnson/Evinrude 6hp. This thrives on regular use, quickly recovers from a total immersion, and is very reliable indeed.

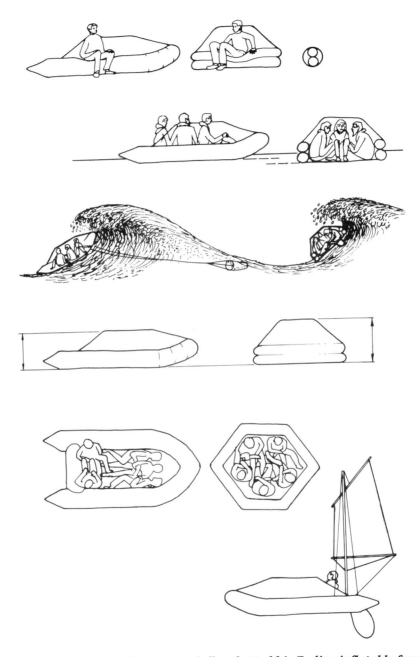

*Fig 14 **Frenchman George Nacam specially adapted his Zodiac inflatable for a sailbome 'life-dingby'. The result had lower overall windage (which combined with greater surface area made it more resistant to capsize), better shape and buoyancy forward for breaking waves, higher freeboard, and considerably improved space for occupants over conventional liferafts. With a simple rig and large rudder it had the capability to sail towards shore or shipping lanes***

The dinghy as a liferaft

The design of the conventional inflatable liferaft is often criticised for its lack of development, poor durability, tendency to capsize easily, discomfort and the heavy ongoing expense of servicing it. For all this, it takes some nerve to dispense with it and go your own way by adapting your dinghy for a lifeboat role.

The ability to sail towards shipping lanes or shore would have saved hundreds of lives in the past, and I believe that most of us would prefer the ability to help ourselves

Foreigner's 'life-dinghy' in sailing mode

in this way to just sitting in a liferaft praying for someone to see us. The boost to morale a moving liferaft would have is important to the success of such an emergency. Many ideas have been suggested in sailing magazines, and the Tinker range of inflatables are a laudable step towards the goal of self-preservation. However, Tinker dinghies are expensive and for just half the amount one could produce good alternative.

One is aiming to achieve many things with a 'life-dinghy', and not necessarily in this order:-
1. It must be seaworthy, unsinkable and be 'rightable' after a capsize
2. It must have room (and buoyancy) enough for the full complement of crew
3. It must have some form of propulsion, preferably a small sail
4. It must have good shelter for the crew
5. Ideally, it should be arranged so that the crew are not sitting in puddles
6. At least one person should be able to sleep with some comfort
7. It must be ready to use at a moment's notice

A 10ft (3.04m) inflatable fitted with some kind of sailing rig is an obvious choice, and wouldn't need a great deal by way of adaption to make it into an excellent life-dinghy. Figure 14 shows an idea suggested by Frenchman George Nacam a few years ago. The attendant photos show our interpretation of what a 'life-dinghy' should look like, based in our case on *Foreigner 2*'s 10ft aluminium dinghy.

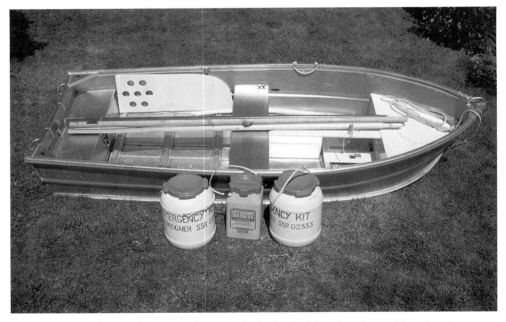

Our present 10ft aluminium tender-cum-'life-dinghy' for Foreigner. The standard dinghy was extensively modified by fitting an Add-a-Buoy flotation collar around the outside, and a hooped fluorescent orange cover. A very simple rig, based around a two-part sailboard mast, was fitted. Before putting to sea, the spars, safety equipment and two emergency packs are lashed inside the dinghy. As such, we are in a good position to rescue ourselves rather than sit in a liferaft waiting to be spotted

16. Spare Parts and Tools

The extent and range of your spare parts determines your level of self-sufficiency and therefore, to some extent, the success of your cruise. A comprehensive parts list should be made as soon as possible, something best done aboard, systematically working your way through the yacht. It will pay later, because trying to find a Baby Blake bowl gasket, Stanley knife blades, or stainless steel washers may be very difficult when you're off the beaten track.

Nevertheless, Sod's Law decrees that you will often not have the particular spare you need, but a plentiful supply of good glues, sealants, rigging wire, miscellaneous plastic piping, studding, seizing wire, nuts, bolts and screws, timber and scrap stainless will enable you to improvise. We took an old lorry inner tube which, cut up, did service in all manner of applications, from water tank inspection-lid gasket to bungy cord for the tiller.

The spares locker should be stocked gradually a long time from the planned departure day, because you get the best bargains by buying out of season (we were able to purchase two years' supply of antifouling at 25% discount) and you also allow yourself time to track down the difficult items. A friend of ours started his collection 18 months before he planned to leave, and each week would go into the chandlers and buy a shackle or rigging clamp. In this way he collected an impressive spares locker but didn't notice the cost in the same way as buying a dozen heavy stainless shackles, half a dozen cans of antifouling, a spare halyard, assorted stainless bolts and a couple of tubes of sealant all in one go.

The question that soon arises over spares is, how much of your capital do you invest in them? Getting even the most basic parts whilst you're overseas is usually difficult and, for marine equipment in non-yachting centres, normally impossible. The cost of having them sent out from home can often be two or three times the price of the part itself, irritating to say the least when you could have bought it easily and comparatively cheaply a few months beforehand. It's comforting to go away with a big bank balance, but a yacht used 365 days a year needs continual looking after and spares of everything will be needed. Balancing these two factors is quite critical, as an imbalance either way could pave the path to failure later on.

Spend some time tracking down plenty of different marine chandlery catalogues (especially the mail-order chandleries) and technical brochures for any slightly

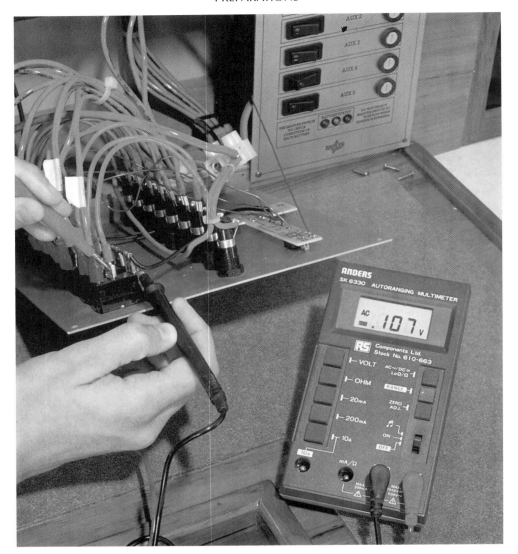

***The cruising man's stethoscope. If your boat has electricity in any form, don't go to
sea without (however basic) a multimeter***

complicated equipment you have on board. Thus equipped you'll have all that is
necessary when it comes to needing precise measurements or specifications, and part
order numbers which are often essential to purchasing the correct item.

A sail repair kit comprising plenty of patching material (a sailmaker will usually
quite happily give you offcuts from his rubbish bin), polyester yarn and a good
sailmakers' palm is essential. Another useful addition to this kit is thirty or forty feet of
one-inch (25mm) wide webbing tape – it is cheap, pliable, strong and can be used in
many applications when a sail (particularly the corners) needs strengthening or rein-
forcing. Also carry one or two appropriate Sta-Lok swageless terminals so that any part
of the standing rigging can be repaired if, as is likely, the damage occurs at the old

terminal. Because modern blocks are so expensive we bought a dozen single and double ash blocks very cheaply from Thomas Foulkes in London. Varnished and fitted with strops, they were forever useful, especially when running in the trades when all sorts of extra blocks and leads are required.

You should understand the basic workings of your engine before you leave and to some extent this will reflect in the spares you carry for it. You can't have enough water pump kits (impellers, O-rings and gaskets) and make sure to have three or four of each type of belt used. For servicing, lube oil can be bought in most places so don't bother cluttering up the boat with it, but filters and elements are not so easy, so buy plenty and keep them wrapped in plastic. If you are reliant on the engine for sole battery charging, and money allows, buy a second identical alternator, and a spare regulator for both. Take any specific hoses, a spare thermostat and plenty of hose clamps. A complete, and carefully stowed, head gasket kit is expensive but worth having, though you'll need to borrow a torque wrench to use it.

Most people take far too many tools, most of which are heavy, and without exception rust terribly. Many jobs can be done with just pliers, three or four different screwdrivers, a hammer and a molewrench, all stowed conveniently but a long way from the compass. Go right through the working parts of the boat and see if any specialist tools are needed. The stern tube will probably need a large spanner. Winches generally need Allen keys, as for example do Aries wind-vane gears. We bought three of each of the Allen keys required for the Aries on the assumption that we would be working on it hanging over the stern and therefore run the risk of losing them into the water, and sure enough on our return had only one set left. The heads might require imperial spanners while the engine needs metric. However, instead of having a complete imperial set for the head, just bring the specific one or two that it requires. Feeler gauges will be needed for the dinghy outboard spark plug or if, after a period of time, the engine needs a bit of re-alignment or the tappets have to be adjusted. If you're stuck, remember Knox-Johnston's trick of taking an inch of pages in a book, then working out the measurements by numbers of pages – it is surprisingly accurate.

A hacksaw with plenty of spare blades will get good use, as will a tenon saw with its teeth protected in an oil-impregnated and grooved batten of wood held on with elastic bands. Obviously the right tools make a job much simpler but unless you plan to earn your living with them later on, approach tool choice with the attitude of how little you need rather than how much.

Take a 12v soldering iron (they're not expensive) because crimped electrical connectors are not reliable and will need replacing from time to time. A simple multimeter will transform the electrical maintenance of any boat that has 12v electricity. If you've anything more than bare essentials, going to sea without one will be like a doctor going on call without his stethoscope – both are essential. Another unwitting victim of Sod's Law and an item to take plenty of is light bulbs and fuses. You can guarantee that when you want them overseas, their fluorescents will always be an inch too long and the monofilament bulbs will be screw-fit rather than bayonet.

17. Preparing for Heavy Weather

Preparing a modern boat for heavy weather is very much easier than in days of old when they were utilising much weaker materials, such as glass for windows, canvas for sails and hemp for cordage. But although the modern boat is built using inherently stronger and more durable materials throughout, in these days of commercialism there's a better chance she will have been built down to a price with carefully calculated strength limits, so that flaws show up as a result.

Preparation for heavy weather must be put into perspective. Over the course of several years' cruising, the number of days a yacht spends at sea weathering gales is surprisingly few. It is therefore counter-productive to make it absolutely bulletproof for these few days, if by doing so the boat is made so uncomfortable and difficult to live in for the rest of the time that the cruise is jeopardised by a discontented crew. Awkwardly-placed companionways and tiny or even non-existent cockpits rank along with turtle decks, watertight bulkheads and miniscule ports in making a boat highly seaworthy and impossible to enjoy. All the same, a yacht crossing an ocean must be capable of withstanding any weather that is thrown at her and a skipper/owner needs no reminding that the whole responsibility of this lays on his shoulders.

Openings

As long as it avoids land, a bottle with a good cork will survive anything at sea and yachts have often been compared to this. For the construction of the 'bottle' you can only trust on the integrity of the men and women who built your yacht – suffice it to say that one rarely one hears of the hulls or decks of modern, quality yachts being stove in by seas, or indeed keels falling off. If you have any doubts, employ a yacht surveyor and carry out any recommendations he makes. The 'good cork' part of the equation - a yacht's ports, hatches and openings – will also depend on her builder but they can usually be improved or upgraded if there are any question marks. Look very closely and critically at every opening in your deck and coachroof.

The Companionway. The normal design of washboard caters for convenience during weekend sailing, but not for heavy weather. All the washboards have to be in place

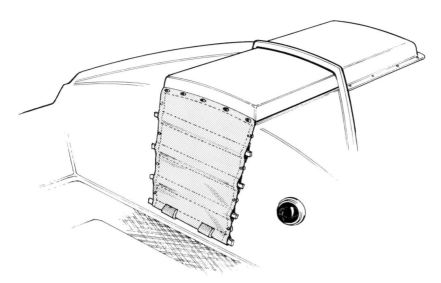

Fig 15 **Wooden washboards are cumbersome in normal sailing conditions. A simple fabric cover, larger than the opening and supported by battens, will save a lot of aggravation when rain or spray is flying about. A small amount of lead wrapped over the lower batten holds it closed**

and the hatch slid shut to hold them in. A number of the problems experienced by yachts in the 1979 Fastnet Race stemmed from just this arrangement. The crews in the cabin didn't want to be locked below, so the top washboard was left out – meaning that the two lower ones could not be secured, and neither could the hatch itself. So when the yachts were rolled their washboards were lost, the hatch could not be held closed and after this they were unable to run downwind with such a large area vulnerable to the seas. The majority of production yacht builders have totally ignored this problem, but the ocean sailor must fit stout individual barrel bolts on each washboard and devise a method of securing the hatch that can be operated from both the cockpit and inside the cabin. The washboards themselves must be strong (minimum 1 inch [25mm] thick per 2sq ft [.185m2] of area) and ideally a bit bigger than the companionway hole they are covering.

Well-tapered companionway entrance slides make using the washboards more convenient, but in extreme conditions those washboards don't have to slide up far before they fall out (assuming they are not secured with bolts), so they are not nearly as seamanlike as parallel-sided ones. If your companionway entrance is not vertical but cants forward slightly, the moment it rains you must put in all the washboards. Irrespective of heavy weather, this is pretty annoying and if you can avoid it, either by extending the sprayhood aft or perhaps making up a battened fabric cover (Figure 15), do so for your sanity, especially as the engine and electrics are often just below the companionway entrance.

Ports/Windows. Nowadays the strength of acrylic windows is such that they are unlikely to give way, but the weak point is the extruded aluminium frame. The subject of storm shutters is frequently raised. They were used a lot 30 years ago when a

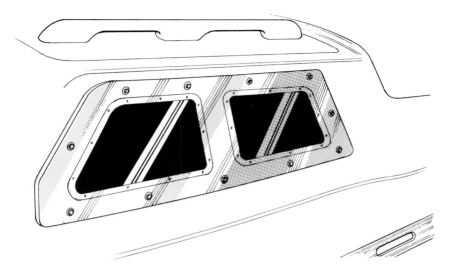

*Fig 16 **If you are nervous about the size or integrity of your windows and ports, a simple remedy is to bolt polycarbonate or acrylic sheets over them; give the cover a generous overlap and use as few bolts as possible, with large washers on the outside***

broken porthole was not uncommon. Now it would be overzealous to have either wooden or polycarbonate storm shutters for every port on a yacht, unless she had really large windows all round, in which case permanent polycarbonate shutters should be fitted (see below). But it's certainly worth the small effort and expense of pre-fabricating one storm shutter, shown in Figure 16, which should be big enough for the largest opening and stowed in an easily accessible place.

Although some people consider it amateurish, a through-bolted acrylic window a few inches bigger all round than the opening is about the strongest arrangement it is possible to have. If you use a material like polycarbonate for the window, it is likely to be stronger than the glassfibre coachroof surrounding it. If you have conventional framed windows which are a little too large for your peace of mind, it is worth considering fitting permanent polycarbonate shutters (Figure 15) which don't detract too much from the appearance.

Under no circumstances have an opening porthole in the hull topsides of a seagoing yacht. They are strictly for big ships. The chance of someone leaving the port open, or of the fastening or hinge giving way as the yacht falls heavily on her side, is too great a risk to take.

Hatches. Reports of modern aluminium hatches failing are almost unheard of, although from time to time they are ripped off when not properly dogged down tight. If one did go, you would have a large and vulnerable opening. A precaution for such an emergency is to choose a stout piece of plywood already in use, like a section of lifting bunk top, and try it out for size over your large hatch openings. If it is more or less the right size, make a wooden strongback as in Figure 16 (window shutters) and drill appropriate holes in the plywood to take the bolts. In this way the only addition is a strongback kept ready with bolts attached.

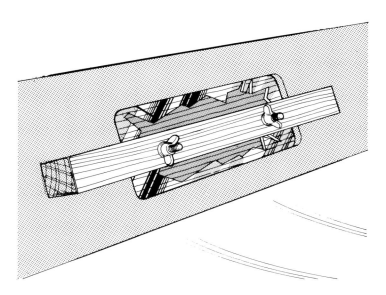

*Fig 17A **plywood storm shutter, as large as the biggest port with a wing-nutted internal strongback, should be located where it can be easily found in an emergency***

The only other potential problem with modern hatches is the manufacturers' tendency to glue the perspex into the aluminium frame. This can fail, and there have been examples where it has happened, so the prudent offshore mariner would be well advised to back up the connection with self-tapping screws.

Cockpit locker lids are undoubtedly the most vulnerable opening on deck and many experienced voyagers prefer a cockpit designed without lockers or lids, the stowage area below being accessible either from the accommodation or a well-sealed lazarette. In bad weather a cockpit can be swept by seas and there is invariably a good volume of water sloshing around the sole. For this reason, removable cockpit floors should never be used because all of them leak sooner or later. Many boatbuilders don't anticipate how vulnerable cockpit lockers are for letting in large amounts of water in heavy weather, and not only are the openings getting bigger each year, but the hinges are nearly always tiny. The ability to dog the cockpit locker lids down tight is of paramount importance. A lost cockpit locker lid could quite easily lead to the loss of the yacht in extreme conditions.

Preparing below decks for bad weather

High fiddle rails, deep sinks, smallish lockers and removable struts to hold in books will make life easier in normally boisterous seagoing conditions. To prepare better than this for heavy weather is difficult, because try as you may items will start flying about. Always carry a bag of rags to stuff into lockers where breakables such as jam pots and crockery are stowed, and don't throw away old socks – they are ideal to put over bottles to stop them rattling.

There is some discussion about fitting barrel bolts to all underbunk lockers so that in the event of a capsize the contents are held in place. Having experienced a severe knockdown in a North Atlantic gale on *Euge* I don't believe that normal catches would withstand the combination of weight and centrifugal forces imposed on them in a knockdown, but the chances of this happening are very rare and chaos will be inevitable however well you prepare.

Three items must be firmly harnessed. The batteries must have either webbing straps holding them firmly in place or a wooden crossbar bridge bolted or lashed down. The gas bottles must also be firmly lashed down because should the working one be thrown on its side or inverted, liquid gas can flow through the regulator. This can cause a seventy-fold increase in pressure on the low-pressure side of the appliance. The cooker must also be firmly attached to the gimbals because many will only swing to 90 degrees before dropping off their gimbals and flying free. As well as having captive gimbals, the cooker must also have a mechanical restraint that prevents it swinging too far and pulling off the gas pipe. A gas bottle should always be turned off in heavy weather (if at no other time) but if this has been forgotten a lot of gas can come through a fractured pipe until somebody can get to the bottle to switch off, and obvious dangers aside, this could make the cabin uninhabitable until the fumes are cleared.

Heavy weather on deck

The kind of strains that are imposed on deck equipment in heavy weather were demonstrated to me in the knockdown we experienced in *Euge*. Our two amidships stanchions, which were heavy-duty stainless steel, were bent down to about 45 degrees, with the other stanchions distorted less (but with two cracked bases), by water pressure alone. The amount of force required subsequently to straighten them out gave me considerably more respect for the sea.

Deck-mounted liferafts are vulnerable and must have very firm wooden or stainless chocks backed up by strong independently mounted eyebolts for lashing down. A far better arrangement is to have the liferaft in a locker, or mounted in the cockpit where is has some protection.

Spray dodgers, if fitted, can be guaranteed to self-destruct unless there is a quick way, as heavy weather approaches, of unlacing them altogether or just disconnecting the lower tie downs, rolling them up and lashing them to the upper guardrail wire. They should be made with at least a 4in ventilation gap between them and the deck so that even in moderately rough conditions when the yacht's rail is immersed they don't trap water and become damaged. An alternative to lacing is to attach their lower edge with Velcro, which will pull free if the sea gets behind them.

Spray hoods are rather difficult because in bad weather they really ought to be folded flat on the deck and lashed down to avoid damage. Yet it is in these very conditions that they give sterling service. Our answer is to make it very flexible, by using a long length of bungy cord as a restraint aft. In this way, even when it was clouted by big seas it gave way and was never damaged.

In really severe conditions a boom needs to be restrained in some way. For centuries seamen have used gallows in various shapes and forms and many yachtsmen swear by them. Others consider them heavy, cumbersome and old fashioned. Gallows advocates maintain that as well as supporting the boom, they are also a stout grab pillar when you are entering or leaving the cockpit, form the frame for a cockpit-only sailing awning, and can't be beaten as a comfortable support for taking a sextant sight. A very simple alternative for supporting the boom in heavy weather is a shaped wooden chock bolted in place at the point where the lowered boom touches the side-deck or cockpit coaming. A simple lashing then holds the boom firmly.

A lot of heavy weather preparation comes back to the Keep It Simple philosophy. Study the ergonomics of the tasks you may have to perform and make sure that nothing is too complex or too awkward or far away to get at.

In heavy weather, ergonomics mean safety. If a self-steering gear has to be adjusted by going aft or even leaving the cockpit, a crew member is being put into unnecessary danger each time an adjustment is made. A headsail roller reefing winch on the sidedeck near the rail on the lee side could result in the watchkeeper overbalancing and going over the side. Faults that are minor irritants most of the time become danger black spots in a storm and should be eliminated.

Harness attachment points must also be laid out with ergonomics in mind. You

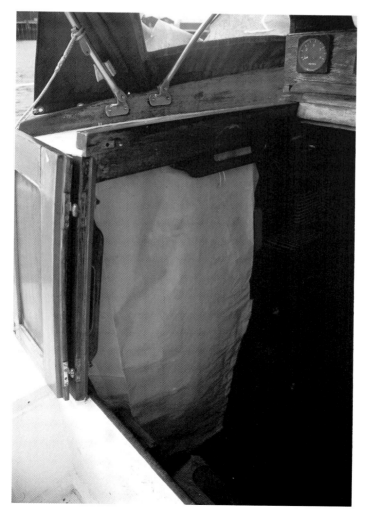

A fine mist of spray always finds its way down below at sea and a feature such as this will protect the navigation area, especially if you have no sprayhood (Peter Nielsen)

shouldn't need to reach a long way for the next attachment place, neither should it be necessary to cross the deck without being attached before reaching the next point. The use of harnesses as a matter of course is a good habit and ease of use makes that habit easier to pick up. The cockpit must have a strong harness attachment point and this is best positioned within reach of the companionway, so in coming on deck or going below when balance can easily be lost if the boat lurches, a person can remain clipped on throughout. This was another cause of men lost overboard in the 1979 Fastnet Race. Although a harness should keep you attached to the boat if you go overboard, getting back on can be very hard, so look for ways of rigging the harness to keep you inboard. A catamaran's wide beam solves this problem because the wire jackstays run up the middle of the yacht, so harnesssed to this it is not possible to stray near the gunwales and go overboard. If the coachroof is not too cluttered the same system can be used on a monohull as long as the harness lanyards are kept short enough. When fitting jackstays make sure they are fairly tight, otherwise when you roll going downwind the wire will scrape and clatter around on the deck, causing chafe and irritating those below.

18. Preparing for Hot Climates

Ventilation

The comfort of living aboard in a hot or tropical climate is in direct proportion to the shade you create and the extent and quality of ventilation. We've met dozens of poor yachties getting even poorer in air-conditioned bars because life was almost untenable aboard.

Good ventilation has to be thought out for each of the many circumstances a yacht will find herself in – at sea with water flying around, lying head to wind at anchor, laying alongside a jetty, and when it is pouring with rain.

There are many tricks to ventilation, but probably the most important single factor to remember is that air must be able to evacuate easily, thus providing through ventilation. A locker with a single vent is only marginally better ventilated than one with no vent at all. One vent hole should be drilled or cut low down in the locker and another high up, so as air warms up it is able to rise, escape and draw in fresh air through the lower vent. A similar thing applies to areas like the after double quarter berth often fitted into modern production boats. There is usually a single small hatch or port overhead but, if an opening porthole were fitted into the transom near the occupant's feet, or into the cockpit side, air could flow right through and transform the cabin. Louvred cabin doors are very good in this respect.

Dorade boxes with cowls are generally good although the amount of air coming down through them is not great. They can be improved by making the modification in Figure 18. Dorades come into their own at sea and when it's raining, when they are often the only method of ventilation. The more you have fitted, the happier you'll be in these circumstances. Unless you have plenty of time to make them in wood, the best way is to use an ice-cream container as a female mould and laminate as many as you require from it in GRP. Rather than make a traditional wooden baffle, cut out a 2in (50mm) aperture in the deck and epoxy-in a short length of plastic guttering pipe. Make sure that the boxes can drain on either tack. Some people (including me) have fitted them to a cambered coachroof and only made drains at the lowest point. As soon as you heel the other way, water collects until it drains through the aperture into the cabin (and hopefully on to the person who made them).

A yacht spends the majority of time in port laying head to wind on her anchor and

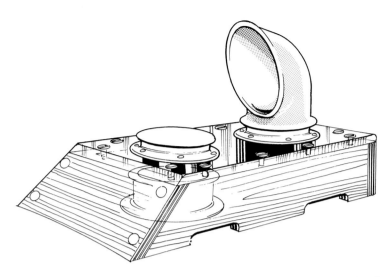

Fig 18 **Dorade vents are essential for ventilation when spray or rain don't allow the hatches to be left open. A second cowl fitting directly over the vent hole can be used to improve flow when it is unlikely to rain. With an acrylic top they let in a little more light below**

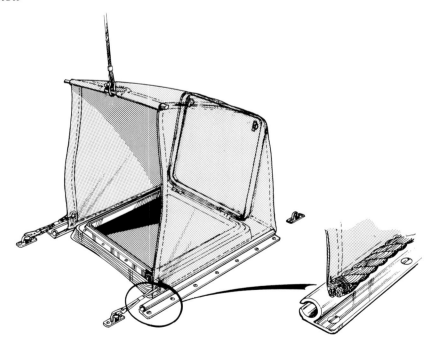

Fig 19 **It must be possible to close a hatch without touching the windscoop. With eyes on each corner, this design (using aluminium extrusions) can be reversed to let in air from the bow or stern and still be left rigged in a rain shower**

Traditionally, deck hatches were hinged along their front edges for safety reasons. With modern materials it is not as important, but if your hatches are hinged thus, a windscoop can save a lot of trouble switching it around

in these circumstances opening deck hatches are by far the best method of ventilation, especially if they're hinged on their after edge. A boat under 35ft really needs one over the foc'sle and another over the saloon, and thus equipped she meets 80 percent of ventilation requirements. On boats over this size, two opening hatches are generally required for the saloon. A small hatch over the heads/shower compartment is desirable. As long as the furniture isn't too ornate and the loo roll is covered up, this hatch can be left open in the rain or at sea, providing ventilation when all other hatches have to be dogged tight.

It is an advantage to have a hatch over the berths. If this is left open at night you will wake the moment it starts to rain, and close it. If not, you will never wake up, let alone get out of bed to close hatches elsewhere.

Opening portholes or windows in the coachroof sides are very handy when the yacht is laying across the wind, and also at sea when the leeward ones can normally be left open. They don't contribute much to ventilation when the yacht is lying head to wind. Unfortunately it is rare to find opening ports that are stout enough to be trusted in very heavy weather, and stand up to being opened and closed regularly without developing leaks. The leaking problem is made worse by the fact that most coachroof sides are angled, so the windows often collect puddles. The French very often use opening deck hatches as coachroof ports in their bigger aluminium and steel designs, having as many as eight or nine. It is an expensive, and probably ultimate, solution to the ventilation problem, although many of them must walk around with bruised shins.

Windscoops can be a Godsend in certain circumstances and it is well worth making one before you leave. If your boat has a centre cockpit and wheelhouse it tends to act as a windbreak, so little air gets into the after hatch and a scoop will be necessary. A scoop will catch the lightest zephyrs and funnel them into your cabin.

Finally, depending on where you plan to cruise, it may be worth considering fitting a couple of electric fans for when conditions are muggy. Make sure they have continuously-rated electric motors and can withstand being left on for a few hours at a time. The protective grilles usually rust unless you buy some spray lacquer and liberally coat them with it before you start.

Awnings

Until you have experienced living in a very hot or tropic climate you may be inclined to put an awning low on your priority list. Don't! This particular piece of equipment ranks in the top three essentials for living aboard a yacht in hot weather.

There are two types of cover to consider – a proper awning extending from the mast right aft and a small cockpit cover used when sailing. The cooling effect a full size awning has on the cabin accommodation is very noticeable. Often we return from a trip ashore longing to get back aboard a cool, shaded and well ventilated boat.

What is needed is an awning that is easy to set, so you don't hesitate to rig it, and one that allows the crew to move around freely without negotiating a cat's cradle of lines, and without being bent double. In many tropical regions the climate features occasional heavy downpours between bursts of scorching sun and the type of awning described below (and in Figure 20) copes with both conditions and allows life to carry on comfortably throughout.

This cover is common in the Caribbean and among ocean cruising fraternities. It features a reasonably flat top with vertical side curtains reaching almost to the guardwires, which keep out the rain and sun and provide some privacy. The curtains can be rolled up out of the way to cut down windage. The flat top has an attachment point in its centre where a halyard or topping lift can be shackled on and hauled tight to create a watershed for rain, also stretching the whole cover for a tight, neat appearance. By installing a plastic skin fitting in the cover near the middle, water can be collected when it rains by lowering the topping lift. If a short length of hosepipe is directed into the water tank filler you can, after five minutes' free flow for cleansing, collect quite a lot of water. The awning for *Euge* collected 15 gallons (68 lit) an hour in steady rain and two or three times that much in a good downpour.

The design of the cover requires the running/spinnaker pole to be threaded through a sleeve forward and a separate, equally stout, pole aft. Twin or divided backstays simplify the setting by fully supporting this after pole. If you have a single

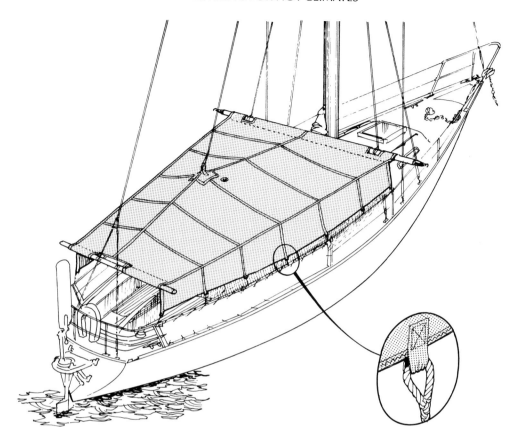

*Fig 20 **Supported by the spinnaker pole forward and a special stout after pole,
this design of cover is very popular in the tropics. The side curtains can be
rolled up and if the centre lifting point is lowered during rain and the drain
fitting is piped directly to the water filler, it makes an efficient water catcher.
Don't use DIY eyelet kits – they rarely last. Better to sew in doubled-up 1in (30mm)
webbing tape (inset)***

backstay you'll need some extra lines to brace each end of the pole. When the awning is taken down, the after pole is unlashed from the backstay and the cover rolled around it working forward. As the after pole will be shorter than the forward one, the ends of the resultant sausage can be folded back and the whole stowed either in a large cockpit locker, on the coachroof or behind a berth.

Using a hand-cranked sewing machine it took Lou Lou a weekend (approximately 12 hours' work) to make the awning, with three or four hours' help from me marking and cutting out, plus splicing up all the lanyards. We used 18 sq yds (15m²) of acrylic material which, although more expensive than plasticised fabric, is longer lasting, better looking, largely unaffected by ultraviolet rays and more pleasant to work with and stow. One simple discovery revolutionised the cover and its fastenings – using 1in (25mm) webbing, available from chandlers, for the longitudinal strengthening (they take the strain off the cloth itself) and also in short lengths to substitute for brass eyelets, which are rarely strong enough in the DIY kits available. These 'tabs' are simply 8in (20cm) lengths cut with a hot knife (we used an old kitchen knife heated red-hot over the cooker flame), doubled on themselves and sewn with a square and cross pattern on to the cover, preferably in the direction of the strain. These enable the cover to be set up very tightly and have never let us down, as eyelets have on numerous occasions.

Tautness is the secret of success of the cover, especially on the fore and aft ridges between top and side. If these are allowed to slacken, the cover not only looks sloppy but will oscillate and flap in a breeze and collect water in puddles rather than in your tank. This ridge line should extend from the yacht's maximum beam at the cover's forward end to the same aft. Resist the temptation to drape the awning over ropes stretched from shrouds to backstays because, accounting for inevitable stretch and the fact the shrouds are normally set inboard, the whole thing ends up looking like the conventional boom-over cover, and collects puddles easily.

One problem with the flat-topped awning is dealing with the boom and topping lift. Solutions vary from boat to boat, but one answer is a boom gallows or crutch and

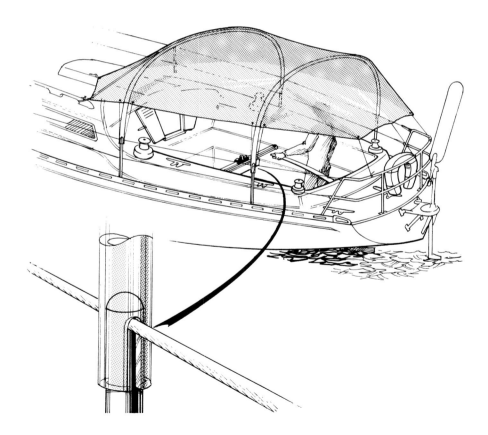

Fig 21 **When sailing in very hot climates, some kind of a sailing awning can be a blessing. This design, made simply with plastic piping, is considerably cheaper than a custom bimini top**

another is to use a short wire strop talurited to the backstay and clipped on to the boom end. We just left the boom resting on the sidedeck, which looks a bit French but doesn't get in the way. Another system is a sewn tab under the cover's central lift point with the boom supported on a short rope strop from this – the topping lift being attached to the cover directly above it. For simplicity's sake it's better not to divide the cover aft to accommodate the topping lift and boom, although with Velcro-fastened flaps a watertight join can be achieved.

Equipped with such a cover it should be quite possible to stay dry in the cockpit on rainy days, or if not then certainly to have the companionway hatch open to promote ventilation.

A cockpit-only sailing cover used in moderate conditions is very pleasant to have and provides essential shade for the watchkeeper over the hottest three or four hours of the day. Rigging such a cover is not easy, though, unless you have a boom gallows forward of the cockpit, because while a pole can always be attached to the backstay or mizzen rigging, finding a place for the forward attachment is difficult without having lines running in all directions – which you can do without when under sail. Also, the mainsheet nearly always fouls such a cover.

One arrangement that seems to work quite well has a strong strut, such as an oar, lashed to a bulkhead handrail right alongside the companionway. Jutting up and firm, this allows the forward batten of the cover to be attached, but there is still quite a lot of complication and string needed. Figure 21 shows two designs that can work. The success of A is dependent on the height and positioning of your stanchions, and B will work if you have a fairly straight bar along the back of your sprayhood, the disadvantage being that headroom beneath it is limited to the height of your sprayhood.

In America they've developed the 'bimini' top, a permanently set-up cockpit cover on a stainless steel frame which is both practical and effective, although hardly improves the look of the boat.

Sun deterioration

It is inevitable, and largely unavoidable, that the yacht, her gear and equipment will deteriorate steadily from the strong ultraviolet rays of the sun in warm latitudes.

The most vulnerable items are the sails, which in a tropical climate won't last much longer than 12-18 months without becoming brittle, unless they are covered at every opportunity. If you make or adapt your mainsail cover to the design shown in Figure 22 it will be quick and easy to use so you will cover the sail as soon as it is lowered. If you expect strong winds, or leave the boat for any length of time, this cover will need copious rope lashings wrapped right around it.

Hanked-on headsails should either be either taken below or left on deck in UV-resistant bags (acrylic is the best, but quite expensive). If you have a roller genoa, it is not really practical to take it off the headstay each time so a 1ft (30cm) wide sacrificial acrylic strip edging to the leech and foot is essential. These acrylic strips unfortunately add quite a bit of weight to the sail in the wrong places and are rather prone to damage, so expect them to be a continuing maintenance chore.

Dark colours will absorb heat and cause quicker deterioration, no matter what the object is or what it is made of. This applies to inflatable dinghies and wooden hulls as

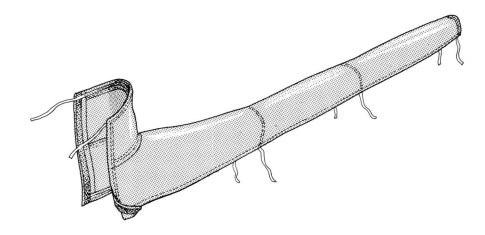

Fig 22 ***A loosely-fitting sail cover that is simple to rig is one that will be used regularly. A Velcro-fastened front and just two or three tapes will suffice in most conditions. When leaving the boat, or in strong winds, a rope lashed around the outside will hold it in place***

much as smaller items. It is essential to use and choose light colours. This is especially so for the deck which will otherwise make the cabin very hot. A dark colour also makes the deck impossible to walk on in bare feet. White might seem bland to many people, but it is the most practical colour for yachts heading for hot climates.

Barometric pressure

One piece of traditional equipment that doesn't strictly need to be aboard an ocean cruiser is a barograph, lovely though it is. If you are given one as a parting gift, or have an ample budget, fine, but don't feel it is necessary. It is a pleasant ornament, but in the tropics barometric pressure becomes diurnal – in other words the pressure varia-tions are exactly the same over a 24-hour cycle and the jaggedy 's' shape will be the same nearly every day of the year with only minor variations, so they are of little help. A barometer however is an essential instrument outside the tropic regions. It will suffice perfectly well and the cost is only a fraction of a barograph's.

19. Emergencies

It requires a huge effort of will to spend a great deal of money on safety equipment that you are probably never going to use. Yet the moment that equipment is needed, any little money you saved by getting slightly cheaper goods seems blind, stupid, and a false economy. You must develop the attitude that prevention is better than cure.

I have had my fair share of emergencies, none of which I'm proud of. I've suffered the ignominy of being dismasted on three occasions, been aboard a yacht at sea with a serious fire, had a boat start to break up in mid-ocean, been driven ashore with a danger of total loss and experienced 'man overboard' both by day and night. Still I sail around thinking it'll never happen to me! Immediately afterwards, the importance of preventing anything similar happening is paramount, but quickly enough that fades away in the knowledge that you came out of it alive and reasonably unscathed. This attitude alone is a bigger danger than the potential emergencies themselves and tiresome though it may be, one of the only ways to overcome it is to develop sometimes mindless routines aboard to help prevent the problems in the first place.

Man overboard

Being of heavy build, I sail with the knowledge that if I were to go overboard and become unconscious, the chances of getting me back aboard are infinitesimal. When Lou Lou and I started cruising we promised each other that we would always wear harnesses when working on deck or when alone on watch. We splashed out on what were then the best and most expensive harnesses, the Ancra, which were high specification, easy to use and with a lanyard that could be unclipped. We quickly got into the habit of putting them on, and the ability to remove the heavy lanyard and carbineer clip meant that they were no discomfort to wear all the time at sea, even when below, as you might a belt. Combining this with plenty of convenient clip-on points and efficiently laid-out jackstays, the routine soon stuck and now we both sleep well off watch in the knowledge that the other can't be lost overboard. We also have a rule that the one on-watch calls down through the companionway hatch if ever they need to go on deck. It may seem unfair to wake an off-watch sleeper when you do, but it beats the shock of waking up hearing clattering on deck above you.

The scoop stern has come of age and is a very popular feature for blue water cruising. Primarily, it is very useful in recovering a person overboard, but for everyday use, it makes loading and unloading the dinghy with provisions, fuel/water or an outboard much easier and makes a handy swimming platform

The above illustrates a routine which two people, who are normally far from keen on anything routine, persevered hard to make a habit of. Now it is a habit, we enjoy our sailing that little more knowing the chance of long, unscheduled mid-ocean swims has been cut right down.

Keeping aboard is an obvious priority, but being prepared for a man overboard situation is just as important. Some advocate trailing one or two floating polypropylene lines astern, attached to the tiller or self-steering in the hope of the one in the water catching them and pulling the boat off course, thus alerting the off watch as she tacks or gybes. It is a good idea in theory, but in practice a boat travelling at six knots covers a little over 10ft a second and unless you are trailing so much rope that you are slowed down considerably, the chances of a shocked and disorientated swimmer being able to reach and locate the rope quickly enough are very slim indeed. Assuming they did, it is unlikely they would be able to hold on even if it was knotted.

A lifebuoy with floating strobe and danbuoy attached still offers the best means of pinpointing somebody overboard and it goes without saying that this should be clear and ready to run immediately. A danbuoy tube, either incorporated into the hull or in the form of a plastic guttering pipe firmly lashed on the sidedeck near the stern, can take away much of the clutter of the man-overboard equipment.

Retro-reflective tape will be the only way to spot a man overboard at night, so buy a reel of it (it is made by Scotchbrite/3M) and sew or glue it to all the life-saving equipment as well as the shoulders and cuffs of all sailing jackets (so an arm in the air might be spotted) and the shoulder straps of harnesses.

Think out how you will get someone out of the water, and practice it. There are now a number of good (and bad) man overboard recovery aids on the market. Most assume that the casualty is in the water alongside, and achieving this is, of course, the biggest hurdle. A stern boarding ladder that extends deep into the water is of great value, but this can only be used with the yacht across the seas, otherwise the pitching motion makes recovery both dangerous and difficult. Perhaps the most significant contribution to safety is the advent of the 'sugar-scoop' stern arrangement which allows a crew member to get close to the water and haul the casualty the short distance into the scoop.

Major leaks

That great ocean sailor, Bob Griffiths, had a particularly pertinent piece of advice about serious leaks. When a leak is discovered your first priority is to find it! 'To use time and energy bailing when the leak might be stopped is not good thinking,' said Griffiths.

This may sound obvious in the cold light of day, but in an emergency the brain doesn't always work so clearly. We were in fairly big seas off Bermuda watching the Tall Ships Race start, with about a dozen people aboard, not all of them seafarers, when Lou Lou calmly and quietly announced to me through the corner of her mouth that the bilgewater was above the floors and we were sinking. We'd been hardened by a couple of years of chartering beforehand, and in comparison it seemed a minor problem. Not wanting to panic the landlubbers I pumped the bilge surreptitiously until it sucked dry, but five minutes later the bilge was full again. As I could pump from the helm position and everyone was distracted by the lovely ships around, nobody noticed that I had to pump all that day until we dropped anchor again in port. The problem could easily have been solved with the most elementary investigation, when I would have found that the bilge water was hot! We'd been motorsailing all day and the engine cooling water was not injecting into the exhaust because the pipe had fractured and was pumping all the water into the bilge.

Most flooding emergencies can be traced to very obvious sources so before you assume that the garboard has sprung or the keel is dropping off, check that the toilet isn't overflowing, the bilge pump isn't siphoning water back in to the bilge or that a hose clamp hasn't loosened on a seacock and allowed the pipe to slip off. Before you head off spend a couple of pounds replacing all seacock hoseclamps and put two clips where there is normally one on every fitting below the waterline. Seacocks are not infallible and next to each one the prudent sailor should have a shaped wooden cone on a rope lanyard, ready to be rammed in the hole if the seacock fails in any way.

Flotsam

The chances of serious damage from hitting flotsam are increasing steadily. Between 1980 and 1983 at least $50 million-worth of containers were washed overboard from cargo ships, many remaining just awash. Hitting one of these would be enough to sink most yachts, except possibly steel ones. Yachts have been lost in the last few years by hitting containers, tree-trunks and even an old freezer held afloat by its insulation material. A cargo pallet, if not piercing the hull, could damage the prop-shaft or rudder. One yacht in the English Channel had her whole propshaft ripped out and the

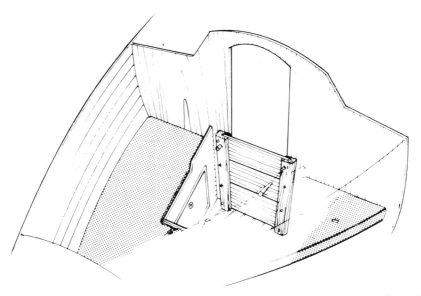

Fig 23 **If you are concerned about hitting flotsam, it is not out of the question to have washboards fitted across the forward bulkhead. They are unlikely to to be completely watertight, but will reduce flow to manageable levels**

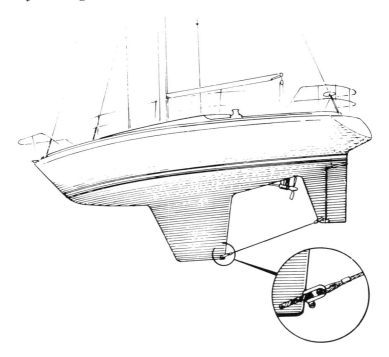

Fig 24 **Fish traps, nets and general flotsam can cause serious damage which might be impossible to repair overseas. With an unprotected propeller, a length of wire fitted between skeg and rudder will avoid many problems**

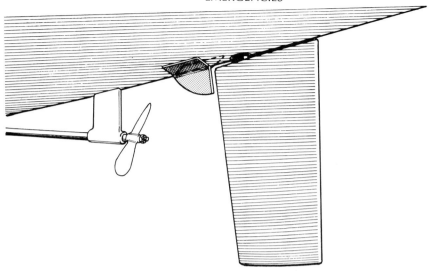

Fig 25 **If your yacht has a spade rudder, a welded stainless steel deflector plate, strongly epoxied in place, will eradicate many potential problems**

inaccessability of the gland meant that she nearly foundered as her crew couldn't reach the leak without removing the fuel tank. The busy areas of Northern Europe are the worst affected. A ship lost 2,400 drums overboard in a Bay of Biscay storm in 1984, a situation made no better by the fact that the skipper didn't report the loss for four weeks.

A watertight bulkhead forward is a good precaution, but a huge sacrifice of space in a boat of less than 40ft (12.19m). Figure 23 shows an alternative that can work with a conventional forecabin arrangement. The plywood washboards would have to be stowed handily, maybe under the forward berths, and any other major holes in the bulkhead, for example heating or ventilation ducts would need to be stopped up. This arrangement wouldn't be entirely watertight, but might reduce the flow to a level the bilge pumps could cope with.

Smaller pieces of flotsam can also be a menace. The fishing industry throws 23,000 tons of plastic packaging into the sea annually, as well as losing more than 133,000 tons of synthetic netting and lines. A grill should be fitted over the engine seawater cooling seacock. If you have a fin and skeg design the suggestion in Figure 24 will help to protect the propeller. Similarly, if you have a skegless spade rudder, the addition shown in Figure 25 can avert the possibility of a rope jamming up the rudder.

Dismasting

To prepare a special jury rig is impractical, because you can only really put something together after the accident when you know what is left of the original rig. The best preparation you can make is to have at least a dozen bulldog grips and a handful of large-diameter thimbles in the spares locker and a coil of wire that exceeds the length of your longest stay. This can be ready to make up a spare shroud if neccessary but will obviously come in handy to start a jury rig with the running poles.

Sailing books of yore talk of cutting away the rigging after a dismasting. This is something that has been passed down from sailing ship days, and from my own experience it is an action one should take only if the mast is in immediate danger of holing the yacht. There in the water is the basis of your jury rig and there is always the remote chance that it can be repaired once you get back to port. If the rig is lost in heavy weather it can make a very effective sea anchor if all the shrouds are disconnected and the forestay and/or headsail halyards left attached at the bows. On the basis of weight, space, expense and lack of use I have never carried a set of bolt-croppers on board.

The main danger in a dismasting is the jagged end of the mast puncturing the hull. Although lifting the mast, with the tangle of ripped sails and spagetti of cordage, back on board can be a Herculean effort and one that shouldn't be underestimated, it is not normally out of the question to get lines attached near to the stump and with sheet winches haul just the end up near to the deck, perhaps getting a turn of rope around a crosstree to help steady it.

Grounding

In many emergencies, quick action can solve the problem quickly and simply before it escalates. The difficulty lies in recognising the fine line between expediency and panic. This is especially so in tackling a fire, but also when a boat hits the bottom a quick bit of action in the right quarter can sort out the problem almost before you know it's happened.

In terms of preparation for going ashore the only things you can do is to make sure that the main anchor and kedge are laid out ready to go immediately. It is an old-fashioned custom to disconnect the anchors from their cables for a long passage, dating from the days when anchors were large, unwieldy and vulnerable on the ship's cathead. There is no need to do this today, and yet a suprising number do. The dinghy must be in a state of readiness (also so that it can be taken in the event of having to abandon ship). A three-bladed propeller may be a bad drag when sailing but is worth having for the power it has in reverse gear when you are trying to back off.

Heavy strandings are few and far between, but a reasonably adventurous yachtsman will have plenty of odd glancing blows and scrapes with coral and rock. If you particularly plan to sail off the beaten track, a sacrificial keel shoe is worth considering. There are two varieties. For a traditional wooden boat a steel shoe can be fabricated, liberally sealed with pitch and bolted in place. As well as protecting from cosmetic damage during the occasional grounding this fixture also has the significant advantage of saving the bottom of a keel, which often doesn't get antifouled, from the danger of teredo worm.

If your boat is fibreglass and has an internal encapsulated ballast the answer is to laminate a ½in (12mm) thick GRP shoe over the bottom 18in (45cm) or so of the keel. Don't worry about the weight, it's in the perfect place! Although the existing keel should be sanded back to the gelcoat, ultra-strong adherence isn't vital as long as the shoe, once laminated on, is screwed in position with dozens of self-tappers. Coral is hard and unyielding and with this sacrifical shoe you can do a fair amount of GRP-ripping and tearing before you come anywhere near the original structure.

Liferafts

It is not within the scope of this book to catalogue the extensive and continuing criticism of conventional liferaft design. Until we start building good dinghies that double as lifesavers, the existing range of liferafts are the only choice we have.

An exception is the Tinker range of inflatable dinghies made by J M Henshaw in England, mentioned earlier. They are not, in my opinion, suitable as the yacht's principal tender, for a number of reasons. One is that an ocean cruiser's tender is a daily workhorse and takes a great beating alongside dinghy stagings, being dragged up and down beaches and so on, and there is a limit to what a sophisticated inflatable such as the Tinker can withstand without putting its liferaft role into jeopardy. I also feel that at present the liferaft conversion and sailing equipment is too complicated and fussy for the dinghy to be prepared as a liferaft for every passage. Although the Tinker Traveller is at least 25 percent more expensive than a comparable liferaft there is nevertheless a strong case for having one purely as a liferaft and, like its contemporaries, used for nothing else.

A modern liferaft and a personally prepared emergency pack constitute a vital combination. One is pretty much useless without the other. Every emergency pack will differ according to the sailing area and crew aboard. The one outlined below is based on my own, prepared for a one-year North Atlantic circuit cruise for two people. It caters for the principal hazards of liferaft habitation, except extreme cold, and gives a broad guide to what is necessary.

Before preparing anything, the first job is to look closely at your existing liferaft and its contents or, if you're about to buy a raft, to inspect the maker's options and plan from there. Don't be tempted to buy a 6-man liferaft when you have just two crew on the grounds there will be more room and rations. The size of liferafts and their ability to withstand capsize is directly related to the human ballast in them. A large raft with few people in it will capsize much sooner and with greater frequency than a properly loaded one, and the capsize factor is an important contribution to eventual survival. Conversely, do not be tempted, on considerations of expense, to buy a model that satisfies the minimum requirements. If you are buying a new raft, one desirable feature, which could make the difference between life or death, is an inflatable double floor, offered as an option on most designs. This will create a much more comfortable base to sit on and, more importantly, it will insulate against the crucial loss of body warmth in colder waters. In the lower latitudes, it also alleviates the aggravation to body sores of fish and turtles rubbing against the bottom of the raft. To have a double floor fitted to your existing liferaft is very expensive, and will add between £70 and £120 to a new model. With a small crew, a more viable alternative is to equip everyone on board with one of the many popular survival suits used by ocean racing crews. Alternatively, have a stowed air mattress like a Li-Lo, or inflatable cushions, ready to be grabbed with the panic bag.

Panic bags

Liferaft manufacturers generally provide basic packs which vary considerably in contents. I will refer to these as 'raft kits'. Whichever you have, it will need to be supplemented. Avon, for example, make no apologies for the limitations of this equipment

Preparation is an essential element of the cruising lifestyle and never more so than when it comes to the compilation of an emergency pack

in their liferafts by stating, 'You must consider what additional emergency equipment is required for your journey and this must be stowed where it can rapidly be loaded into the liferaft.' The contents of the British RORC standard kit gives the most basic survival items (listed below) while the more expensive emergency raft kits include a small quantity of water and a couple of parachute flares. The contents are based on an anticipated rescue time of around 36 hours.

As well as preparing an emergency pack, it's a good idea to make a list of four or five items which see everyday use aboard but must be taken into the raft in the event of the yacht foundering. Our list comprises sextant, almanac, flare pack, oilskins and extra water. Paste your list to the inside of the loo door so you read it every day.

Water. Whilst some raft kits contain water, it is generally a very small quantity – sometimes as little as half a litre (one pint) per person, which doesn't go very far. Water must therefore be taken aboard the raft in addition to your prepared emergency pack. Twenty litre (4½ gal) containers have the advantage of high capacity but, weighing around 20 kilos (40-45lbs), are heavy and unwieldy for a tired and frightened crew member, so a number of 10 litre (2 gal) containers would be better. Keep these in an accessible cockpit locker to form part of the ship's normal supply, ensuring they are refilled regularly with fresh water. Water containers should never be filled to the brim. A little air left inside creates enough buoyancy for them to float. Have bright yellow containers that, in the event of the boat going down quickly, could be pitched into the sea with a better chance of spotting them from the raft.

Looking on the bleak side, if rescue hasn't arrived before this water is finished, rain collection and storage has to be anticipated. A rectangle of waterproof material, about 6ft by 4ft (185cm x 122cm) with many eyelets around its edge can be very useful as a shade, makeshift sail, blanket, pillow or rain catcher. As well as being able to catch water, you must have somewhere to put it, if you have been unable to get water containers on board the raft. My emergency pack includes six bags taken from the inside of wine boxes. These take up little room when stowed and give an extra 18 litres (4 gal) storage capacity. Solar stills are very useful, as Steve Callahan found during his 70-day drift across the Atlantic after his yacht sank during the Mini-Transat. A graduated water cup is usually included in the raft kits and should be added to your bag.

Food. Food is not included in any raft kits. Naturally as much food as possible will be taken from the stricken vessel, but the emergency pack should contain a supply of sugary foods. If adrift for any length of time, fish will provide a protein-rich diet, but its digestion requires a lot of water which might not be available. Sugary foods are not as demanding in this respect and are more suitable. The Baileys, who survived 117 days adrift in the Pacific, recommend compressed glucose and vitaminised survival biscuits.

Shelter/Health. These items are dealt with together because they are closely related. Exposure will lead to death much faster than hunger or thirst. Protecting your body from cold in higher latitudes and the sun in hot climes should be an initial priority of liferaft occupants.

Survival suits are ideal but, if these are unavailable, oilskins should be included on the loo-door list of extra equipment. A small foldaway umbrella for shade, if for any reason the liferaft canopy is damaged, could double up as a rain catcher. A pair of heavy gloves will keep hands warm in cold weather and can be used for handling fish and turtle catches.

The emergency pack should contain a first aid kit including sunblock cream, Vaseline and seasickness tablets. Most raft kits include these, but make a point of adding more. Seasickness must be guarded against in the unusual motion of a liferaft as the body loses precious fluids through vomiting. Special personal medicines for those aboard, like heart pills, must of course be taken and a supply of multi-vitamin tablets included and taken regularly.

Signalling. Attracting attention is a high priority and you need every practical means available. The invisibility of small craft in bad weather was illustrated during the sad loss of Graham Adams' *Adfin's Rival* in the Western Approaches of the English Channel in September 1983. Although the crew were able to communicate with a nearby ship on only 1 watt VHF power, the ship could not find them.

I put my faith in an EPIRB, as their success record has been impressive. Years ago the best EPIRBs transmitted not only on 243Mhz but also on 121.5Mhz, the civil aviation distress frequency, which all civil airlines monitor. However, whilst still operational, these older EPIRBs have been eclipsed in efficiency and functions by the new breed of 406Mhz EPRIBs. Much more sophisticated, these can transmit coded information which makes the rescue authorities' work much easier. Transmitted to satellite is information such as the type of vessel, nationality, and even, in some sets, the nature of distress. Positional accuracy is also better than the old 121.5Mhz sets – 3.1 miles compared to 12 miles, insignificant perhaps except that in terms of ocean to be searched the comparison is 20 sq miles with 406Mhz against 452 sq miles on 121.5Mhz.

Alongside our emergency pack is strapped a comprehensively equipped RORC flare pack. Our other means of signalling are a hand-held VHF in a waterproof bag which is probably 100 times more effective than the heliograph mirror, torch (with spare batteries) and whistle which we also carry just in case.

Survival. Those making long passages should take special care in their preparation of survival items, although much of it is also necessary for the coastal emergency pack. Survival equipment in the RORC-standard liferaft includes a rescue quoit, sea anchor, knife, bellows, repair kit, baler, two paddles, rescue signal guide and general instructions on how to survive. The extra raft kits usually supply tin openers, plastic bags, basic fishing kit, sponges, spare torch bulb and batteries. To these should be added extra fishing equipment (if possible, take a small harpoon), extra knife, many small (30cm x 30cm/12in x 12in) plastic bags and a spare torch which uses the same batteries as the first. Plenty of extra lines and rope should be thin and strong. A Swiss Army knife is a perfectly adequate 'toolkit' on a liferaft.

Mid-ocean navigation is likely to be basic, but necessary all the same. Quartz wristwatches should give accurate time and date, and a hand-bearing compass is a must. Sextant and almanac will enable a meridian passage to give your latitude. A timed 'equal altitudes' sight either side of noon provides longitude to quite acceptable accuracy without the need for any plotting.

Last but not least for the emergency pack is an Admiralty routeing chart. At the start of any long voyage, I always slip the appropriate month's routeing chart into the emergency pack. This is vastly superior to an ordinary chart, giving shipping lanes, currents and wind and climate data which could be vital information for survival.

Morale. Seemingly unimportant items may contribute to morale, which is a vital factor in survival. For instance a food obession is common in those conditions. The Robinson family dreamed of and planned the restaurant they would open on their return home. Similarly, the Baileys fantasised over the preparation and consumption of various dishes and made sketches of the dreamboat they subsequently built. Therefore include pencils and notepad in your survival gear, as well as a pack of cards. Instruction books, like *Survival At Sea* by Bernard Robin (Stanley Paul) and *Safety And Survival At Sea* by E C B and Kenneth Lee (Cassell) may be useful.

Having accumulated the contents of an emergency pack, it is necessary to decide how it is best stowed. With just one container, there is the chance that, if lost, all your eggs are in one basket. However, two containers are more difficult to handle in an emergency and Sod's Law guarantees that if one is lost, it will contain the most important equipment.

The emergency pack must also have some form of attachment, like a snaphook or rope tail, so that it can be positively secured to the raft while other things are being passed down from the yacht, or to prevent loss in bad weather if the raft is capsized.

Even if it takes up prime accommodation space, the emergency pack must be situated as close to the companionway as possible and not stuffed up in the quarterberth. The higher it is the better, in case flooding makes it difficult to find or remove. A good alternative with a sealed container is to stow it in a cockpit locker, ideally the one the extra water containers are in.

The emergency pack, like the liferaft itself, is something few of us are ever going to use and it's therefore easy to satisfy one's conscience by purchasing a liferaft only, and praying you never have to use it. However, the next time you go to a boat show, visit a liferaft stand and inspect the contents of the standard raft kits and decide whether you could entrust the survival of your family or crew to them.

Fire

There are dozens of easily combustible materials all over a boat and speaking as one who has experienced a serious fire at sea, the best possible method of dealing with it is nipping it in the bud by swift and immediate action. A fire blanket right next to the galley is the simplest first precaution, then lots of BCF/Halon fire extinguishers, available within hand's reach all over the boat, so no one can be trapped below without firefighting means. The reason I suggest carrying so many fire extinguishers is because of the difficulty of having any serviced at their correct intervals, which may mean some becoming defective.

Controllable discharge fire extinguishers are a great boon for the ocean cruiser because if you handle a small galley fire, it can be out in seconds whilst the firefighter is training the remainder of the one-shot extinguisher over the side. This is frustrating and possibly dangerous because you're cutting down your fire-fighting ability should you be unfortunate enough to have another fire before you have the opportunity to replace the extinguisher.

Intruders and pirates

In the last few years half a dozen rather grisly incidents have put the spotlight on this unpleasant subject, but they have perhaps been reported out of proportion. Rape and robbery happen anywhere and most cruising areas are no worse than anywhere else. Nobody with any sense goes looking for trouble spots in any country. Certain regions of the world though are undoubtedly dangerous, especially with drug-running being so prevalent. The South China Sea has a bad reputation, as do Colombia, West Africa, the waters surrounding the Philippines, Indonesia and, to a lesser extent, the Red Sea. The Bahamas is a massive drug trafficking centre, but yachting goes on quite happily as long as you don't stray into certain islands or anchorages that any local will name for you. Most potential problems can be avoided by steering clear of large cities.

Some ocean voyagers take the precaution of carrying guns but this is a step needing very careful consideration. A yacht carrying a gun will be expected to declare and surrender it in 95 per cent of countries she visits. To hide the gun is taking an unacceptable risk. If it is found on a search, penalties are harsh in tiny 'banana republics' and not only will you end up in a local jail or with a high fine, but there is a good chance of having the yacht permanently confiscated. That effectively confines the use of the gun to when the yacht is at sea, yet the need for it is five times more likely to be in harbour.

My belief is that unless you are professionally trained in weapons, you would be in danger of becoming a bigger liability to yourself and your crew. If you are armed and confront a pirate at sea who is pointing a gun at you, he'll be more used to the situation than you and, staring down your barrel, he is likely to pull his trigger first. If you are not pointing a gun at him, there is the chance, however small, that the situation can be salvaged.

I make no apologies for putting a one-sided argument over this matter, and speak with some experience. I also baulk at the idea of everyday people incapably toting slightly rusty and ill-maintained firearms with possibly old and damp ammunition.

Lou Lou and I came close to an unpleasant incident in Castries, St.Lucia when we interupted thieves on our boat in the early hours of the morning. Both were very well-built West Indians, one with what looked like a rifle, the other wielding a 3ft machete. We climbed over the stern of the yacht and within seconds blind fear had wiped away the effects of the evening's rum drinks. If we'd had a gun aboard we couldn't have got at it in the cabin, and knowing how much both of us were quaking at the time it was fortunate for everyone we didn't have one. Fortunately for us, they got away with virtually nothing except my spear gun which, in the darkness, was the rifle I thought one of them was carrying. We gave chase for long enough to get a good description of them and their boat – information the local police showed not the slightest interest in.

The interesting thing about this incident was the aftermath. Without our knowledge or anyone interviewing us, the story reached the British press. We didn't recognise the story when we finally received cuttings. It was one of four similar incidents concerning yachtsmen in the three-year period we were in the Caribbean. The other three were far more serious, but ours was ultimately embellished to the extent that I'd been stabbed and my wife raped too . . .

None of us like things that go bump in the night, even at home. It is no different on a yacht and one of the best methods of scaring away an intruder, sometimes without even getting out of the bunk, is to have the Aldis or similar lamp at your bedside. Within the confines of a cabin, this suddenly blazing out at an intruder will scare the living daylights out of them and with the bright light blinding them they are likely to retreat.

20. Domestic Life

Cooking

Bottled gas has now almost entirely taken over from paraffin (or kerosene), which was always the traditional choice of galley fuel. Paraffin has advantages in that you could easily stock up for a year if you had a good-sized tank, but its availability and quality have diminished significantly, converting even staunch supporters of paraffin cooking to the ease of liquid petroleum gas (LPG). Both fuels are potentially dangerous, but as one person put it 'I'd rather die with one big bang from gas than be slowly burned to death with paraffin'.

No yachtsman needs reminding of the dangers of gas, and because it is so trouble-free and easy to use it should never be taken for granted.

The availability world-wide of both propane or butane is very good. The Camping Gaz brand is marketed in over a hundred countries, but the bottles do not stand up to the marine environment well and rust and pit badly when left on a boat for a long time. Unless carefully maintained, this puts them out of the question on safety grounds, not to mention the fact that Camping Gaz agents won't accept them back in this condition and you have to buy an expensive replacement bottle. Calor gas is a brand name which is well known in Great Britain but not so much elsewhere. Each country has its own brand name, but fortunately the actual contents will always be either butane or propane.

Butane is commonly used in many European countries,except Scandinavia. With the exception of Brazil, propane is by far the more popular everywhere else and yachts are best geared up for this before leaving. With a propane system, you can easily adapt to butane, but not vice versa, because propane is stored at a much higher pressure than butane and might explode in the wrong bottle. Although they are built to very high specifications, never have a blue Calor or especially Camping Gaz bottle filled with propane. Check your appliances to be sure, but most cookers and heaters will run just as well on either gas. In Britain, propane containers are the red Calor bottles and can be obtained in 3.9kg, 13kg and 19kg sizes. Before you leave, make sure on your last swap that the shop-keeper gives you brand new bottles – it'll be the last time you exchange canisters and those ones will stay with you for the whole cruise.

The trick to having an adaptable system is to bulkhead-mount your propane regulator (37mb) with a flexible pipe leading to the bottle. In this way, if you can't get your own bottles filled, you can use local ones temporarily and only need to change the bottle connector on this pipe to run on the new bottles. After a while you build up a stock of connectors, which is very handy. Always carry a spare length of approved high-pressure flexible gas piping so that as your pipe is worn out it can be replaced. We have never had trouble finding cooking gas, although it is invariably necessary to go to the central gas plant, normally in the main port, to get bottles filled. We would generally hire a car to do this run, rowing around the anchorage first collecting everyone else's bottles and asking a share of the car hire. This normally worked out cheaper than a taxi. When you have bottles recharged, make sure that the operator doesn't over-fill them. The limit is 70 percent in hot places, 80 percent in temperate climes. This can be ascertained by weighing the bottle with bathroom scales or a spring balance and deducting the 'tare' (ie empty) weight stamped on the bottle's collar. This should be no more than the gas fill figure also stamped on the collar. We always found three of the 3.9kg bottles perfectly adequate. If your gas locker will accommodate extra, by all means have it, but four small bottles are much handier than two big ones.

A gas solenoid shut-off switch is obligatory on all American boats and seen more and more on European ones. After a year or two reliability can be a problem, for most are made of ferrous metals and can seize solid with rust. They are another drain on the battery, although at around 0.3/0.5 amp this is not too serious. A Gas-low pressure device, which monitors gas pressure between the bottle and appliance, is well worth having. By turning off the bottle you can find out very quickly if you have a gas leak by seeing if the pressure is maintained. This should be done daily, no matter how good the system seems to be.

Refrigeration

Despite everything that has been said about keeping things simple, there is no doubt that a refrigerator in a tropical climate is mighty nice. The big drawback is their huge power consumption, so one of the first considerations when installing refrigeration is the method by which you provide that extra power. A custom-designed, properly installed small fridge (not freezer) will draw a minimum of 40 amp hours daily in the tropics. A more typical stock model can easily consume between 120 and 145 amp hours a day. The alternative is an engine-driven compressor pump, but again you are looking towards a minimum of two or three hours engine running a day.

All the same, more than half the ocean cruisers sailing the world today are fitted with some form of refrigeration but most forget about having a freezer. The greater differential between ambient and box temperature for freezers gives them a voracious power appetite and you can easily become a slave to feeding them. Most of us have a large fridge at home which is loosely stuffed with a lot of food and drink that doesn't really need to be there. On board, you can get away with a small volume (1-2cu ft), only putting in it what you need cold that day and not using it as a general store. You must also learn to open the door as few times as possible.

Yacht refrigerator efficiency is more related to its installation than its cost and whilst bought-off-the-shelf fridges will work in European climates, they can't cope in a hot climate without using a great deal of power, largely because few have more than 1-2in of insulation. The design of the box itself has to be good. British designs tend not to be reliable as there is little experience of what is needed to remain efficient in the tropics. By keeping the box small you will have more room for insulation. You can't overdo this, and if your fridge is situated in an area under or behind which there isn't much usable room, fill the entire space with two-part polyurethane foam. The absolute minimum should be four inches all round, but thinking about all the power you'll save in the long run, there's nothing stopping you putting in 12in if you can.

There are three broad categories of refrigeration applicable to yachts. The first is thermo-electric, operating on the Peltier principle that a cooling/heating effect occurs when a DC current is passed through junctions between certain semi-conductor materials. Cooling is achieved and, if polarity is reversed, heat is created to warm up the contents of the box. This solid state principle is reliable in that other than a fan to dissipate heat, there are no moving parts. However, in terms of power consumption they are poor, drawing between 2-5 amps continuously and rarely achieving more than 25°C below ambient temperature. Satisfactory for weekending, this type of refrigeration is not to be recomended for serious use.

The second type is absorption, which works on the basis that ammonia refrigerates on being heated. That heat source can be provided by 12vDC, 240vAC or gas, creating a system which, on the face of it, is adaptable if nothing else. Unfortunately, employing 12vDC is far from efficient, so most users run their absorption fridges on cooking gas which doesn't work too badly. Unfortunately for the long-distance cruising yachtsman, absorption refrigeration has a number of drawbacks. It doesn't like to be out of alignment or heeled over which pretty much limits its use on most boats other than multihulls. It also generates a great deal of heat, so good ventilation is essential. Finally, as absorption refrigerators were really designed for the mass caravan market where physical space is limited and a regular power source pretty much guaranteed, the yachtsman has no choice but to use the manufacturers' minimally-insulated front-opening boxes which go totally against the grain of hot climate yacht living.

Many years ago manufacturers such as Electrolux used to provide absorption fridges powered by paraffin. They were used extensively in the Third World where power supplies were unreliable or non-existent. The Hiscocks used one for years and reported that it worked well. Using only a pint or so of paraffin per week, the above-mentioned efficiency losses were inconsequential. It would appear to be the perfect solution for yachtsmen (apart from the non-heeling aspect) but unfortunately their safety record was not good enough and eventually they were withdrawn from the market.

Type three refrigeration, using a compressor to pump a refrigerant solution around a closed circuit (as used in domestic fridges), is really the only answer for long distance yachts. This type of refrigeration is simple to understand in principle and with some basic knowledge and a stock of spare driers the average yachtsman can troubleshoot his own system.

Most use the refrigerant Freon 12. This takes a continuous circuitous route first through the high-pressure side of the system, then the low-pressure, before arriving at the compressor pump to start the cycle again. The compressor pumps Freon into the high pressure piping. Being compressed, the gas leaves this pump heated and makes its way into a heat exchanger, known as the condensor, where that heat is extracted (either by a 12v fan or salt water piped from the engine cooling water intake). The nature of the gas is that as it cools it condenses into liquid form. It continues its route, still cool but under a lot of pressure, through something called a drier which is like a water filter on the engine – it removes both impurities and any moisture from the Freon. After this operation, the Freon is forced through a tiny orifice (the expansion valve) and is squirted into the cold plates, or evaporators, in the actual fridge box, now on the low-pressure half of the system. The expansion valve matches the performance of the compressor against the efficiency of the evaporator, thereby maintaining a balance between the high and low-pressure sides of the system. The sudden drop in pressure in the evaporator plates immediately changes the liquid Freon back to its natural state, a gas, and at the same time there is a rapid drop in its temperature. As the now very cold gas flows through the plates it absorbs any vestiges of warmth that comes from them, which in turn has come from the fridge box. Finally, the gas, now warmer, continues its way to the compressor pump to re-start the cycle. A fridge is therefore just a heat pump which sucks warmth in through the evaporator and expels it through the condensor.

There are many variants, and if the components are properly matched it will usually dictate the efficiency of your system. First of all, the compressor pump can either be driven direct from the engine or from a 12v motor. There are several variations of heat exchanger. Firstly, a straightforward 12v fan can be used, although power consumption will be increased by 0.5 amp. This is a very common method, although not very efficient unless the compartment which houses the condensor is well ventilated. On the bigger, engine-driven compressor models, the motor's raw cooling water is usually tapped (before entering the engine) to take away some of the condensor heat. Friends of ours, Richard and Cathy Cottier, fitted their condensor in the yacht's main water tank (in the keel, itself naturally cooled by ambient seawater outside) and by cutting out the 12v fan reduced their battery drain. On the low-pressure side, the efficiency of the evaporator's heat absorption is directly proportional to the length of the piping and, therefore, surface area. Steve Dashew in his excellent book *Circumnavigator's Handbook* describes his 'finned evaporator' which, for a small increase in cost, greatly improved his system by having fins on the piping to increase the surface area.

Eutectic plates are simply a snake of evaporator piping immersed in a sealed box filled with a combination of water and an anti-freeze-like solution (mono ethylene glycol). Sometimes called holdover plates, they are used primarily with engine-driven compressor refrigeration systems when you will only be running the engine for two or three hours a day. They're like a block of ice that freezes at a lower temperature than water. The refrigeration is run for a couple of hours and the eutectic plate freezes. Like a block of ice, it keeps everything cool for a period of time (normally up to 12 hours) before needing freezing down again by running the motor and refrigeration, thereby maintaining a steady supply of cold. The smaller the eutectic plate, the less time it'll keep frozen and the more often you'll have to run the engine, so the more plates you have the better. However, the compressor capacity has to be matched to the demands of the plates.

Alternatively, a number of 12v-driven compressor units also use eutectic plates with an intelligent control unit. The control unit senses when there is plenty of power available (ie voltage above 13v) either from wind generator or solar panels or, more likely, when the engine is running. At this point it lets the compressor work hard, letting the eutectic plate act like a savings bank of coldness. During interim periods the box is partly fed by the eutectic plate and partly by the occasional running of the

12v compressor. We have such a system, the Isotherm 3000, in *Foreigner 2*'s custom box and it works extremely well, the Windbugger supplying its needs (plus all others aboard) comfortably when we're in the tradewind belt.

If you decide to go ahead with refrigeration, the name that comes up time and again for efficiency, reliability and economy is Danfoss. Many other brands use Danfoss components and I've heard nothing bad about them.

Provisioning

The mountain of tinned food tradionally associated with long voyages is the first to forget unless you are planning to make a singlehanded circumnavigation non-stop. We made this mistake first time and we've spoken to dozens of others who've regretted taking on a massive stock of food. The boat disappears even deeper into the water, there's not a free inch of stowage space and trying to find anything entails dismantling and re-assembling a three-dimensional jigsaw puzzle. After all, the longest passage is perhaps five or six weeks and you can buy most provisions at either end. There is also something unromantic about lying to an anchor in a perfect crystal-clear lagoon with tree frogs chirping away ashore, the palm trees silhouetted against an impressive tropic sunset, a local rum drink in your hand and then being served Fray Bentos steak and kidney pie with Co-op tinned peas (on Special Offer at 22p). Of course, it pays to carry enough food on board for emergencies. You may take a lot longer to reach port than you had bargained for, so never provision just for the days you expect to be at sea.

Fresh fruit and vegetables come aboard for an Atlantic crossing. Careful choice of every piece, allowing for its state of ripeness at the outset will make a big difference to the pleasure of an ocean crossing

If you shop in port as and when you need to, you are likely to eat more fresh food and enjoy local delicacies. There seems little point in stocking up with cases of tinned fruit such as peaches and pears if you are heading for the Med where fresh fruit is cheap and plentiful. On the other hand, do make sure you take plenty of your favourite things as some of them may prove prohibitively expensive abroad, if available at all.

Tinned versus dried food

Dried food can often only be purchased in bulk at the wholesalers, which can mean less variety if you have to buy it in 100-serving packs. It is light to stow but it must be kept absolutely dry and you may have to increase your water capacity to rehydrate it. It is not as easy to prepare as tinned food, which can be made into a delicious meal in minutes on a stormy night just by emptying a few tins into a pot with some shopped onions and heating through. Depending on how dry your stowage is, the length of time you intend keeping them and your thoroughness, tins can be protected against rust by varnishing. This is another of those tradional long-voyage chores that not many people bother with now. It has been found by experience that tins will last quite long enough as they are. As long as a tin hasn't 'blown', it's amazing how well the contents are preserved in a tin whose outside looks dreadful. It is quite sufficient to rip off the labels and mark the contents on the top with indelible pencil, them store them in as dry a place as you can. If possible, try out a small quantity of everything before you buy in bulk. It will save you a lot of tasteless meals.

Food stowage

Fruit bruises easily and must be stowed in trays with newspaper wedged between each piece. Vegetables need light and air and a good place to keep them is in hanging nets. Another way of storing veggies is to have a big ventilated bin lashed on deck, the sort of thing bakers use to deliver loaves of bread in, with a cover over it to keep out spray. If you can spare it, lettuces stow very well with their base submerged in fresh water which is changed regularly. Tomatoes should be completely wrapped when green to slow down the turning process. Lemons will keep indefinitely if wrapped in aluminium foil.

Eggs are usually recommended to be protected with vaseline, which is horribly messy and time-consuming. They keep well without protection for 3-4 weeks, but you can prolong the life of half a dozen or so by putting them in a wire basket and dipping them in boiling water for 30 seconds. Dried eggs are available, which are great for cakes and scrambling and help to stretch out the fresh supply a bit longer.

Butter is a problem in hot countries as even tinned butter goes rancid quickly above 70 degrees. Margarine is a good substitute and in the tropics they sell a peculiar tinned substance, sometimes called Glo-spread or Oleomargarine, which has been specially processed to stop it melting. It is good for cooking, but we would rather go without than spread it on bread. Cheese keeps well if bought in its wax or covered in silver paper and stowed in the coolest place possible. Cured ham, salami, and sausages all make a pleasant change from corned beef and can be stowed strung up as in the delicatessen.

After a few weeks at sea, one is usually craving something crunchy and we have always had great success with sprouting beans. There are a great many to choose from. Mung, toh foo, and even chick peas all sprout well and mixed with a tin of sweet corn, some rice, oil and vinegar they make a refreshing change when all the lettuce has been eaten.

Do not overlook the possibility of preserving food as you go along. We have met many people who have dried their own fish by cutting it into strips, hanging them out like washing until completely dry and then packing them between layers of salt in air tight containers. Lou Lou has successfully bottled fruit and vegetables using a pressure cooker and kilner jars when we've arrived in a port and found a glut of some local speciality going cheap.

In the galley

Buy a good quantity of bay leaves as these help to keep weevils out of lentils, flour, rice and pasta. Dry commodities like these store best in wide-mouthed plastic containers. In deciding where you will be stowing your food, don't forget that, apart from being handy to the galley, you will want to get at it without continually disturbing the off-watch crew members or unseating the navigator. Above all, make sure it is in a dry place.

Most cruising cooks rate their pressure cookers as their most important piece of equipment on board. If you take one (and they certainly save fuel) don't forget spare gaskets, relief valve rubbers and weights (these always get thrown overboard with the washing-up water!). It is a good idea to buy stainless steel replacements for all your cooking utensils as these last much longer.

A minute timer in the galley is a useful item, not just for cooking but reminding you of the noon sight and watch changes. It may not sound very seamanlike, but it is very useful to take along a granny basket (one of those shopping bags on wheels) for carrying provisions, gas bottles etc, because the car you have always taken for granted will not be there. We had a cheap steel one but it rusted badly and next trip, we shall treat ourselves to a specially-made stainless or aluminium one with good-diameter plastic wheels.

Toiletries and cleaning materials are expensive in certain places abroad. Shampoo is a must for sea water baths as it lathers beautifully in salt water, we bought 10 family-sized supermarket shampoos for this purpose. An all purpose cleaning fluid such as Flash serves many uses aboard so will also be needed in big packs.

21. Everyday Life Afloat

Future maintenance

Messing about with the boat can be very pleasant and there will be plenty of it, with everything receiving much more wear and tear than ever before. But you don't want to become a slave to it, so it is worth taking a few precautions before you start to keep future maintenance to a minimum.

In warm, tropical waters, osmosis in glassfibre hulls is much more likely, aided and abetted by the strong sunlight in the waterline region. To reduce the risk, strip the antifouling off and coat the undersides with the latest two-part epoxy anti-osmosis treatment. Technology is changing fast, so research what is considered the best at the time you need it.

When you antifoul, one job that will save you hours and hours of toil in the future is to raise the yacht's waterline by at least six inches, preferably nine (but no more, as inflatable dinghies will constantly smudge them). Not only will your boat inevitably sit a little deeper in the water with all her stores and extra gear, but from time to time she'll be out of trim and raising the waterline will save a lot of scrubbing off of weed (which grows quickly in warm climates) from the first few inches of the topsides. Also, it is unavoidable that you will sometimes have to moor in dirty, oily harbours, and raising the waterline saves your topsides from the resulting yellow stain that can be so hard to remove.

In the interests of preserving your topsides (either gelcoat or paint), a simple fender curtain approximately one third of the boat's LOA and coming to within 6 inches of the waterline will save a lot of grief when lying alongside little stone quays or oily harbour walls. When berthed for a short time anywhere where fenders have to work hard for their living or get filthy or damaged, go ashore and find a couple of old car tyres, ubiquitous in ports the world over, and use them as fenders for the duration of your stay alongside, with a fender curtain totally protecting the topsides.

Exterior varnishwork is best kept to a minimum. Sacrilegious though this may seem, it may be worth getting the varnishwork on areas of a wooden boat like coachroof sides and cockpit coamings to a good standard with lots of coats, then paint over it. You then always have the ability to revert to the varnishwork when the cruise is over. Americans seem to make the best varnish and several of the Caribbean charter fleet

Don't waste too much time making the yacht look prissy and immaculate; a hard-working life and many oily or weedy waterline scrubs will remove the shine

It's heartbreaking to see the state that immaculately-kept yachts can get into in filthy commercial harbours; this happened in Tenerife, an island otherwise noted for its tourist appeal

operators, who are genuine experts on maintaining varnishwork, use the US Pettit products, the Bak-V-Spar varnish being highly recommended with UV filters. When you get to the States or Caribbean it is worth buying in a stock of this. The difference in your varnishwork will cushion the blow of its price. In the tropics varnishwork has to be recoated every 8-10 weeks for it to remain looking good. This may sound horrific, but once the brightwork was up to this standard it needed only a very light rub down before being recoated, preferably early in the morning before the sun becomes too hot and the varnish too sticky to apply.

Photography afloat

The environment afloat is about the worst possible for delicate camera equipment. It needs cushioning against the chance that it could fall out of a locker at sea and fly for a few feet. A smallish but robust aluminium camera box, looking like a suitcase and padded inside, can be purchased in any camera shop and affords good protection. Ask in camera shops for any silica-gel cachets they had spare. All camera equipment comes

Photographic equipment and the seagoing life don't mix easily; here the author's Olympus is put to work earning its keep before it finally gave up the ghost

from the manufacturers packed with these silica-gel bags and shops often have some lying around. They are the best way of keeping moisture away from the equipment, and toasted under the grill every six months or so to dry it out, it will remain effective.

There is a huge choice of highly sophisticated, electronically operated cameras. I went for the basic and hard-wearing Olympus OM-1 with Zuiko lenses, fitted with 'sacrificial' UV filters for protection against scratches. It lasted four years afloat but had to be written off after that. I chose something similar next time round. Make sure to take along three or four CdS batteries for the light meter. You'll never find them overseas.

Processing films abroad is a constant problem. The various laboratory processes, even with well known names like Kodak, often mean that a film bought in one country can't be processed in the next. Black and white is almost impossible unless you are lucky enough to find a keen amateur to process it for you and colour slides are equally difficult. Kodak publish a booklet listing all the their offices and agents all over the world, plus all laboratories that accept Kodak, and other makes. It is available, free, from Kodak House, PO Box 66, Hemel Hempstead, Herts HP1 1JU. It may be less bother in the long run to make an arrangement with someone at home to have your films developed and send on the results.

In terms of transparency films, Fuji 100 and Agfachrome CT18 is widely available as are Kodachrome 25 and 64 and Ectachrome ER. The longest time you can hope for film to last is six months on a boat in hot weather. Keep it as cool and dry as possible and inspect expiry dates on the box carefully when you buy.

Earning money overseas

On first impressions, this can be fraught with difficulties involving work permits and entry visas and many a cruising yachtsman has been thrown out of a country for illegally working. In reality, cruising work can be had in many places, on condition that you go out and find it – it rarely comes to you.

A high proportion of yachtsmen finance their cruising life by working along the way and some come back at the end of three or four years with more money than they set out with. The beauty of it is that the overheads of living aboard are a fraction of those doing the same job living ashore, and you have become used to living a little frugally, so you need only work for four or five months to support the next year's cruising.

The best possible way of earning money is by using a specific skill. We met two dentists in the Caribbean who'd sailed their 26ft sloop down from New York and were holed up in Bequia, filling the neglected teeth of grateful yachtsmen as fast as they could. The quarter berth had become the operating table, the patient propped up with pillows and the yacht's spotlamp wedged into the bulkhead bookshelf to shine into their mouths. A diver's air bottle provided power for a drill and a fierce Jabsco water pump had been adapted to vacuum the mouth. They were making a fortune!

Competent diesel mechanics are always in demand, as are refrigeration experts, and electrical engineers who can repair radios, autopilots, or general electronics will have an easy time of it. We made a corner in sail repairs, upholstery and cover-making and our dear Reeds Sailmaker sewing machine paid for itself time and time again. However, the work will never come to you unless you gain a reputation. Our best advert was making a really good awning for ourselves so that as people went by in dinghies they'd ask where we got it. In this way we had dozens of orders, including a 700sq ft all-over awning for an 86ft ketch, which was made entirely in our 34-footer's saloon with a hand crank machine, evidence if ever it was needed that you'll do anything when you're broke. In the charter centres of the Caribbean and Mediterranean, there were always expensive crewed boats wanting a new sailcover, windscoop, or cockpit cushions.

Unfortunately this form of earning money is very popular now, but those who are really good still manage nicely. A South African friend of ours started making trendy but simple Bermuda-type shorts out of nylon spinnaker material for her husband and within a short space of time she couldn't churn them out fast enough. Another friend crocheted bikinis in the Caribbean, and with a lovely figure herself to show them off never had problems selling them at vastly inflationary prices to tourist shops. Clearly one has to aim for the richer cruising areas, especially where there are big boats, but when finances are starting to run down this must be embraced as part of the cruising plan.

Writing for magazines is a possibility if writing comes easily and you are a good photographer, but be prepared for the fact that editors receive three or four manuscripts about ocean cruising topics for every one about home waters cruising, because the blue water yachtsmen have more time to write. The trouble is that 95 percent of the readers are coastal sailors who like to dream occasionally of blue water but are generally more interested in home waters. Diary-like accounts of voyages are almost universally rejected. It is far better to take a small incident or experience and examine it, perhaps for entertainment value, or for the lesson there is to learn.

If you plan to submit articles, write to the magazines and ask for their contributor's guidelines. Most have a printed resumé which will give a clear idea of the sort of subjects they like to see, the type of illustrations they can use, and the sort of article length they prefer to accept.

Chartering is many a yachtsman's idea of a dream come true until they've tried it. If you have a boat of 45ft or more, it seems an obvious way to make money, but as a general rule it rarely pays off. Cruising boats make lousy charter boats and vice versa. Chartering has to be a business. You must have equipment and accoutrements that have no place on a long distance cruiser and you must be established with a US or European agent and have a good brochure. It is easy to see that anyone contemplating a costly holiday with all the air fares will be more easily attracted to the well-presented, established boats, even if they cost more. So you won't get sent charters by the agents, who will have dozens of other yachts on their books, until you are proven with happy guests in your wake, and you can't gain that reputation until you've done some charters. Clearing this hurdle will take years rather than months, and a better alternative is to get a job with a charter company and lay your own boat up temporarily.

A charter boat also needs paraphernalia to be attractive. It is the norm to have nine or ten sets of snorkels, flippers and masks aboard (so there is the right size for everyone), one or two windsurfers, diving equipment, along with a big and stable dinghy with powerful outboard for skiing. Charter guests straight out from a cold climate need permanent protection from the sun for the first few days, so a bimini or permanent sailing awning is required. They also generally use a great deal of water and electricity, which must be replaced. Six charter guests could be going through 100 gallons of water a day.

Day charter can be lucrative in holiday areas, but recognising this, authorities have

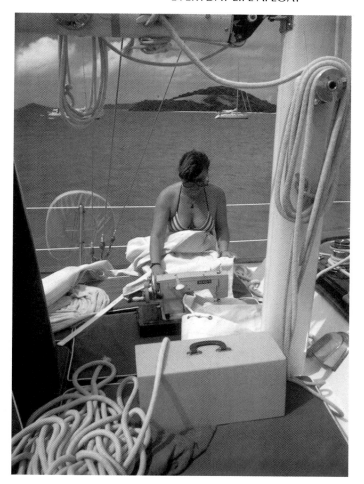

Repairing sails with our Reeds Sailmaker. Expensive to buy initially, the machine has paid for itself countless times over

imposed clamp downs and only issue licences to locals. You can certainly pick up the odd illegal day charter from time to time, but it is risky. In the Canaries, the routine among yachtsmen was to anchor off a holiday beach. Within minutes you could be sure that a tourist had swum out and was engaging you in conversation. With a little subtlety, it was not difficult to get them to come for an informal day sail with you, bringing along a few friends. However, this is not something one could do regularly without risking a lot of trouble. The rules are the same the world over in all holiday areas.

The blue water bookshelf

The essence of ocean cruising is self-sufficiency and independence. It used to be said that there should be absolutely nothing aboard that the skipper or crew couldn't repair, but that may be going a bit far in these high-tech days. However, the right books to refer to may save you a lot of frustration and money. Given that you will also want to take a library to read for pleasure, there will be space limitations, but the following is a basic list of books I have found helpful.

Boatowner's Mechanical and Electrical Manual by Nigel Calder (Nautical). No long-distance cruising yachtsman should head to sea without this bible. It is expensive, but will pay for itself immediately when it allows a job to be completed by the yachtsman that might otherwise have required a professional. Our copy is dog-eared, well-thumbed and referred to at least weekly.

Yachtsman's 8-Language Dictionary by Barbara Webb (Adlard Coles). You would have thought this book would have been invaluable for long-distance sailors, when in fact it is very rare indeed that you can buy sailing equipment in foreign countries and therefore don't need to know what a cranse iron is in Portuguese. For Mediterranean sailing it is likely to get more use.

Anchoring and Mooring Techniques Illustrated by Alain Gree (Adlard Coles). This is a mine of excellent information, and whilst it is likely to be of more use in preparation than practice, it is nevertheless a nice one to have aboard.

Marine Diesel Engines by Nigel Calder (Ashford Press). Much of the information in this is duplicated in the above-mentioned *Boatowner's Mechanical and Electrical Manual*, but well worth buying if you don't buy the former.

Complete Canvas Worker's Guide by J Grant (Ashford Press). As its name suggests, this book is useful if you either plan to earn some money or if you want to save money by making awnings etc yourself. It describes how to make just about everything that's canvas/fabric aboard, from sea anchors to flags and harnesses.

Flags of All Nations (Brown, Son & Ferguson). This is one of a number of similar books. Make sure you have an up-to-date one as flags are constantly changing and not only is it annoying to spend a lot of time making an out-of-date one, it goes down like a lead balloon with the authorities when they see it flying proudly from your crosstrees.

Meteorology at Sea by Ray Sanderson (Stanford). Again, one of a number of very good books available on the subject and undoubtedly helps to get the most efficient weather forecast in many regions of the world – by doing it yourself.

Safety and Survival at Sea by Kenneth Lee (W W Norton). Hardly gripping or fun reading, but an essential for the emergency pack.

Sails by Jeremy Howard-Williams (Adlard Coles). Universally recognised as the Bible on sail handling, care and repair.

Self Steering Without a Windvane by Lee Woas (Adlard Coles). We carry this aboard for one reason only: if our windvane breaks down in mid ocean. On this basis alone, it is cheap insurance.

Ships Captain's Medical Guide (HMSO). There are several yachtsmen's first aid books around, but none have come anywhere near the standard of this work. Some of its information is inappropriate to a yacht (it was written for ships' captains) but it is nevertheless comprehensive.

Cruising in Tropical Waters and Coral by Alan Lucas (Stanford Maritime). Written by an extremely experienced sailor, this book will be of particular interest to yachtsmen who plan to sail beyond the Caribbean and into the Pacific.

Boat Data Book by Ian Nicolson (Nautical). A thoroughly practical little tome that unearths endlessly useful information if ever you plan to modify (in whatever way) the boat.

Then there are the the navigation books, many of which are unavoidable for safe seakeeping. These include:-

Ocean Passages of the world/World Cruising Routes
Relevant Admiralty Pilots
Celestial Astro for Yachtsmen
Sight Reduction Tables for Air Navigation, Vols 1-3
Choice of Almanacs
Admiralty List of Lights
List of Radio Signals
Admiralty Catalogue of Charts and Publications

Traditionally, ocean cruising yachtsmen have bought *Ocean Passages for the World*, which is far from suitable but the only thing available for passage routeing. Now Jimmy Cornell has produced an excellent substitute called *World Cruising Routes* (Adlard Coles) which, although not totally precise in its information, is far preferable to *Ocean Passages*.

Admiralty Pilots are expensive and often inadequate for the yachtsman, but one would be foolish to sail without them. When cruising the Atlantic we only used one of our eight volumes on a single occasion, and then it didn't describe the bay we were entering. Instead, we always used commercial yachting pilot books and guides. For the Pacific and high latitudes, they are perhaps more use, but a stock of commercial yachting pilot books and guides for the area you are visiting will be needed. More often than not, they are not on sale anywhere but the particular area.

The **List of Lights** and **List of Radio Signals** are in theory essential. In reality, the information they contain is invariably out of date for the lighthouse or RDF station you are wanting to check. It is far better to determine the local situation before leaving and never rely on the information in these books, but use them as a guide.

Charts – carry a copy of the Admiralty chart catalogue. Though bulky, it will enable you to order your charts from overseas. Even so, they are expensive and it is easy to get carried away and spend several hundred pounds. Another address well worth keeping is that of Bluewater Books and Charts, 1481 SE 17th Street Causeway, Fort Lauderdale, FL 33316, USA (Tel: [305] 763 6533/Fax: [305] 522 2278 or Toll Free in USA 1-800-942-BLUE). They stock over 20,000 charts and books and their prices are a tiny fraction of those in the UK.

It is best not to plan too far ahead. If you want to circumnavigate, for example, buy charts as far as Panama and if you still want to continue, wait there a month or so while new charts are ordered and sent to you.

Everybody faces the same expense and often you can swap charts and pilot books with someone sailing in the opposite direction to you. Another dodge is to talk to big ships in harbour. They are very friendly and all have a cancelled-chart drawer where sheets with more than six corrections are written off. Even so, they may be newer than the ones you are carrying from home. From time to time the contents of this drawer are dumped, so make sure you get to see it first. Alternatively, you may be allowed to take a tracing or photocopy of somebody else's charts. This is a definite risk, but if you were stuck for a particular chart it would be the lesser of two evils, and used with caution, considerably better than nothing.

Documentation

This is more straightforward than most people think. For a British yacht all that is needed is either the old-fashioned formal Certificate of British Registry, or if your boat doesn't have this, the Small Ship's Registration (SSR) document from the DVLA. Make sure it is made out in your name. SSR is accepted all over the world and its former administrators, the RYA, report that they've never heard of anyone having problems with it. We have never been asked for the licence for our VHF radio, but it would do no harm to carry it just in case.

Thereafter, documentation is only what's generated in individual countries. You will often be asked to fill in myriad forms in triplicate and produce them for whatever reason as you clear out again. As long as you have valid passports and the correct visas, nothing else is required, except sometimes your clearance from the last country. If you arrive in some West Indian islands without outward clearance from your last port, it is not unknown for them to send you back for one.

It is always advisable to toe the line with bureaucracy, which is worse in smaller countries. In some the customs officers, who are very often also the police, have a great deal of power and there is nothing to stop them from putting you in jail, or even confiscating the yacht if you don't do things exactly as they wish.

A small tip is to buy postage stamps and stick them on the back of your registry documents. Always have made a ship's rubber stamp, suitably grandiose, and print it all over the postage stamps. This may sound infantile, but it gives a document credence in some countries!

Mail from home

Mail takes on a completely new complexion when you are far from home. The arrival of letters is a great excitement, but you have to brace yourself for plenty of disappointments and lost parcels.

Giving someone a blanket instruction to forward all mail will mean spending a lot of money shipping worthless leaflets and mail-shot brochures around the world, so you must trust whoever you choose to forward your mail to open everything and be selective.

Poste restante addresses vary considerably in efficiency and are generally regarded as a final resort, unless there are good reports about them. The normal routine is to find out through the cruising grapevine where there is a reliable address ahead, and if possible send a card there asking them if they would mind holding your mail. Few ever object and you can then phone or write home with the new forwarding address. Airmail nearly always arrives within two weeks anywhere in the world. If you can't find an address ahead, wait until you arrive in a place you plan to stay for a while and seek out a forwarding address then. Embassies, harbourmasters' offices, cafes, boatyards, hotels, and banks will all help.

Friends will always want to write to you in an exotic location, but it is better to encourage them to send to your home-base address for forwarding. Otherwise letters will forever be arriving too late to catch you before you sail on and may never catch up.

The home base and finances

The obvious person to handle your affairs is a relative. If they have your Power of Attorney this might save problems and it would be easier if you make them signatory to your bank account. However, relatives are not always available to do the job and some ocean cruising people use their banks to provide a similar service. Despite the fact that in financial terms we were lousy customers, we found our bank manager and his staff interested in our movements, which probably make a welcome break from everyday routine, and although we didn't formally use them as our home base, they were very helpful with money matters.

Getting cash overseas can, at times, be a frustrating affair. There are no hard and fast rules, as regulations and facilities change constantly. We have found that credit and charge cards, especially Visa, Barclaycard and American Express can be used to either obtain cash, make purchases or buy traveller's cheques in many places and this is about the most reliable system. However, in many third world locations such niceties are worthless. They are only interested in the US dollar note. It is wise to have as many different ways of obtaining money as possible and never let yourself get low on cash before sending home for more. Keep the number of transactions to a minimum and transfer money in largish chunks. Cashing money overseas can be a very expensive affair, whichever way you approach it. One ocean voyaging friend solves the problem by taking all his money with him. It may seem outrageous advice but he has cruised for years and used to spend many frustrating hours trying to have money forwarded from home. With his present system he has no problems, no bank statements, is never overdrawn, always knows exactly how much he has left, and gets no bank charges. He claims that before he lost more money in forwarding transactions and bank charges than ever he made in interest. The money was very well hidden (not under the bunk mattress), and although his boat has been broken into on a couple of occasions the intruders never found his cache. Those cruising on a fairly tight budget without much income going into their home account might find the simplicity of this system makes sense.

22. Common Worries

Medical preparation by Dr Nigel Pearce
This does not purport to be a comprehensive health text

Just as properly preparing a yacht for an extended cruise is vital to the success of the enterprise, so also is preparation and prevention essential to the crew's physical and mental wellbeing. When you're a long way from immediate help, good health requires effort and a little learning – so start now.

You need some first aid training, a First Aid kit and a good First Aid reference book. You will need to be familiar with these before you depart, so don't leave them till the last minute. And you'll need some basic medical understanding and, again, a medical reference book and a medical chest with a few useful drugs. You do not need to weigh your boat down with an enormous medical chest. Time and care in choosing a few relevant drugs could be a good investment.

Everyone needs a dental checkup in good time to have any remedial work done. The optician should also be visited, for spare spectacles and a copy of your prescription. I'd advise a general check-up at your doctor's – expensive multi-system checks are only occasionally of benefit, but a few minutes having your blood pressure and urine checked and getting some personal medical advice from your own GP is time well spent. Try to discuss everything that is relevant in your own past medical history. When he hears of your plans, your GP will probably be interested, helpful and jealous! If you are taking children along, or have a pre-existing medical problem, consulting a doctor is especially important. You should also glean all the information you can from other medical professionals, like nurses, physiotherapists and pharmacists, and perhaps have a private tutorial.

Beware of gratuitous advice from laymen. Medical anecdotes may be amusing and interesting; they might also, occasionally, be relevant, but they often are not representative of the common problems. Preparation needs care and objectivitiy, so beware the medical loudmouth. Like the crew you choose, the one with the big ears for listening and the small mouth for talking may have greater sense and more pearls of wisdom.

Other preparations revolve mainly around commonsense items. Make sure you take plenty of contraceptives. Go on a First Aid course. Medical costs overseas can be very high, so make sure everyone carries insurance.

You should remember that many serious illnesses appear long after they are actually caught, even if the correst preventative drugs have been used. Hepatitis, HIV and malaria are among these. Therefore, always seek medical advice if you have any symptoms after returning home, and emphasise to your doctor that you have been abroad.

The following books are recommended for reference.

The Ship Captain's Medical Guide (HMSO). Every yacht should have one.

Preservation of personal health in warm climates from the Ross Institute, London School of Hygiene and Tropical Medicine, Keppel Street, London WC1E 7HT

Travellers' Health by Dr Richard Daywood, Oxford Universtity Press

ABC of Healthy Travel from the British Medical Journal

The skipper's responsibilities

The skipper is responsible for the safety of his boat and his crew. He should thoroughly check on his crew's present and past mental and physical health before taking them on. Don't rely on their answers alone; don't be afraid to play the amateur psychologist. Beware if there a history of past mental ill health (this, of course, applies equally to a crew appraising a potential skipper). Physical ill health or disability is not necessarily a barrier to long-distance sailing. With careful preparation disabled people can fully benefit from pleasures of life at sea. But the skipper must bear in mind that this places more responsibility on the able-bodied members of the crew.

The skipper carries the responsibility for the medical equipment and drugs. These must be carefully packed and labelled, and it must be emphasised that they are strictly for medical use. Any medical event should be recorded in the Log. Either the skipper, or an appointed crew member, must be in charge of First Aid and medical matters. For obvious reasons, all the responsibility for this should not rest with one person.

I have already suggested that everyone on board should be insured against illness and accident. Skippers should bear in mind that litigation is becoming more common these days. In one case, an American crew member broke his ankle on a British yacht. He then had the yacht arrested in France on the strength of an American writ for US$300,000. You should, therefore, consider a Disclaimer and an Agreement of voluntary acceptance of it.

Finally, the responsibility for the crew's psychological health rests with the skipper. A happy crew needs a reasonable routine, acceptable tasks and reponsibilities, interesting food and drink and enough of it, a variety of books and music and time to themselves. They also need faith in their skipper's knowledge, seamanship, judgement and fairness. Do not underestimate the problems that can arise from incompatibility.

Immunisations

Immunisations are essential and useful, but they are not absolute. They reduce the chance of catching certain illnesses and if not, should reduce the severity of that illness. They are, however, only one aspect of prevention. Six months before you set off, you should contact your local surgery to arrange an immunisation schedule. Give them a rough itinerary. In the United Kingdom the Department of Health produces a regularly updated 'health advice to travellers' brochure, which among other things gives specific immunisation advice. It is free and I thoroughly recommend it.

There are many nasty diseases about. There is the ever-present worldwide hepatitis risk; there are new killer diseases like HIV and the re-emergence of older ones like TB. Luckily, there are some new immunisations available such as against Hepatitis A (the type you get from contaminated food and water) and against Hepatitis B, the killer transmitted via blood and sexual intercourse. However there is one vaccine, the anti-cholera one, whose effectiveness has to be seriously questioned. The main line of defence here has to be prevention – careful eating, careful drinking and a bar of soap and a scrubbing brush.

On long trips some immunisations may need updating. These may best be achieved during any brief return visits to the UK. The alternative, an injection in a foreign country, may best be left to your discretion and bank balance.

There is as yet no immunisation against malaria. This disease continues to kill and, as travellers to foreign climes, we must take every possible precaution. Drugs recommendations often change so it is best to consult the Malaria Reference Laboratory (Tel: 089 600350). Start taking the drugs at least a week before arriving at a location where malaria is present, and for at least four weeks after leaving. Even so, there is still a chance of contracting malaria and it is important always to tell the attending doctor that you have been to a malaria area. Wear long-sleeved shirts and long trousers after sunset in malarious areas. Insect repellents containing Deet are useful and mosquito nets around the bunks at night are essential. Some other diseases are also spread by insects and ticks.

Contacts: The travel clinic at the Hospital for Tropical Diseases (Tel: 071 637 9899); the Medical Advisory Service for Travellers Abroad, c/o London School of Hygiene and Tropical Medicine (071 631 4408); British Airways Travel Clinic (071 831 5333).

Coping with heat

For many of us, leisure and pleasure are synonymous with warmth and sunshine. Unfortunately these carry with them some pitfalls, which can only be avoided by exercising care and common sense.

As we sweat and lose body fluids we dehydrate a little. There is, therefore, a reduction in the serum, the liquid part of the blood, but the solid red matter stays at the same level so overall the blood becomes thicker. As there is less blood in total, the blood vessels will close down a little, so we have thicker blood going through narrower tubes. This requires more effort from the heart and contributes to an increase in heart attacks. Also, the blood becomes stickier and the cholesterol level rises, which increases the chance of a thrombus (clot) forming, especially if the blood vessel is furred up. This furring-up process is associated with obesity, smoking and old age, and the clots cause strokes as well as heart attacks.

There is nothing to fear – prevention is easy. Drink more fluid than you think you need, and keep fit. Also, obtain advice about the suitability of any heart medication before you go to the tropics. Some blood pressure tablets are diuretics and therefore are designed to cause fluid loss. Alcohol is also a diuretic, and therefore can be dangerous in the tropics. Enjoy a little but compensate by increasing consumption of other fluids.

It takes time to acclimatise to hot weather, as much as several weeks, which means a sea voyage might not be long enough. The core temperature of the body needs to be remarkably constant, about 37 degrees, for it to function optimally. The body obeys the laws of physics, obtaining and losing heat by radiation, conduction and convection. In addition, however, it can gain heat by digestion and muscular work. It loses heat by the evaporation of sweat. We must be able to sweat through our clothing and, ideally, let air circulate around us. We therefore need loose cotton clothing. Those long, baggy shorts that characterised military personnel in the 50s were actually very sensible.

Hot, humid conditions require longer acclimatisation. Sweat losses can reach up to ten litres a day. The guide is the same for all of us: we must drink more than we think we need. The sensation of quenching thirst is not sufficient. We should keep passing plenty of pale urine. Some additional salt may be necessary, especially when first acclimatising. Avoid hard physical work in the midday heat, that is the time for a siesta in the shade. Incidentally, the younger, slimmer and fitter you are, the faster you will acclimatise.

Failure to follow these guidelines can lead to serious conditions such as heat stroke, where the body fails to sweat, and there is headache, confusion and a rising temperature. As in all heat problems there must be cooling and fluid replacement. Heat exhaustion is caused by dehydration and depletion of body salt. Again, it is serious and the patient must be kept cool and given copious quantities of fluid. If someone has recently arrived in the tropics, the cause could be salt depletion so extra salt should be given. Remember that fevers could possibly be caused by infections not related to heat.

Whatever the cause, fluid replacement is paramount. If you are severely dehydrated or are dehydrating as a result of gastro-intestinal disturbance, then it is not only water that is required, but also some sugar and salt. You can buy sachets of rehydration powder to mix with water, or else make your own rehydrator by mixing 8 level teaspoons of sugar with a litre of water and adding just one level teaspoon of salt. Sometimes the fluid has to be given as just a teaspoon at a time, but if this is repeated every half minute or so, the volume soon adds up. Small, frequent quantities of liquid are not an adverse stimulus to the guts and therefore do not aggravate vomiting or diarrhoea in the way that a pint, swigged straight down, would.

This is only intended as a brief introduction to heat-associated problems – please refer to a full medical text for comprehensive information.

Saving your skin

A slight suntan is attractive, but with the way the incidence of skin cancer is soaring, brown bodies are out. Some of that warm, caressing sunshine is ultraviolet radiation (UVR), which can cause sunburn and lead to certain types of melanoma (skin cancer). Fair-haired northern Europeans are particularly at risk. People who have been sunburned will run a greater risk, later in life, of contracting malignant melanoma. A mole which is increasing in size, or is itchy, crusty, irregular in shape or dark, needs a doctor's opinion.

Although the skin adapts by tanning, this protection is not sufficient and the damage caused by over-exposure is cumulative. This gives rise to the familiar thinned, wrinkled, aged skin, and can also lead later to other skin precancers. UVR is strongest in the middle of the day in summer, when the sun is high. It is stronger nearer the equator and it is greatly increased by reflection off the sea. It is not absorbed by light cloud cover and it penetrates water. A pleasing wind might feel cool but it does nothing to prevent sunburn, and actually worsens the problem, perhaps leading to wind burn.

To prevent sunburn, make sure that exposure to sunlight is slow and never excessive. Wear a broad-brimmed hat and loose cotton clothes. Beware of thin cotton with a very open weave because it might let too much UVR through. Have a good harbour awning. Use UV-absorbing sunscreens or even a reflective sunscreen on the lips and nose, and wear UV-filtering sunglasses, as UVR can damage the eyes and lead to cataracts.

The skin is prone to damage in other ways – abrasions, cuts, and infection. In hot climates skin easily becomes septic and takes longer to heal. Fungal infection, such as the classic athlete's foot, can appear anyplace where two skin surfaces rub together, such as axillae, groins, under the breasts, and also on exposed skin surfaces. It is often good to use some hydrocortisone with the antifungal cream. Other skin infections need to be kept moist with antiseptics or coloid dressings until they are clean. Then you can allow a scab to form.

Coping with cold

We do not acclimatise to the cold. We must eat and drink more, be more active and have better insulation. Hypothermia (low heat) is the serious condition in which the core body temperature has fallen by just 2 degrees, to 35 degrees. If uncontrolled, hypothermia leads to death. Core temperature must be measured by a thermometer in the anus or under the armpit for five minutes.

The combination of wetness and wind, the wind chill factor, can enormously increase heat loss. Water is a fabulous conductor and the cold sea is an extremely effective heat-extracting environment. Acute accidental hypothermia from immersion in cold water is a dire emergency requiring medical help. Unfortunately, the immediate panic and over-breathing make the situation worse. The care of hypothermia involves drying, protection from the wet and cold, dry insulation, rewarming, hot, sweet drinks and medical help.

There have been some amazing recoveries from drowning and hypothermia. In resuscitation, therefore, work hard and long before ever giving up. Victims of near-drowning or water inhalation can later develop pneumonia.

Another danger from the cold is frostbite, which can especially affect the face, hands and feet. These, and the head itself, are tremendous heat loss areas and need extra protection. In frostbite, the initial pain and tingling give way to numbness as the flesh is damaged and freezes. Thawing must be slow, avoiding massage.

There is obviously a lot more than this to cold-weather problems. If you are sailing to cold areas the subject of hypothermia must be thoroughly researched. The Royal Navy is one of the world leaders in hypothermia research and knowledge. Prevention must rule absolutely – there are no shortcuts. We must stay dry, keep active, well-fed and watered, and wear the best clothing, footwear, gloves and headgear in layers.

Remember too that clothing gets wet from the inside – sweat – as well as from the outside. Whatever the source, wetness reduces insulation.

Hypothermia and hyperthermia (heat) both affect our mental ability and receptiveness. If you suspect a crew member or indeed the skipper is suffering, then you should give orders, not suggestions. Alcohol should be avoided either way: in hypothermia it increases heat loss, and in hyperthermia it increases fluid loss.

The importance of water

Insufficient food is a demoralising nuisance. Insufficient water can be disastrous. Water is essential for survival and we need three to five litres a day (or even up to ten if working hard in a hot climate). Choose your water sources carefully. Water from a tap is not necessarily safe. Wells and springs are usually good sources of water, but rivers, expecially in populated areas, can easily be contaminated. Your water tank should both be clean and easy to clean. Some filters can give effective treatment, but beware of false claims. They are a useful first step for chemical treatment with iodine or chlorine. Water is best stored in the container in which it was treated. Filters containing activated charcoal can remove the chemical taste from water just before it is used. If in any doubt about water quality, boil it for five minutes to sterilise it. When ashore, if you are not sure about the safety of the local water, stick to hot drinks and well-known brands of bottled or canned drinks. Avoid ice.

Food and hygiene

Food is not just a fuel. Good food, well presented, should be a pleasure, a social asset and a catalyst for a happy ship. Today, with careful planning and provisioning, and a versatile galley and cook, a balanced diet is possible even many weeks into a passage. Only on the longer, endurance-testing passages should vitamin pills be useful.

There is an old saying that travel broadens the mind but loosens the bowels. We need good personal hygiene, a clean galley and care with raw food. Contaminated, uncooked food can cause problems. Vegetables and fruit should be washed thoroughly in a strong solution of iodine or chlorine. Strictly speaking, meat, fish and other seafoods should be well cooked.

We can be seriously poisoned by eating some species of fish. Ciguatera poisoning is nasty and can occur anywhere from 35 degrees south to 35 degrees north, but is particularly prevalent in the tropical Pacific and Caribbean where certain fish accumulate Cigua toxins from their foodstuffs. The fish themselves, which are predominantly the barracuda group and snapper, are not affected by the toxins. The appearance of ciguatera is ill-undertsood. Symptoms are abdominal pains and vomiting, and nerve symptoms such as shooting pains.

Scombroid poisoning can occur anywhere in the world and is associated with mackerel and tuna. To avoid this, the fish must eaten while still very fresh, or refrigerated immediately. Puffer fish are supposed to have delicious flesh but their roe, liver and skin contains a lethal toxin. As well as these specific examples, hundred other species are poisonous or venomous. Take care, learn from the locals and buy a good fish identification book.

Because of their eating and filtering habits, shellfish are easily contaminated. Such contamination can easily pass on dysentery, typhoid and other illnesses. Cooking will destroy these bacteria, but if this is not acceptable, then you must rely on obtaining your shellfish from reliable and clean sources.

Special problems

Being pregnant, very young or very old are no bar to life at sea. There are, however, physical limitations to such states and extra advice and preparation may be necessary. A little knowledge and a good reference book should help in childhood illnesses.

There is widespread fear of catching AIDS through contaminated needles or trans-fusions while abroad. There is a real chance of this in a country with suspect medical standards. Before travelling, it is useful to know your own blood groups and get advice on who can give blood to other members of the group or family. It is then worth carrying needles and intravenous giving sets. However, Sod's Law would no doubt make sure that you never had the equipment with you should disaster occur! If you are contemplating very isolated areas of the world, you can consider carrying intrave-nous fluids. You must then, however, either have the expertise to use them, or hope that you can get the necessary expertise in the very unlikely event that this becomes necessary. You would need full medical advice in the selection and operation of such equipment. You may consider carrying stitching equipment – sutures – and perhaps paying a casualty sister or doctor to show you how to use it. It is really very simple, but there are a few important principles. Pig's trotters are useful for practicing suturing.

Diagnosis

Classically, we medics listen to someone's complaints, ask a few questions to narrow down the posibilities, and look at the patient in toto, including an assessment of their psyche. Then with our own eyes, ears and hands we look, listen, feel, prod and poke and hope to make a diagnosis. Sometimes further tests and investigations are needed before we can come to a firm diagnosis and advise on treatment. At sea or far from civilisation it won't be quite the same. You will have to rely on your common sense, your training, your knowledge and your own medical reference books. You will also have your radio and your medical chest. As part of your general preparation you should have a radio which is usable in your chosen part of the world. You should be thoroughly familiar with your medical references, and you should enter the basic per-sonal and medical details of each crew member in the log. You can then give the best service to a crew member in need.

Medical help and the radio

The basic personal and medical details should be entered in the log. As part of your general preparation you should have at least one radio which can used in your chosen part of the world.

If there is an injury or illness at sea you initially will have to rely on your onboard knowledge and equipment. In an emergency the international distress radio channels should be used, with PAN PAN repeated three times. Less urgent advice can also be obtained via local radio stations and other ships. This latter also implies that if you are carrying medical expertise you should be prepared to help others. You can also get medical advice around the clock, through Portishead radio, from experienced Royal Naval doctors at the RN Hospital at Plymouth or Portsmouth.

To get the best advice, be ready to impart as much information as possible to the listening doctor, and know what drugs and equipment are on board. Publications such as *The Ship Captain's Medical Guide* give good directions.

First Aid

Everyone should know how to deal with an unconscious person, or with someone who is choking, and be familiar with resuscitation procedures. Everyone on board should have some basic First Aid knowledge. Attend a course at an Adult Education Centre, or St John's Ambulance or the Red Cross. This is time well spent, one day the knowledge may save a life. You must carry, and be familiar with, a good First Aid book.

The following should be considered for a first aid kit. They should be in a water-proof container, clearly marked and readily accessible. A lot can be learnt from a medic whilst making a kit.

Airway	Micropore tape
Adhesive plasters and tape, strapping	Non-adhesive dressings
Antiseptic solution and cream	Pile ointment
Antihistamine tablets (Triludan, Piriton)	Rehydration powder
Antidiarrhoea tablets (Loperamide)	Safety pins, scissors, forceps
Antiseasickness tablets (Stugeron)	Scrubbing brush
Bactigras dressings	Scalpel and blades
Calamine lotion	Sodium bicarbonate
Crepe bandages	Surgical spirit
Eye pad	Steristrips
Flamazine (burn) cream	Sunscreens & lip salve
Granuflan dressing	Thermometer
Hydrocortisone 1%	Triangular bandages

Possible additions to the First Aid kit are an injectable kit for anaphylaxis (life-threatening severe allergic reaction – take adrenaline, hydrocortisone, piriton), and a stitching kit. If sutures are carried, you will need Lignocaine ampoules, needles and syringes for anaesthetising the skin. A dental kit comprising oil of cloves and temporary fillings is worth taking.

Medicines and drugs

The body recovers well from many minor illnesses without the need for drugs. Sometimes drugs are useful or essential but they are only part of an overall treatment of a condition. The patient must always be well hydrated – ie keep passing lots of pale urine. Drugs can cause many side-effects – some serious, but mainly rashes, diarrhoea and nausea. Before taking (or giving) a drug always check the recipient's history of allergy to drugs. Always take plenty of fluids with drugs and avoid alcohol.

A drug has a generic or chemical name. There is also the name that a particular manufacturer gives to its own brand, the proprietary or brand name. Thus the same generic drug may be made by several manufacturers, look quite different and have a different name. There are also, of course, different strengths of the same drug, and frequently a particular tablet or medicine is a combination of several drugs. The name of the manufacturer also appears on the packet, so you can get three different names on one drug and still not know what it does. It is best to obtain medicines in your own country prior to departure. This way you will get explanations in your own language. Hopefully, you can rely on the quality too. Drugs vary enormously in cost, quality and availability from country to country.

When more than one drug is taken, they can interfere with each other. This could just mean that one or the other drug works a little more or a little less. It could, however, have serious consequences, such as failure of the contraceptive pill or causing a dangerous heart rhythm. Use your reference books and ask for medical advice.

Children should not be given the adult dose! Do follow the manufacturer's guidelines. Very roughly, you assume an adult weight of 70kg and give a 35kg child half a dose, and pro rata. Some drugs are not advised for children.

For the boat as a whole, some drugs will be needed depending on the time away, intended goal and degree of isolation. Individuals also need a supply of medicines relevant to their present medical state, and past weaknesses. The drugs should be labelled and stored in waterproof containers. They need to be kept cool but reasonably accessible. You should keep a list of drugs in the container and a further list (and usage directions) in the log book or chart table. Usage should be monitored and supplies replenished as necessary. Remember that drugs deteriorate over time and with heat.

This drug list can form the basis of your discussion with your GP before you set off. They should be used in conjunction with medical references and medical advice. The MIMS magazine which is given to doctors lists the drugs, their alternative names, mains usages and dosages, and special precautions. Pregnant women should try to avoid all drugs, especially early in pregnancy.

Painkillers

Ibuprofen 400mg (Brufen) – for pain and inflammation, up to three a day
Paracetamol 500mg – for mild pain – up to eight a day
Dihydrocodeine 30mg (DF118) – strong – one every four hours, beware nausea
Diclofenac (Voltarol) – suppository 100mg – one daily
Diclofenac Retard 100mg (Voltarol Retard) – one daily

Antibiotics Generally one type for about five days
Amoxycillin 250mg (Amoxil) – a penicillin – one three times a day
Cotrimoxasole 480mg (Septrin) – two twice a day
Metronidazole 400mg (Flagyl) – one twice a day
Metronidazole (Flagyl) – suppository
Erythromycin 500mg – chest, venereal disease – one three times a day

Antihistamines

Terfenadine 60mg (Triludan) – one or two twice a day
Chlorpheniramine 4mg (Piriton) – for severe allergy – one three times a day. Also injectable, 10mg

Seasickness

Cinnarazine 15mg (Stugeron) – two stat. then one eight-hourly
Prochlorperazine (Stemetil) – 5mg tablet or suppository, up to 4 a day, or 12.5mg injection twice a day
Hyoscine
Promethazine (Phenergan) 25mg – up to three a day

Other useful drugs

Mebendazole (Vermox) – one tablet only for threadworm, one tablet daily for three days for threadworm
Loperimide (Immodium) 2mg– for severe diarrhoea
Cimetidine (Tagamet) 400mg – for acid stomach – twice a day
Bisacodyl 5mg – tablet or suppository for constipation
Salbumatol (Ventolin) 4mg – one every eight hours for wheezing
Prednisolone 5mg – for severe inflammatory reaction, as directed by doctor
Chloramphenicol – eye ointment or drops
Gentisone HC – ear drops
Lignocaine (xylocaine) gel – to anaesthetise the skin
Betnovate N – strong steroid skin cream for bad inflammation (not infection)
Cicatrin – powder or cream for skin infection
Micanazole – powder or cream for fungal infections
Diazepam (Valium) – for sedation
Canesten – cream for fungal infections
Adrenaline – for life-threatening allergenic reaction
Magnapen 500mg – very strong penicillin for severe infections

Thieves

The value of items you have aboard is greatly increased by the fact that many of them are irreplaceable without returning home and this alone should sharpen your precautions against theft. Taking an expensive yacht into poor areas inevitably puts temptation in the way of those ashore, who see a potential goldmine sitting in their midst. Simply locking up will not keep out determined, professional thieves. Their crowbars will make short work of any resistance a yacht can offer and only if you have a well-prepared steel or aluminium boat do you stand the slightest chance that they might give up.

You have certain things in your favour. Few thieves want to run the risk of confrontation. They are generally fairly hyped up and nervous themselves as they work, so will avoid bumping into someone if possible. After our confrontation with thieves we always left the companionway hatch wide open with one light and the stereo cassette on whenever the boat was left during an evening. The cassette player was the auto-reverse type that played alternate sides of the tape automatically, so would provide constant music until turned off. With the hatch open, light on and music playing softly it looked as though somebody was on board. It could have been coincidence, but we never had a problem afterwards. A second dinghy, perhaps a cheap inflatable, trailing astern would complete the ruse.

Use your knowledge of your boat to trick potential thieves. Every boat has dozens of little hidden nooks and crannies, behind linings and in lockers, that could house an envelope with important papers and travellers' cheques or cash. A friend of ours kept all his cash in an old Duckham's grease tin, impeccably cleaned out on the inside and put amongst the other maintenance materials in the paint locker.

Unless a padlock is situated in a specially-designed tight corner where a thief can't get a crowbar or hacksaw at it, it will be useless and certainly won't stop anyone with the slightest determination from getting down below. A better method is to do away with padlocks altogether and have a strong stainless steel pin inside that drives right up through the strengthened companionway. We made one using bungy cord as a spring and with a light control line leading back into an aft locker with camcleat, it looked quite unobtrusive.

Most aluminium hatches can be ripped open within seconds. A better arrangement is to have closely-spaced steel 'prison' bars put under the deck protecting the opening. Leave the hatches undogged and in this way they won't be damaged. In a steel or aluminium boat the bars can be welded in place, but on other forms of construction if they are welded to a single strap which itself is bolted right through the deck. This stands a good chance of holding if the bolts are beyond arm's reach from the hatch. The forehatch must have a removable frame of bars, as the crew are likely to use this for access. One system, suggested to me by George Taylor, is a steel foc'sle ladder which swings up under the deckhead, covering the opening at the same time.

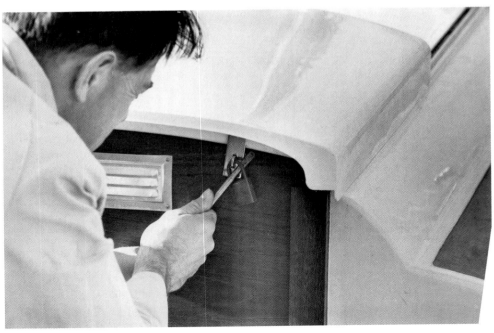

A determined thief is very hard to stop, although a little psychological as well as physical deterrent can do wonders

COMMON WORRIES

Wooden companionway washboards sitting in wooden slides can be broken into very easily by splitting the wood. If you are serious about preventing thieves, the best way is to replace these is by using heavy sectioned aluminium or stainless steel U-channel bolted or welded in place. A single or perhaps two washboards can then be made by using aluminium sheet with plywood screwed on to add bulk and stiffness.

A built-in safe, particularly on a steel or aluminium boat where it can be welded in, seems like a good idea at first, but Mark and Amanda Wilson, cruising their 43ft steel cutter *Hanne IV* in Brazil, found to their cost that when a thief finds a safe he will look no further and once in the cabin out of sight will work until he opens it. Having been completely cleaned out, they now recommend hiding places instead, but don't put all your eggs in one basket or money in one place.

Dinghies, particularly those with outboards, are prime pickings and it's a sad state of affairs that in some cases the culprits have been other yachtsmen. There can be quite a trade in tenders. The transient nature of their owners means that a thief only need hide a dinghy and outboard for a few weeks until the owners have gone. If he then steals another and hides it he can often enough sell the first to the new losers. Inflatable dinghies like Avons and Zodiacs are so common, and often indistinguishable, that they are as good as currency, several hundred pounds tied only with a bowline to the harbour wall. Sometimes the best answer is to do some local enquiries and put the word about that you're prepared to buy your dinghy and/or outboard back. This may take some swallowing, but the inconvenience of losing a dinghy is great, not to mention the fact you might wait months before reaching somewhere to buy a replacement.

There are two ways around the dinghy dilemma. One is to have a dinghy that is so disreputable as to be not worth stealing, another is to make sure the outboard is firmly locked on and the dinghy is always attached with a stainless-steel wire painter whether it's ashore or alongside the boat.

Personal security ashore is not easy either. We were robbed in Lisbon and it all took place so quickly and smoothly we hardly knew it had happened at first. The best answer is to carry as little of value on you as possible and don't look too rich (by local standards, not yours) with a lot of jewelery, cameras and so on. Buy a good money belt, but don't take from it in conspicuous places. If you sew in an extra Velcro fastener it makes a noise, so you hear someone trying to steal from it. In dodgy surroundings we adopted the routine that Lou Lou walked in front of me carrying any valuables. If there were any problems I could see what was happening and had a start on the thief.

Finally, that great old seaman Joshua Slocum said 'it is well known that one cannot step on a tack without saying something about it'. He therefore sprinkled carpet tacks over *Spray*'s decks in the Magellan Straits when he expected trouble, and sure enough late one night he was woken by howls and splashes as natives discovered them and pounced over the side. In these days of sophisticated burglar alarms this may sound simplistic, but one person we know cut out a couple of pieces of old carpet to fit the cockpit seats and companionway entrance. She then liberally pierced them with hundreds of carpet tacks from underneath and lays them out before going to bed. She lives in fear of the night she ever starts sleep-walking, but otherwise these adaptations of Slocum's methods are worth considering. The tack-laden carpets are rolled up and put away each morning.

Chafe

Happily, with modern materials like stainless steel, plastic pipes and synthetic ropes and sails, the chafe on an ocean cruiser is no longer the major problem it used to be. By the end of our 11,000 mile Atlantic circuit trip in *Euge* we hadn't put a single stitch into any of her sails. Although by then they needed to be valeted, with odd little bits of damage and stitching sorted out, ostensibly there was nothing wrong with them because we always watched carefully for chafe. The same applied to all her sheets and lines. We had stainless 1 x 19 standing rigging, which is very smooth for a sail to rub against. Stainless standing rigging is considerably more expensive than galvanised, but the reduction in future chafe is well worth the outlay. The alternative is plastic pipe sleeved over the wire before splicing, but this increases the windage by two or three times.

Spreaders should be checked for any roughness and the spreader ends well parcelled with thin strips of mattress foam, well taped up. Other than this, the key to cutting out mainsail chafe is an easily-rigged tackle as a preventer which is always used when sailing off the wind. Removing the topping lift when the mainsail is being used significantly reduces irritating stitching and batten-pocket damage on the leech. Always hoist and lower the mainsail when on the wind, or in such a way that it wasn't dragged up against the standing rigging. The first two or three slides at the head of the sail get more strain than the others and the best method of attachment is with narrow webbing tape wound around several times, then sewed along its edges (see Figure 26).

Headsail chafe is a completely different ballgame. The most prominent design error is to have spreaders too long and which press into the genoa when it is hauled in tight. This is prevalent on many amateur and home-build plans. There are many ways around it. Though ocean cruisers don't generally need to go to windward much, when they do it's generally in anger and for a good purpose, so don't kid yourself that the problem doesn't exist. The first test is to determine how much performance is lost if

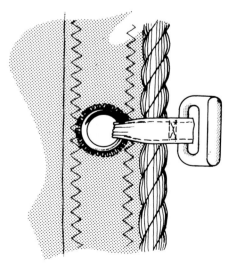

Fig 26 **The top few sail slides on a mainsail should be bound on with narrow webbing tape, finished off by sewing along their edges**

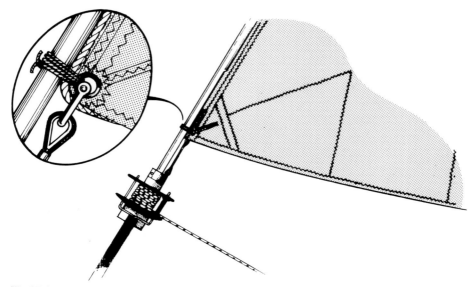

*Fig 27 **A common point of chafe on a roller headsail is where the luff tape enters the extrusion, especially if there is any distance between the point and the drum. Lashing the tack to the extrusion solves the problem***

the sail is eased enough for it to stop rubbing. Check tacking angles and boatspeed with the sail in tight and eased out. If this is insignificant, the spreader tips can be well parcelled and the sail have a sacrificial patch sewn on. Under way, make sure to check it regularly as fluctuating wind strengths can cause enough stretch and contraction in the sail to start the chafing when the wind drops slightly. If the performance loss is just too much, the only alternative is to shorten them, but don't do this without consulting the designer or a naval architect.

A common problem area for genoa chafing is the pulpit. Working sails can often be set on a strop high enough to clear the pulpit, but genoas on boats less than 40ft nearly always touch the pulpit when eased out. Attack any rough stainless welding with a file and if there are any sharp protuberances or fittings for the sail to rub against, such as the terminal fittings and welded eyes for the guardrails, a piece of plastic pipe, split and sewn in place, can cover many of them. If the sail or stitching starts showing any signs of wear or damage, again a sacrificial patch will be necessary.

There is nothing you can do about headsail hank wear short of using high quality fittings, such as the French Goiot brand, from the outset. If your boat has galvanised rigging, make sure that the forestay is stainless, otherwise you'll have rust problems very quickly. With a roller-furling headsail, boltrope wear can be quite a nuisance especially if the gear is getting old and the extrusions are slightly worn. Sacrificial tabling works to an extent, but one is always limited by the width of the groove. Filing the edges of the extrusions can help to a degree, but ultimately one is faced with having to replace the extrusions. Figure 27 shows a simple method of easing a chafing problem common on many gears.

Chafe on lines can be eased, but rarely totally eliminated. The bowlines on the clew of a headsail, for example, are susceptible to wear. Make the sheets over-length so that every couple of years, after end-for-ending, they can be trimmed slightly to lose the chafed section. The same goes for halyards, especially for the spinnaker.

Chafe occurs throughout a boat and it is worthwhile buying a few feet of half-round brass or stainless strip and fitting it in potential problem areas – all around the existing mooring fairleads, on the foot of the companionway, where self-steering lines rub slightly (these are killers – moving constantly) or maybe where the wire jackstays pass around the forward corner of the coachroof. Line up the lead of the kedge warp from stern fairlead to sheet winch and see if brass or stainless strip is required where it rubs on the cockpit coaming.

A short length of chain, to wrap around harsh mooring objects or over the edge of quaysides, will save your mooring lines but so will the way you use the warps and fairleads. In wild conditions a mooring rope that is taken through a tight bend will chafe away to nothing very quickly, no matter how smooth the fairlead or how much chafing gear you parcel it with. If you are moored in bad conditions watch tight corners, both on the boat and ashore where a large radiused bollard is much more preferable to a steel eyebolt.

23. The Last Six Months

The first time around, I'd imagined that the final six months of our workaday lives before cutting ties and leaving would be a matter of pleasant evenings spent drawing up provisions lists, dreamily ticking off the charts we'd need on the Admiralty chart catalogue and making sure the boat had a well-stocked bosun's locker. Then as the big day approached, we'd tie up all those little jobs, stow the pile of food just delivered on the quayside, say goodbye to friends and then sail off into the blue yonder. Little did I know . . .

It wasn't until we were almost ready to go that I realised how much time and money could have been saved had we attacked the last six months' preparation in an orderly and logical fashion. We considered the period very carefully, but still ended up keeping everything in our heads, and tackled jobs and problems as they arose. Had we taken stock of everything that needed doing from square one and listed jobs and their priorities, our lives would have been much simpler.

Very few people are in a position to drop everything suddenly and disappear to sea for a long period, so for the majority the idea will have been nagging for many years. It's not usually until eighteen months or two years before leaving that the plans come into focus and fixing the approximate date becomes possible. From this period the commitment to the project accelerates quickly and the disposal of house or flat and contents and a large chunk of your possessions and straightforward home comforts becomes quite hard. The extent of devotion to the dream becomes apparent during this period and it is the point where many projects founder.

You will probably have an approximate departure date in your mind, so when you get to within 8-9 months of this the first move must be to fix the initial cruise plan, stage one. Having broadly decided where you want to go, buy a set of monthly routeing charts and start juggling the stage one cruise plan with dates, to establish D day (departure day) to within one or two weeks. Give yourself two or three weeks in hand to allow for the inevitable last-minute hold-ups.

Having decided the date you can start working out the amount of money you are likely to be able to get together before leaving and link this with terminating your employment and completing other business matters. In Great Britain, if you technically emigrate before you've earned a certain sum in that financial year you may be entitled to a substantial tax rebate, so this could influence the dates you fix.

Unfortunately the money side of cruising is crucial for most of us and a liberally allowed-for financial strategy covering the preparation period is imperative from an early date. This must be monitored carefully because the final six months is a highly expensive period, and before you know it things can get frighteningly out of hand, as a thousand and one small costs and expenses you never dreamed of start cropping up.

Tackle officialdom as early as possible. Find out early how you personally stand in terms of maintaining stamp payments, pension schemes, life insurances and so on while away, because when you venture into these paperwork empires with an out-of-the-ordinary request, months can pass waiting for a satisfactory answer. On our first trip we wanted to carry a Verey pistol aboard for distress signals (and, neophytes that we were, for the possibility of piracy that we had been advised by 'experts' we would undoubtedly encounter). What should have been a fairly straightforward process of getting a Firearms Certificate through the local police became prolonged and complicated when a police messenger dropped our application off the motorbike on his way to the local government offices. This single incident held us up for nearly a week when we were otherwise ready to go and, had it not been for their later kindness and efficiency, could have taken much longer. We had applied for the certificate in plenty of time but had not allowed for such slip-ups.

Now aware of the extent of administrative work that will need clearing up, and with much of it in hand, it is important to review health in general. This, and inoculations, are dealt with by Dr Nigel Pearce in Chapter 22, but time is of the essence, and looking on the bleak side, they may tell you something that could alter your decision to leave. First aid and a basic medical understanding is important in a yacht that could be at sea for weeks, so enrol at least two crew on a comprehensive first aid evening class. The Cruising Association at Ivory House, St Katharine Dock, London E1 organise excellent yachtsman's first aid courses. Although you need a strong stomach to look at some of the colour slides, the lectures teach you how to cope in an emergency and deal with the more common cuts, burns and ailments. Local adult education centres and yacht clubs also run similar courses, so seek out the best in your area.

The days before you leave will be hectic, and you will probably spend a great deal of time achieving very little, so it is important to get as much done on the yacht as possible, a few months in advance. If her refit is incomplete, she needs modifications, engine servicing, sails checked, or any alterations, plan to complete these in plenty of time. Otherwise, as the final weeks approach, the jobs simply don't get done. Head the list with the jobs that affect seaworthiness. If she hasn't been painted, or items of inessential new gear haven't been fitted, don't worry. You can always stop for a quiet month or two further south and finish things off.

Get important sea trials done early as well because the last thing you'll have time to do in the last few weeks is go sailing. One of the last jobs on *Foreigner's* refit was to build and fit new rudders, which, in itself, didn't take long. However, we made the foolish mistake of leaving until late the fabrication of the new pintles and gudgeons. When we 'phoned the only galvanising plant within 75 miles, the company was closing down for a two-week summer holiday the following day and could not treat our fittings. We finally managed to get them galvanised, but it wasn't without a lot of persuasion and a long fast car drive, which wasted the better part of a day.

About six weeks before you are due to leave, order all your charts, pilots and any other literature. This leaves it late enough to maintain relatively up-to-date charts and publications, but not too late for the chart agent to get any he doesn't hold in stock.

At this stage as the tempo begins to rise, you remember a host of little items that need seeing to, affairs that need clearing up, awkward spares to get hold of, provisions waiting to be collected, plus chasing the non-delivery of other items. A small notebook and pencil should live in your pocket so as soon as you remember something you can jot it down immediately.

To add to the confusion, you'll probably experience little nervous doubts and with long hours of working and sleepless nights going over everything in your mind, the temptation to rush through everything and be away from it all finally is very strong. Despite this it pays to plan your timetable to leave the final two weeks theoretically completely clear. At the start of our first venture we still had one or two things to buy and do but on the whole we left the period free. We considered ourselves and our yacht well prepared, but nevertheless during the final two weeks we were rushed off our feet and never had a minute to spare.

Somebody had mentioned our plans to the local newspaper, which subsequently put our faces on the front page, having the effect of summoning just about everyone we'd ever known to come and visit. However, on the positive side, it was only being recognised from the newspaper at the police station that procured us our Firearms Certificate, a document which usually takes about three or four weeks to process, in less than three hours!

There is no need to over-emphasise the level of activity during the final weeks, and this can be eased considerably if you have a car available. More by accident than intention, we still owned our car during the week before we left on our first voyage; a seasonal slump in car sales meant we were unable to sell it and it was absolutely invaluable. The fact that I drove over 1,000 miles in short trips during our last seven days speaks for itself. Although I wouldn't advise keeping your own car until this late, if you have access to another it is well worth using it, and in the interests of keeping to schedule, even justifiable to rent a car or van for the final week or so.

Finally, as you sail out of harbour, the months of hard work are over and you begin to unwind – and almost immediately remember the things you've forgotten, the business you've left unfinished, the chandlery you've ordered which probably arrived the day after you sailed and a host of other minor items that would be better cleared up. It is a good idea to pre-plan, as an extension of your preparations, a rendezvous with an informed friend or relative about a week after you've left, and a little further down the coast, rather than heading out into deep water immediately. You can arrange with him or her over the telephone to bring any hangover mail, late deliveries or anything else you may have left behind. We did just this and sailed from the rendezvous with completely clear minds.

The overall success of a project involving tearing up so many roots and leaving home waters for a future with so many variables and unknown factors is very closely related to the integrity of the initial preparation. The Slocum Society researched, some while ago, the number of people who actively planned to go away on an extended passage within a year and later compared it to those who actually went. Of 105 people who planned to leave, only five got away. While there were individual reasons for each failure I am sure that most of them stemmed from the fact they simply were not ready, either materially or psychologically, and put the trip off until next year – and the next, and the next. Without the need for the sometimes unrealistic attitude of 'get everything finished in good time', if your preparation and its priorities are assessed and planned from the very beginning there is no reason why you should not be one of the five.

Index